CW00674501

Juicy Guides ltd
13 Arundel Rd, Kemp Town, Brighton
01273 672020
www.juicymapminder.co.uk

Registered Office:
Registered in England and Wales with registered number 4991076
Registered office; Middlesex House, 34-42 Cleveland Street,
London W1T 4LB.

ISBN: 1-903320-04-6
written and compiled by Gilly Smith and Jed Novick

Research assistant: Vanessa Austin-Locke
IT support : Mark Sutton @ Fearless Computing 01273 547600
www.fearless.co.uk

Researchers from The University of Brighton's BA (Hons) Information and Media/Library
Studies: Sarah Bolton, Monica Schiza, Sara Nash, Alan Foley

Contributors:
Gay Brighton: Lucy Kamper, Stephanie Lam and Indra
Teenage Brighton and Hove: Lara Hassell, Elly Novick
Additional copy: Anna Dewis
Shopping: Helen Paine Smith
Neighbourhood consultants:
Paul Bonett of Bonnetts: 01273 677365 (Kemp Town) 01273 775900 (Hove)
David Andrew at Raymond Beaumont :01273 550881
Barrie Alderton: 01273 570242
Ted Skinner @ John Hilton: 01273 608151
Glen Mishon @ Mishon McKay: 01273 821800
Astrology: Jessica Adams, with thanks to Brighton and Hove Museum and Library for their
assistance with the city's horoscope

Maps courtesy of www.mapminder.co.uk © Mapbyte © Telmap © 2004 NavTeq

Design by Will Harvey will@willharvey.co.uk

Published by Juicy Guides Ltd
Distributed by Portfolio Books

THE JUICY TEAM

Gilly Smith's background spans radio (BBC GLR), TV (Big Breakfast, Food File, Kilroy) and print. She now concentrates on writing books – mostly on food and travel. Working with chefs such as Marco Pierre White, Jean-Christophe Novelli, and Pierre Koffman, on her first book, The Mediterranean Diet (Headline), and Australia's top 22 Chefs in her last book, Australia, New Food from The New World (Andre Deutsch), she developed a critical edge to her love of good food. .

Jed Novick's 20 years in journalism has included editing the arts pages for City Limits, The Observer, Time Out and The Guardian. He was TV editor at The Independent and music critic and feature writer at The Express. He is also the author of seven books on popular culture and TV heroes including Michael Palin's first authorised biography, The Life of Michael (Headline). He is currently commissioning editor of Sorted, a new national monthly teenage boys' magazine based in Brighton.

Will Harvey trained as a fine artist before becoming art director at titles as diverse as Observer Life, The Daily Mail, The Sunday Times, The Erotic Review and Manumission. He is now Art Director at Sorted magazine and runs his own marketing company, WHDP.

Vanessa Austin-Locke is Juicy's young blood. Educated across Brighton, from Steiner to St Mary's Hall, from Sumo to Koba, she keeps Juicy juicy.

Publication Details

First published in Great Britain in 2004 by Juicy Guides Ltd

Copyright: Juicy Guides Ltd 2004

The right of Gilly Smith and Jed Novick to be identified as the author of this work has been asserted by them in accordance with the Copyright, Designs and Patents Acts 1988.

A catalogue record for this book is available from the British Library

ISBN 1-903320-04-6

Printed by Cambrian Printers Ltd, Aberystwyth.

INTRODUCTION

People from Brighton and Hove believe they are blessed. Whether it's by Buddha or the Rabbi, by God or Allah, by the planets, the Ley Lines or the fresh sea air is irrelevant. We're right. People move here, stay here or come home after their adventures because Brighton (and increasingly, Hove) has a sexy charm that makes everything seem possible. Come here for the weekend and dive into a fantasy world of boutique hotel hedonism or feather boa and G string clubbing, or move away from the big cities to the calm of the seaside, and the effect is the same, a sigh of satisfaction that says that you made the right choice.

So is it real? Is it marketing hype or the ramblings of well-meaning folk who've spent too long in the sun? In this fifth edition of The Juicy Guide, we'll show you the city's best bits, the restaurants, clubs, bars and activities.

You'll find everything in Brighton and Hove on www.juicymapminder.co.uk, our new sister site with maps on how to get there, and user reviews to tell everyone why those not in the guide should be. We'll be constantly updating our reviews on the site, and as you've bought the book, you've got a quarterly subscription for free, so use it.

Guide to symbols

💳 Credit cards accepted	♿ Disabled access
✖ Child friendly	📺 TV in room
⟊ Outdoor seating	🅿 Parking
	⚔ No smoking

IT'S ALL IN THE STARS

Brighton and Hove is a city exploding with character, and as we go to press, we imagine her painting toes in readiness for The Festival and consulting her stars over coffee in the morning. What do you mean a city can't have a star sign?

We asked Rottingdean's Jessica Adams, astrologer for Australian Vogue and psychic for UK Cosmopolitan, to draw up Brighton and Hove's chart for us to see just what and who makes this city tick.

Now, in order to do a chart, you need a birthday, and Brighton and Hove, in imitable style, can claim a few. But indulge us here, and let's say that we'll deal with the city of Brighton and Hove with her big ideas and fancy double barreled name. "Born" on Thursday February 15 2001 with an announcement from The Queen proclaiming her brand new city status, Brighton and Hove is an Aquarian, an alternative, non-conformist with a lot more tricks up her sleeve than collapsing piers.

Brighton and Hove's Aquarian makes room for us all. Maybe that's why it's a welcoming bosom to alternative comedians and bands, to the kind of comedy clubs that attract international awards and a thriving Fringe now happily sharing a bed with the biggest Festival in the UK. Anyone can be anyone here.

According to Jessica, her Moon, Mars and Pluto in Sagittarius means that her arms are open to outsiders and foreigners, and with Jupiter and Neptune in trine aspect, she encourages people to come here to follow their big dreams. "The helpful, positive trine aspect means they get away with it too", says Jessica. No wonder then that it's a haven to relocators, one of the UK's most popular tourist destinations and a major foreign language centre.

Sagittarius rules universities – and we've got two, as well as The City College of Technology, and The Sussex Innovation Centre which was set up to offer budding graduate talent an opportunity to keep their ideas within the city.

Sagittarius also rules publishing. In a city of 250,000, we've got more than 30 publishing companies – and how many cities do you know with three guide books?

It's the Fire and Air signs – Aries, Gemini, Leo, Libra, Sagittarius and Aquarius itself – who get the most out Brighton and Hove. Norman Cook (Leo), Paul McCartney (Gemini), Zoe Ball (Sagittarius) and Chris Eubank (Leo) have all made happy homes here. Those who manage the message spookily also have the right credentials; The Editor of The Argus is a

Leo, star brother to the brains behind Luv magazine, Latest Homes and its previous incarnations, The Latest and The Punter. The editor of The Insight is an Aquarian, as is the public face of the city, the earring wearing and openly gay chief executive of the Council.

Even the publications which make the grade have been kissed by the stars; anyone would think that Cherie Blair had planned the launches of this is Brighton and Hove (Libra) and the newly styled Argus: born on January 26 2004, it's an Aquarian.

Those behind events such as Burning The Clocks, The Children's Parade, and Carnival Collective, are Leo and Libra respectively. Pride, August's most flamboyant gay bash is so Leo it makes the entire city roar with pleasure.

But look below the surface, said Jessica. Pluto, ruler of dark and mysterious Scorpio, has a strong presence – which means that Brighton's seedy underbelly is never going to go away. Quite right, too.

But if the earth and water signs don't get a look in, they're probably not the types to care and are far more likely to be found on the beach or in the clubs, getting on with life in this dream of a city. Like we said, anyone can be anyone here.

ARRIVALS AND DEPARTURES

BRIGHTON IS THE SEXIEST SIREN in the sea, and there's no more brilliant idea on a sunny day than to pack the boot and head off to the seaside for the weekend. But, even if the will is there, Brighton is not yet set up to deal with its enormous fan base, and you'll spoil a perfect trip home if you don't plan your journey. Just watch the faces on the hapless clubbers making their weary way home on a Sunday night up the gridlocked A23 to remind you of the wonders of the train and the coaches.

Brighton and Hove Council is busy planning a traffic free zone in the centre of the city, with Park and Ride schemes and a bus based rapid transit system along the coast road and through the main thoroughfares to stop the grid locks, and to allow our kids to breathe again. It's an ambitious project and involves a culture change; leaving your car on the junction of the A23 and A27 and taking the Park and Ride into town sounds all well and good. But consider dragging the sleeping kids out of their cosy car seats and getting them to stand in the rain at Waterhall or Braypool as the coach whizzes off into the distance filled with happy campers.

The powers-that-be know that most of us would have to be pulled kicking and screaming out of our cars, and would never haul our suitcases into a grotty old bus to begin our weekend of bliss. They want visitors' first impression of this swinging city to be glittering enough to bring them back again, so the coaches will have to be swanky and the service smooth enough to win us over. We'll be sped through Brighton's bus lanes, with traffic lights waving us through in pro-environment high tech splendour, and nose thumbing those who stubbornly refuse to leave the car at home. It'll take a while, with different political parties lobbying for and against the Park and Ride sites.

We've got links on our website www.juicyguides.co.uk to the train network so you can plan your journey, and if you're driving, use www.juicymapminder.co.uk.

TRAIN

National Rail enquiries: 08457 484950
www.nationalrail.co.uk
South Central customer service: 0870 830
South Central Disabled Assistance: 0845 123 7770
www.southcentraltrains.co.uk
Thameslink customer service: 0207 620 6333
Thameslink disabled: 0207 620 6376
www.thameslink.co.uk

PRICES

Day return arriving in London after 10am: £17. Tube included: £19.50 A weekly travelcard : £72 return or £83.50 including all Tube zones. Monthly travelcard: £276.50, or £320.70 inc the Tube pass. A yearly pass, allowing you to arrive in London before 10am is £2880 without tube, and £3340 with

COACH

The EasyJet of the coach industry, www. megabus.com now has a route between Brighton and London and is unbelievably cheap. Departs Pool Valley at 08.10 and arriving at 10.30 costing £3 and 15.25 arriving in London at 17.45 costing £1. National Express 08705 808080, www.gobycoach.com Day return tickets: £15. It takes two hours.

PLANES

Cabs to the airport (01273 581581). Single fare between £32.50 and £60 Coach to all airports: Jetlink (08705 808080, www.gobycoach.com) TraveLine (0870 6082608) for buses from Brighton across the country. Sky Leisure, based at Shoreham Airport (01273 464422) offers a myriad of treats from flying lessons to day or weekend trips, all pre-arranged. You can call at an hour's notice to book a flight anywhere in the UK and Northern Europe; a trip for one person to London costs £550 and takes half an hour. A family of four splashing out on a day out will have to pay around twice as much.

TAXIS

01273 204060; 747474; 205205 (Brighton) 01273 202020 (Hove) 01273 414141 (Portslade)

BUSES

£1.20, or £2.40 for an all day fare.
A pack of five-day passes costs £12, £13 for a weekly saver. Kids over six get to pay 10p for any journey with a free ID card and a ticket buying adult. All tickets from the Post Office, newsagents and One Stop Travel Shop at the Old Steine.

CYCLING

Contact Roger Simmons, the Council's walking and cycling officer (01273 292475) for information on routes.

FERRY

Newhaven to Dieppe Transmanche: 0800 917 1201. www. transmancheferries.com

SEACAT

Hoverspeed: 08705 240241 www.hoverspeed.com

History Past and Future

BRIGHTON AND HOVE IS A CITY OF OPPORTUNITY, full to bursting with new people, new ideas and new energy. From the students grafting and sweating at university to the endless stream of removal vans from London and beyond, it's a city which welcomes and thrives on new blood. But if you imagine that it's only in the past 10 years that it's been such a honeypot to out-of-towners you misunderstand where Brighton comes from.

Entrepreneurs have been seizing the day since the great storms of 1703 and 1705 when disaster struck and the lower town and most of the shore was destroyed. The population dropped to 2,000 until a gaggle of entrepreneurs spotted a golden opportunity to take advantage of the falling house prices and begin acquiring property. Sound familiar?

Where do you start when you're telling the story of a city that has had more facelifts than Michael Jackson? There's evidence of life in the Brighton & Hove area dating back before the last Ice Age (a flint axe was found by Black Rock). We could go back to the Neolithic settlers who set up shop on Whitehawk Hill. We could go back to the Romans or to the Saxon village of Bristelmestune. Or the 14th century village of Brighthelmston, when the town grew up around the burgeoning smuggling trade.

Probably though, the best place to start is back in 1750 when a Lewes doctor published a treatise in 1750 advocating the revitalising properties of sea-water bathing, Dr Richard Russell's snappily titled bestseller "De Tabe Glandulari Sive De Usa Aquae Marinae In Morbis Glandularum Dissertatio" - loosely translated as "come and relax. It'll do you good". Thus was born the trip to the seaside.

Brighton's reputation as a resort grew with the development of the Pavilion. The story began in 1783, when the Prince of Wales, the future King George IV, rented out the building when it was just a farmhouse. Four years later, architect Henry Holland extended

it, but it was between 1815 and 1822 that things really happened. George became Prince Regent in 1811 and instructed John Nash to enlarge the building and create the Indian style palace as we know it today. Nash was sacked for spending too much money, but Brighton's most famous icon was born. Decked out like a playboy's bordello, it became the place for aristocratic hangers-on and the Prince's arty entourage to spend their spare time.

Finished in 1821, George IV had little time to enjoy his playpen. He died in 1830, and the Palace was passed to his successor, William IV who in turn was succeeded by Queen Victoria who didn't share his love of Brighton. Victoria announced her intention to sell the Pavilion in 1846 and over the next two years stripped many of its contents. Fearing it would be demolished, the people of Brighton petitioned Parliament and the town acquired the Palace.

In 1841, the opening of the first London to Brighton train line made Brighton accessible to ordinary folk and day trips to the seaside took off. The first trains took one hour 45 minutes (it was supposed to only take 54 minutes but there were delays at Three Bridges...) and cost the equivalent of 40p for a second-class ticket.

In the 20th century Brighton cemented its reputation as the civic equivalent of someone you wouldn't want your daughter to marry, and the famous have flocked to Brighton, drawn by the attraction of a town that

believes in live and let live. Lilly Langtrey, the famous Edwardian actress and Edward VII's mistress, lived in Brunswick Square. Lewis Carroll wrote Alice Through The Looking Glass when he was living in Sussex Square, inspired by the vision of his protégé, Alice, wandering in its beautiful gardens and disappearing into the secret tunnel that runs from the lower gardens directly to the sea. Rudyard Kipling, lived in nearby Rottingdean and his house is now open to the public. Oscar Wilde and Bosey frolicked on the seafront. Max Wall was born in Kemp Town and there are whispers that a statue in his honour will soon be erected. Laurence Olivier lived in Royal Crescent. Ivor Novello and Noel Coward composed their music whilst staying at the Lanes Hotel in Kemp Town... You get the picture.

In the post-war years, Brighton became a byword for notoriety. From Graham Greene's book Brighton Rock (later a film with Richard Attenborough) to the infamous seafront clashes between the mods and rockers, Brighton was seen as slightly shabby and seedy. Not somewhere to take your mother. The violence reached a peak on the Whit weekend holiday of 1964 with the

only British city the Carry On film team ever went to? Manchester? Liverpool? With respect...

Maybe it's not so surprising. Most places grow because of industry or a strategic position. Brighton is a city that was reborn after a doctor declared that the waters had healing powers. The very reason people first came here was to feel good.

And then there's the Prince Regent who built the Royal Pavilion as a haven for his decadent mates and their wild parties. It's said that he secretly married his mistress, Mrs Fitzherbert here and tales abound of secret underground tunnels that ferried his lady friends to his boudoir. There was a tunnel for Mrs Fitzherbert that was so big she could travel to see him by horse and carriage.

Brighton's reputation as a living Parental Guidance sticker grew in the early years of the 20th century. Back in those days, if you wanted a divorce you had to prove that your other half had been having an affair. The common practice for couples wanting to take this route was to come to Brighton where friendly lawyers would not only 'arrange' for the husband to be caught in flagrante with a prostitute, but they'd also 'arrange' for the liaison to be witnessed. The origin of the dirty weekend?

In the post-war period, Brighton's slightly louche image made it a Mecca for homosexuals, a community which was still persecuted by law. In 1947, the annual Sussex Arts Ball started in the ballroom of The Aquarium and soon became a magnet for cross-dressers - including a flamboyant drag artist, Betty Lou, who

"Battle Of Brighton" - an event immortalised in Franc Roddam's 1979 film of The Who epic Quadrophenia.

Seedy. Shabby. Faded elegance. These words have forever been synonymous with Brighton. It's a curious aside, but interesting to note that when Thomas Read Kemp sold the land of his estates (now Sussex Square in Kemp Town), he built the facades beautifully but left the backs bare.

Like the set on a western film, it looks great from the outside but don't look beneath the surface. To stretch the metaphor, the architecture may dazzle, but behind the glitter there has always been the poor struggling to survive.

SEX AND THE CITY

It doesn't matter how many buildings get turned into "luxury New York style loft apartments". It doesn't matter how many chic restaurants and exclusive bars open. It doesn't even matter whether Brighton & Hove Albion get a proper stadium, Brighton will always be synonymous with - nudge-nudge, wink-wink - sex. A very particular type of sex. British sex. The sex of Donald McGill's seaside postcards. Listen, what was the

regularly stole the show.

These days the boutique hotels with their lovesexy rooms and exotic erotica might dress themselves up as chic and trendy, but really, are they anything more than a Donald McGill cartoon with better clothes?

THE WEST PIER

Ah, the West Pier. Talk programmes crackled with outrage, newspaper headlines spat their horror and Brighton stood by as the sea casually gulped down the heart of this 130-year-old, Grade 1-listed pier in the first winter storms of 2003. Then – and this is terrible luck – two fires hit the pier within a couple of months of each other. (The spiritual and the cynical might, for different reasons, surmise that someone or something doesn't want the West Pier to survive). That no-one has helped her up has become something of a symbol of the city's careless bureaucracy.

Back in 1866, The West Pier, designed by Eugenius Birch as a reflection of the Royal Pavilion, was simply a place to practice that popular Brighton pastime, the promenade, but soon grew to hold a theatre, a bandstand and a concert hall. Closed in 1975, it is now home to a thousand starlings that flock around it like vast swirling black clouds.

The saga of the West Pier in Brighton took what you'd think is bound to be its last twist in January 2004 when the Heritage Lottery Fund (HLF) made a shock decision to withdraw its multi-million pound promise to fund its restoration. Having pledged around £14m to restore the Grade 1 listed monument to its Twenties glories, HLF announced it was pulling the plug after requests for a further £5m by owners the West Pier Trust and developers St Modwens.

Maybe it's sad that The Pier will almost certainly die, but from death comes life and architects are using the opportunity to come up with a new look for Brighton and Hove. This fantastical AROS design would float while tethered to the seabed and respond

Plans include a 60m high viewing tower with a cable car running the 750m length - which means that we could get a horizontal London eye for Brighton. And it's environmentally friendly too; "We're currently developing structural concepts and material technologies" says Nick. "The massive potential energy available through tidal change will be harnessed and used to partially power the pier."

BLACK ROCK

Not so long ago, the bit of wasteland now used by sk8erboys and student film-makers was a stunning lido. Built in 1934-36 and designed by architect, David Edward in a popular modernist Deco style, it was not alone; lidos had became all the rage in the 30's, with Rottingdean and Saltdean also replacing the bathing huts. But it was short lived, and by the 1970s, most of the fun had been zapped from Brighton's spirit after a long period of cultural rape and pillage by the town's bosses.

to the changing tides. "Spaces would open and close as the tide rises and falls, just as beaches change size and shape" says Nick Readett-Bayley of AROS. The walkways would be a mix of commercial space, leisure facilities, water taxi transport interchange, impromptu performance spaces for busking, skate board ramps, windsurfing jetty and a man-made surfing beach. We'd be able to walk above, on and below the surface of the sea, and even live on it.

Black Rock is a natural sea-cliff, now isolated from the sea as a result of the Brighton Marina development. The cliff is unlike any other geological site in the country and cuts through an ancient fossilised coastline – showing the shore, a pebbly beach and cliff from some 200,000 years ago. It also yields fossil evidence of the mammoths and woolly rhinos that lived where Brighton

now stands

But the millennium is breathing life back into the seafront, and the plan to transform Black Rock into a palace of wood and glass housing an Olympic skating arena – as well as a second rink for the plebs – and seating up to 11,500 is due to be completed by 2007. At a cost of around £45 million, it will also be a new replacement for the hideous Brighton Centre with pop concerts, exhibitions, conferences and tournaments.

The building will be barely visible from the coast road and the roofline will be softened by planting, with species able to sustain the salty winds. Former Olympic skater and local resident, Robin Cousins, backed by his mates Torvill and Dean, is behind the plan. "Although the building will take up the entire area the council is offering" he says, "the seating area will be sunk below ground level". One of the other worries is traffic impact, and Park And Ride and special bus services from the station to the arena will be arranged for big events. Far more exciting is Cousins's idea for water taxis to bring visitors to Black Rock from Shoreham Harbour and Worthing.

Throw the new Black Rock into the mix with Aros' new pier, the revamped Marina with its smart skyscrapers, the Beautiful Stadium, a home finally for the Albion tucked into the hillside (although perilously close to our National Park) and Bilbao's architect, Frank Gehry's vision of the King Alfred with its 38 storey seafront building, stir in a little imagination at Shoreham Airport and we could have a world class city.

BRIGHTON AND HOVE ALBION

One day the Seagulls will have a proper ground. No disrespect to the Withdean Stadium which is lovely and all, but it's a little... how shall we say? Small. Falmer is where the ground should be and there are fab plans for a stadium there. All we need is Deputy Prime Minister John Prescott to say "Yes". By the time you read this it might be so. On April 9, all the 'interested parties' will have responded and the decision should be made. But it's a curious thing how often the word 'decision' is preceded by the word 'in'.

KING ALFRED

The King Alfred is one of those buildings that town planners have to be restrained from pulling down with their bare hands, which architects dream about on Caribbean beaches, and for which locals would lay down their life – borne not so much out of a love for the building but a fear of what might replace it. Maybe the local resistance to change at the Alfred is because this is

where Hove lives.

Generations of Sundays have been lazed away there and they're damned if some posh architects are going to get their hands on it. But life doesn't work like that, and the site of one of the first car washes – in the world, ever – will become the city's showpiece after next year.

Four futuristic towers will be beamed into Brighton and Hove, housing a modern sports centre costing between £25 million and £30 million and funded by 400 flats. Council policy now insists that 40 per cent of the homes would be aimed at key workers or people from the housing waiting list, while the executive pads would pay most of the bill.

CITY TOURISM – THE GRAND PLAN

This new city of Brighton and Hove is now so grown up that it even has a 10-year plan to maximise the benefits of tourism. The Big Idea is to create the Britain's premier cultural capital, attracting conferences and tourism. If it all goes to plan, it should increase the 13,000 currently employed in tourism by 12,000 and inject £200 million a year into local economy.

Blue Flag beaches, cleaner streets (although how the Council intends to bring the seagulls on message is a question) and a balanced evening and night time economy are on the cards. Crucially, we need a better transport system (see the Arrivals and Departures chapter), and the rapid transport link along the seafront and main arteries of the city would reduce the traffic gridlock significantly.

Safety is already improving, especially in the clubs. Only Brighton's police force could have thought of something as left-field as Operation Marble, which has been in force in the city centre and seafront clubs since May 2003 and has already brought clubbers to heel. Its formula for success? The idea that these anti-social hooligans need little more than a bit of bedtime TLC, a lullaby and a lollipop. No, really... a combination of providing food in the clubs to fill their tummies, childhood music to call time, and a lolly as they leave the premises to keep them from their natural inclination to head-butt their neighbour, seems to have done the trick.

It all bodes well; by 2014 Brighton and Hove should have dusted off her disasters and retained her sparkly best, no longer luring her visitors with a siren's song but graciously meeting them at the door. There'll be plenty of cranes around the spoil the view until then, but look at where she's come from in the last 300 years and believe that when the bandages come off, Brighton and Hove will still be the most glamorous seaside landlady of them all.

A WALK ABOUT TOWN

THE LANES

Brighton's beating heart, a warren of narrow streets and piazzas alive with colour, music, jugglers and street performers all year round. The Lanes is what many tourists think of as the city-by-the-sea, and leave The Lanes only to try their luck on The Pier and suck some candy floss on the beach. In many ways, they're right. In fact the earliest map of Brighton shows a little town about one quarter of a mile square bordered by North Street, West Street, East Street and South Street, the main boundaries these days of The Lanes. Well, apart from South Street which is under the sea.

With the original fishermen's cottages framing it

on the seafront, The Lanes was where life happened. Allotments grew hemp for the fishermen's nets, and the original Lanes started as pathways between them, with Middle Street becoming its centre in 1500. The first theatre in the town opened in North Street in the 1770's, Brighton's second free school opened in Duke Street in 1779, and The Assembly Rooms, scene of the first Juicy Awards in 2000, was built in Ship Street in what is now The Old Ship Hotel.

These days, there's a happy balance between old and new, with some of the most gorgeous shops in town joshing for space in buildings desperate to tell their stories. If you want to hear them, track down Glenda Clarke whose tours of the spookier side of life have been entertaining locals and tourists for years. (info@brightonwalks.com 01273 888596)

Way before The Lanes was a pleasuredome of chic living and designer shopping, it was the playground for the court of The Prince Regent which had packed its bathers and set up seaside home in a new palace fit for a king. Even the French aristocracy fleeing the Revolution found their spiritual home here as debutantes and English society built their summers in Brighton into The Season.

More Zadie Smith than Emily Bronte these days, it's a mix of homeless drug addicts and designer shopping, alfresco café society and buzzing tourism, although the ghosts of Brighton still lurk. Watch out for the famous twittens, the tiny little allies squeezing between ancient buildings that suck in unsuspecting tourists and spit them out where they least expect. Be particularly careful of the twitten running from outside The Cricketers pub, itself aching in history, that will deposit you at the door of She Said, the erotic lingerie shop in Ship Street Gardens.

for everything from designer kitchen ware to student garb, antiques to collectible comics, only finding time to stop when you stumble across any one of the excellent cafes and bars along the way. Its recent reinvention as a major leisure activity has hit the smaller shopkeepers badly, with more visitors inclined to spend their cash on a latte than a posh watering can. With cafes perched over shoppers' heads, this is a laid back, people watching kind of Brighton, although by the beginning of December, you can't move through the fake fur and biker boots as London tips into The North Laine to do its Christmas shopping preferring the city's compact selection of top notch bargains to the hustle and bustle of Christmas in the Capital.

KEMP TOWN

Set off the seafront between Brighton Pier and The Marina are the streets of St James and St George, with their retail therapy and gay discos, high class delis and European style cafes. The gay capital of the city, this is where trannies and grannies shop happily together in the most bizarre Safeway in the country and where the boutique hotels vie with each other for most decadent welcome in town.

For many visitors, Kemp Town is their first eyeful of Brighton and Hove. Many of the local boutique hotels have sharpened up their act to compete with Blanch House and with the seafront a hop and skip from their bow fronted windows, Kemp Town is becoming the city's finest advertisement for this arty tarty glamourpuss of a city.

SEASIDE

The seafront, the peeling balustrades stretching back from the Brighton Pier against the shimmering whiteness of the Regency squares on Marine Parade, the Volks railway, deckchairs, pebbles and naturist beach give off the mixed signal of decadence and decay, which is Brighton's charm. The fish and chip bars on Madeira Drive are a glitch in the council's plan to create a San Francisco in Sussex, but somehow a perfect reminder of what British seaside towns should be about. In a city where the best summer clubbing

THE NORTH LAINE

Sitting on the North of Brighton's central arts venues, The Theatre Royal, The Dome, Brighton Museum and Art Gallery, The North Laine less touristy than The Lanes, more a honeypot to creatives. As much as the sea and the piers, The North Laine is the spirit of Brighton. From hippy, dippy, grunge gear, to post-modern garden equipment, you can get it here, and if you want it in pink day-glo fake fur, all the better. Sit in any one of the chic cafes or bars and watch the world go by; it's better than anything you'll see on telly.

This is where you'll find one of Brighton's artiest residential communities, although it's more trashy Camden than leafy Belgravia. Unlike the older, more traditional Lanes, The North Laine avoids twittens and hidden squares and goes for the straight lines of Bond Street, Gardner Street, Kensington Gardens and Sydney Street, making shopping a breeze. It's even car free at the weekend.

You can spend all day in The North Laine, shopping

tips straight out on to the beach at dawn, caffs like The Madeira Café also provide an important service: breakfast starts from 3am. It even does a vegetarian breakfast in this veggie capital of the UK.

There are clubs and pubs, cafes and bars, stalls selling rings and books and sarongs. There's basketball, a kiddies playground with paddling pool, bungee jumping, crazy golf and a Mary Poppins carousel. If you can't find something here, I'd go and see a doctor and get them to check your pulse, see if you're still alive. For a great way to take in the seafront, hire a bike and head down the cycle track to Rottingdean. You can hire bikes from Sunshine Bicycles (under the corpse of the West Pier) - £3 for one hour, £5 for two, £8 for four, £12 all day. You'll need £20 deposit and some ID. They do family bikes with all the seats and buggies and things. If rollerblading's more your game, you can hire them from Pulse (23 King's Road Arches, just

underneath Alfresco - 01273 720788) - £3.50 an hour, £5 for two hours or £10 all day.

BRIGHTON PIER

It's the joy of Brighton that you can go from a chic café to the tacky pier in just a few steps. One minute you can be sipping an espresso discussing that arty something you saw last night at The Duke Of York's, the next minute you're rolling balls in the Dolphin Derby desperate to win a fluffy alien key ring.

The Brighton Pier with its palm readers (invariably out to lunch) and candy floss and fudge (don't do it. It doesn't matter how much the little ones bawl, don't do it) has mercifully enclosed its brain-shattering arcade in a noise-proof bubble, leaving you free to wander out to sea, or take a quick ride on the Waltzer or the trampoline that can be found in a cage on the edge of the pier before stopping for lunch at the fish and chip restaurant standing grandly in the middle of the Pier with its offer of a glass of champagne to accompany your mushy peas.

BETWEEN THE PIERS

The row surrounding the West Pier's use of lottery money which finally led to its untimely demise last year (see History chapter) didn't extend to the beach between the piers where it was used efficiently to transform what was a rather tacky line of fish and chip booths into an alfresco pleasure dome.

From the Mary Poppins carousel to the children's playground beyond the West Pier, the seafront has enough to keep the kids happy, while a stretch of cafés serves the grown-ups. The sandy volleyball court gives the girls and boys something to watch as the sun goes down, and the town's best clubs, The Beach, The Zap and the Honey Club entertain sun-drunk, pre-clubbers on terraces leading out to the sea. Even the hippies have got wise, and in high summer the beach is lined with stalls selling Thai trousers, sarongs, ankle bracelets and fruit stalls. If the beach were sandy, we could be in Goa.

THE PEACE STATUE AND HOVE LAWNS

Heading west away from Brighton Pier, past where the boys play basketball (more Venice Beach than hippy India), past the West Pier, life on the beachfront gets

a style makeover. The manicured Hove Lawns stretch out for young lads with their footballs while the less energetic get out their summer picnic hampers. Evening rollerbladers glide towards the Peace Statue - an angel which smiles down at the mini-shorts and crop tops - and an air of tranquillity really does seem to descend. The breathtaking architecture of Brunswick and Palmeira Squares leaves the showy, gaudy anomalies of Brighton's seafront like the Brighton Centre and the tacky eateries paling into insignificance. It all looks impossibly grand, the sort of place where time moves slowly, where if there's a by-law it should be about constant sunshine.

HOVE BEACH

A promenade along Hove Beach is a see and be seen stroll-zone past the multi-coloured beach huts (which you can rent for the summer. Ask us via www. juicymapminder.co.uk; far too much of a secret to publish to the nation). From The King Alfred and a brief stop at Marrocco's Ice Cream Parlour, mosey down past the boats and the fish shop on the beach to The Babylon Lounge, a bright blue blotch on the landscape which is both an oasis – a bar right on the beach where you can have a cool beer while the kids frolic – and a disappointment because, frankly, it could be so much nicer. Much more fun is Babylon Lounge's weekend alter-ego – the home of that hen night frenzy, the Adonis

Cabaret. Tristan flashes what the Sun newspaper prizes as "The Rear of The Year" (and much much more), and Richard plays a canvas piano with his waggling willy while the hens cackle with delight.

The other new development that's raised Hove's profile is the increased popularity of water sports, like kiteboarding. Go behind the King Alfred Centre when the wind's up and there they are, slightly mad types, all dressed up and flying through the air. And if they're not somewhere up in the sky, more than likely they'll be in The Alibi pub talking about the thermal that got away.

THE FISHING MUSEUM

The Fishing Museum celebrates what Brighton used to be (and still is to the tiny minority of fishermen). The museum strews its fishing nets and boats across the beach in a bid to catch the tourist trade if the cod is less willing. The fish shop next door sells fish straight off the boats (Rick Stein swears by it), while another sells smoked fish which it will sandwich up for you if you fancy eating it right then and there. Look out for the Blessing of the Nets as part of the Brighton Festival in May (see The Season chapter) when the first mackerel catch is barbecued and sold to a salivating crowd. If you fancy hiring a fishing boat, ask at the museum for a list of skippers who are willing to take you out.

BLACK ROCK

East beyond the buzz of the beaches between the piers the mood changes. The cosmopolitan feel gives way to something much more rooted in Old England. The harsh would call it shabby; the romantic would say it's a throwback to the days of Donald McGill postcards and Carry On films. Here, it's a universe away from ideas like City Of Culture and any pretensions of Eurochic. Even in the height of summer there are less people here than anywhere else on the beach. The pitch and putt and new children's playground provide a quieter amusement away from the Pier and are largely aimed at younger children. Planet Cycle and various kayaking shops hire out bikes and boats.

But things are changing for what even Kemp Towners don't yet call Kemp Town Beach. Duke's Mound, the once dirty scrubland that tried to keep itself respectable with its climbing plants and bushes,

but is more of a cruising haven for the local gay community, has been scalped, and the shelter is up for a different kind of rent these days. Plans are to turn it into a smart café and several bids are being considered as we go to press.

Black Rock, the wasteland serving as a coach and car park at the end of the beach, originally marked the boundary of Brighton, although the Marina now lies beyond it and calls itself part of the city. Back in the Thirties it was the site of an open-air swimming pool built on the site of a terrace garden, but it closed in 1978 and only now has its redevelopment been put out to tender. In a rather bizarre move, the UK's skating fraternity have finally won their 40-year battle to persuade the Council to build an ice-skating centre on Black Rock. Former ice skating champion and local resident Robin Cousins, has taken up their baton and backed the bid for the double rinked centre, with one rink for professionals and the other for a wobbly Brighton public.

And where there's a public, there'll be a café or two, and before you know it, this stretch of unfulfilled potential will link arms with one of Brighton's best clubs, Concorde 2. Apart from the very fine Volks Tavern (see Clubs for details), until the new development reinvents this part of town, it's the only reason why anyone would go down by night unless you're going to sit on the beach and look at the stars.

THE NATURIST BEACH

The Naturist Beach at Kemp Town is awash with deep-sea swimmers, kayakers and naked bodies (mostly men) throughout the year. As soon as the sun shines, they're out, making a stroll on a balmy February afternoon a surreal experience. Brightonians turn the other cheek as naked men parade their wares, sometimes a little too close for comfort, but those of a nervous disposition should stay well away. The built-up shingle is a thoughtful gesture by the Council to shelter the naturists from the stares.

THE MARINA

Beyond the meditative fishermen lined up on the sea wall lies the extraordinary expanse of Brighton's Marina, a world unto itself that looks like something out of The Prisoner, a south coast Portmerion of almost spooky box-like conformity where nothing is quite as it seems.

What you actually find are million-pound Princess yachts and their owners, young business folk doing deals over dinner at Café Paradiso, The Seattle Hotel's rather lovely waterfront fine dining experience, a floating Chinese restaurant with roof tiles shipped all the way from China and McDonalds. A new collection of chain restaurants has stretched lazily along the boardwalk, including Pizza Express, while the new bars Ebony Room and Karma glitter with stilettos and champagne glasses and a perma-tanned clientele waiting for those yachts to come in.

An enormous bowling alley is packed by day and night with Whitehawkers and children's parties, a swanky David Lloyd health club with café/bar looking out to sea attracts the young and beautiful, an eight-screen Virgin cinema complex pulls in all the locals, and a casino for the property tycoons and their molls. The huge Asda superstore is Cate Blanchett's local while out of towners prefer the collection of designer factory outlet shops that make up the town square. On a Saturday night, you can't get near the great new Indian restaurant, Memories of India as the fashion junkies celebrate their bargains before a night at the Casino.

For seagoing folk, The Marina offers much more (Marina enquiries: 01273 819919). For those popping in from Barbados en route to France, there's a boatyard, with a 60-ton travel hoist and separate crane to deal with those essential repairs, as well as storage facilities, direct sea access and berthing for 1,300 craft. There's also a launderette, showers and washrooms for berth-holders and 24-hour security, which covers the Barrett complex. Apparently in its 21-year history there's never been a single burglary.

If you want to charter a boat for anything from a stag or hen party to a wedding, corporate do or ash scattering, Mike Snelling (07973 386379 or 01273 307700) is a local skipper who will put you in touch with charter-

licensed boat owners. Some of the boats are wheelchair-friendly too. He's also the man to call if it's a beautiful evening and you fancy a trip out to sea to watch the sun set. During the festival, you can take a trip from the West Quay at 6pm every night (6pm and 7.15pm on weekends) for £12. Book at the Dome Box Office (01273 709709).

The average price of hiring a boat is £40 per hour, but as it's just a matter of chatting to the boat owners, it's all open to negotiation. Each boat can take up to 12 people, and some skippers are happy to do a last-minute, four-hour trip up and down the coast on a nice evening for about £150, provided they haven't got anything on. Mike warns that if you want to book a boat for the day in mid-July, you'll have to book six months ahead, but if you fancy a sunset trip in February, five minutes notice will probably be enough! Of course, you can always splash out on your own Princess Yacht, or pop down to the harbour to dream; the Marina is home to the largest sales office in the UK. Prices range from £140,000 to more than £1million.

THE SEASON

Visit www.jucymapminder.co.uk for the latest information and reviews of the Season's festival.

MAY

THE FESTIVAL

How exciting is it to live in a city which wakes up in spring like some doe-eyed, long-limbed teenager after a night on the town, and emerges into the sunlight, sparkling with the knowledge that it's the most beautiful of all seaside towns? Spring comes early to Brighton - you can feel it on the seafront from the first sniff when the shops and cafes start to tart themselves up, and smug locals sip their hot chocolates, leaf through the Festival brochure and consider how lovely their lives are. Even the restaurants throw their tables onto the streets to get a better view.

England's largest arts extravaganza and a carnival to match the likes of the Edinburgh Festival, the Brighton Festival kicks off on May 1 when 71 of its 83 schools parade through the North Laine and The Lanes to the beach. This year the theme is Children's Classics (although Harry Potter is forbidden) and, as we went to press, school offices across the city were piled high with cardboard, sequins and PVA glue. By May 1, those Go Cat and Honey Nut Loops boxes will have become giants' shoes and gingerbread houses, while the sequins will be dressing the city's teenagers as they sashay their way through the streets to the backbeat of their school samba band.

Now in its 38th year, the Festival runs through to May 23 with more than 700 performances, high-tech multi-media performances in dance and theatre and live world music and jazz, pulling crowds of over 300,000 from in and out of town.

Among the music giants on the programme this year... New local resident Nick Cave heads a concert in recognition of Leonard Cohen, and Asian Dub Foundation accompany Battle of Algiers, the controversial Sixties film about urban guerrillas with their live score - a world first. Dance and drama comes in every form from Teatro Kismet at The Gardner to the hip-hop musical Slamdunk at The Theatre Royal and Liz Agiss's dance installation at The University of Brighton Gallery.

The Book Festival is packed with the biggest names in the literary world with afternoon and evening debates across town and into Charleston Farmhouse down the road near Firle. Jo Brand examines the art of Comedy and Writing with Jeff Green, Sean Hughes and Owen O'Neill. Ragah Omaar (BBC Iraq war correspondent) discusses Politics in Writing and Harold Pinter examines Freedom and Independence.

The second weekend (May 7/8) is the Streets of Brighton, the festival's regular appointment with over 200 international performers throughout the daylight hours. In the evening, four major productions bring a heady mix of cranes, live music and serial performance

to town, with the entire community coming out onto the streets to watch. It's worth keeping the kids up for this; last year's Bollywood extravaganza had a life-size steel elephant leading the procession of Indian dancers.

Even Whitehawk takes to its own streets this year with its own version of the Spanish pyrotechnic spectacular, Las Fallas. Giant papier mache statues will be parading through the estate before the effigies are set alight in a huge firework display in East Brighton Park on the Saturday evening.

On Sunday May 16, the Dieppe Market comes to Bartholomew Square selling French produce, and Brighton goes back to its roots as the first mackerel catch of the season is paraded on the beach for a massive lunchtime barbecue outside the fishing museum.

The Blessing Of The Nets, an old Pagan custom, is little more than an excuse for a party for the local fishermen and their families, but this year will again revive the Christian interpretation with a blessing of the catch by Brighton's community vicar. Brighton's and Dieppe's mayors join in with the sea shanties, hymns

and readings, and as the mackerel is thrown on to the barbecue, a Punch and Judy show reminds us of what the seaside is all about.

Throughout the Festival, Cottle and Austin's Circus Festival will be entertaining children and adults in Preston Park. The unlikely venue of Brighton Marina plays host to the grand finale – The Big Splash, a mix of street arts, theatre, music, dance and comedy, Carnival Collective, Brighton's voluntary community samba organisation gets things going with an infectious stomp, bringing leading bands from the UK and Europe

in the second Samba Encounter in a mass procession along the seafront. More details are available on www. brighton-festival.org.uk

GLYNDEBOURNE

For opera fans, Glyndebourne offers its theatre space for the Festival line-up. Glyndebourne itself is only open during the summer, with its own festival running from May 20 to August 29, and it's a fabulous sight to see the succession of DJs, evening dresses and picnic hampers all heading through the gates of the

real world - in his own home. The aim was that visitors could have a chat while they gazed over a glass of wine, and have the chance to be a sociable human in a warm home rather than some isolated being in a cold gallery.

Across town, other groups copied Ned's idea and it has now become the biggest show of contemporary art in the south east, attracting 15,000 visitors, international art collectors and critics. This year, more than 200 homes across Brighton and Hove will be exhibiting paintings, stained glass, sculptures, ceramics, photography and furniture. Everything's for sale and it's great fun, whether you want to buy, chat, or just have the opportunity to nose around other people's homes. Check the routes on www.juicymapminder.co.uk and to plan where to meet your mates for lunch along the way.

CHARLESTON

The Charleston Literary Festival rounds off the springtime feast of culture with a host of luvvies discussing their oeuvres in the grounds where Vanessa Bell hung out with her sister Virginia Woolf and their Bloomsbury chums. Charleston is a treat of a literary festival, not least because of its extraordinary setting. The garden is one of the gems that stud the Sussex landscape and much of the festival takes place in a marquee on its lawns. Visitors are encouraged to take tea in the grounds and breathe in the spirit of an era that still lives on in the farmhouse's museum. This year it runs from May 15-23: Clive James and Joan Bakewell discuss their memoirs, Jeanette Winterson discusses new work with Graham Swift, and Christopher Ondaatje and Caroline Moorehead explore the relationship between Martha Gellhorn and Earnest Hemingway.

Glyndebourne Estate on a hot summer's day. Call 01273 812321 for more information.

OPEN HOUSES

If you're one of those people who feel stifled and put off by the oppressive silence of art galleries, but still like to gaze wistfully at other people's creations, this is for you. The Open House season is a unique idea peculiar to Brighton, which has grown and grown over the past 20 years. Local artist Ned Hoskins had the bright idea to exhibit what his work looked like in the

Open from April to October, Charleston itself houses the astonishing collection of artworks that Vanessa Bell and Duncan Grant, her lifelong partner, amassed throughout their lives. Look out for Gouache table tops, experimental painting on the backs of doors and picnic plates, Picassos and Matisses abandoned in dark halls, and some of the first post-Impressionist work casually scattered throughout the house, illustrating the spontaneous creativity, which characterised their lives.

This summer Charleston will be running a series of four workshops for children and young people in art, poetry and filmmaking, which include Breaking the Boundaries (July 3), Secrets and Lies (August 3), Hung Out to Dry (August 24) and Making Moves (August 31). Contact Charleston on: 01323 811265 for more information or check out their website www. charleston.org.uk

BRIGHTON FRINGE

The Fringe , now The Brighton Festival Fringe, is back side by side, if only in space and time, as the Brighton Festival. It seems only yesterday that the dastardly Dome was flexing its triceps and blocking the feeble Fringe from even using its own name. Don't you just love local politics and egos? But at Christmas drinks last year, they all stood hand in hand to tell the world their war is over. This year, the arrival of a Spiegeltent, a travelling dance hall of the 1920's and 1930's with mirrored pavilions and a glorious past, allows the Fringe a prominent and glamorous space in Pavilion Gardens, and doubles up as the Festival Club by night for anyone who buys a ticket to any show.

RALLIES

Every weekend sees some sort of rally along Brighton's popular Madeira Drive, from time trials for exciting sports cars to the Beetle maniac and the Mini obsessive parading their motors, through to the simply odd, like the rally for the 50th anniversary of the coach-spotters on April 17-18. Most famously, there's the London to Brighton Bike Ride (June 20) and the RAC Veteran Car Run (November 7) which inspired the 1950's classic film Genevieve.

The Pioneer Motorcycle Run (March 21), the Morris Minors (April 4), the Jaguar Car Run (April 25), the Historic Commercial Vehicle Rally (May 2), the MG Regency Run (May 9), the Mini Owners' Rally (May 16), National Speed Trials (September 11) all tickle different fancies.

JUNE

THE FOOD FESTIVAL
June 10th-20th

Last year, The Food and Drink Lovers Festival didn't quite manage to capture the attention it deserved despite the battle of the bars, the cook-offs between all three Tin Drum chefs, and Loch Fyne's oyster tasting on the beach. If our postbag is anything to go by, people in this town really are interested in finding out the best places to eat and drink, but want to smell it on the streets, have treats dangled and secrets whispered. Pulling the best finds out and putting a flag over their roofs, tempting tourists off the beaten track and piling up the column inches is all good for the big picture, and so we're right behind it in its second year.

THE PEACE FESTIVAL

Still waiting to be confirmed as we went to press was this year's Peace Festival in June, a small-scale cross between Womad and Glastonbury and all in our own front yard, with enough tents full of kid's activities, live bands and things to do to keep you thinking about Peace all day long. Again, check www.juicymapminder.co.uk for more updated details nearer the time.

PARTY IN THE PARK 2003

Southern FM's pop extravaganza is on June 27 this year from 12noon to 4pm. It is a ticketed event and though tickets are free you have to listen to Southern FM to find out how to get them. It attracts around 60,000 people to Preston Park to hear this year's pop poppets mime to their latest hit.

JULY

STELLA MOVIE CLASSICS

On July 23 & 24, the beach fills as those very nice people at Stella Artois erect an enormous screen, hand out the bevvies and show a few thousand people a couple of very cool movies as the sun sets past what's left of the West Pier. Of course you can't hear a word, but that's really not the point; it'll make you weep to be part of such a chilled community.

EUROPEAN BEACH SOCCER CUP

Over 400 tons of sand is brought onto Brighton beach to create a playing surface for the best of Europe's pro beach soccer league including Portugal, France and Italy. A purpose built, 3,000 seat stadium will play host to the Kronenbourg Cup between July 30 and August 1.

THE BIG BEACH BOUTIQUE

Plans come and go – as we were writing this, the Boutique was on... no, it's off... no, it's on... The latest is that it's off, but we'll see. It would be a mighty shame. Last year's event was (despite what you might have read in the press) a largely fantastic night. Especially when you consider the number of people there and the lack of organisation. The plans include ticketing the event and keeping it open only to those with BN postcodes. There was a Big Beach Boutique event in Rio earlier this year which was hugely successful – and if they can do it properly in Rio with no problems, Brighton should be a breeze.

AUGUST

PRIDE 2004

On 7th August, just after the Gay and Lesbian Film Festival at the Duke of York's, Brighton and Hove celebrates its title as Britain's Pink Capital. 10,000 of the town's most flamboyant residents and fans parade from the seafront through the town centre to Preston Park in August. Pink in the Park is where the floats come to rest, offering seven hours of dance, champagne, performances, as well as funfairs and market stalls. The theme for the 2004 parade will be "The Hit Parade".

OCTOBER

THE JEWISH FILM FESTIVAL

The only UK 'you don't have to be Jewish' Jewish Film Festival (www.bjewish-filmfest.org.uk) is an annual event held in late October for two weeks at The Duke of York's Cinema at Preston Circus, the intimate Cinematheque at the Brighton Media Centre and other venues around town. Feature films, documentaries and short films combine to create a programme of films with themes that relate to the humour, the laughter and the tears that make up Jewish life in all its many guises and disguises throughout the world.

NOVEMBER

BRIGHTON FESTIVAL OF JEWISH MUSIC

Held from November 10-16, this will only be the second Festival of Jewish Music held in Brighton aiming to unite a wide audience in celebration of traditional and contemporary Jewish music.

LEWES FIREWORKS

It must be something in the Sussex air, but the wild party spirit spreads even to the gentle suburban town of Lewes - once a year anyway. Lewes has an underbelly still gurgling with the dissension of its Pagan days and violent history. On November 5, unhealed memories of religious persecution and war are ripped open to fuel a fire that burns throughout the town in a terrifying display of tar barrel races and pyrotechnics. Effigies are even erected and burnt at the stake. Everyone goes to Lewes on Bonfire night so if big crowds in small spaces make you feel uncomfortable, steer clear. Street crime is also a problem, so we recommend a picnic high on the hill above the town where you can watch the entire proceedings in safety, or wait until the following weekend and take the kids to see the tamed-down version of the same procession in the neighbouring East Hoadley.

DECEMBER

BURNING THE CLOCKS

Local street artists, Same Sky, who are behind anything large and made of papier mache in this city, celebrate the Winter Solstice by leading the thousands of locals and visitors and their giant clock lanterns through the Old Steine to the beach for the Burning the Clocks. A firework display follows the burning of the beautiful clocks in a huge funeral pyre on the beach.

NEW YEAR'S EVE

The Old Steine becomes the focus for Brighton and Hove to get truly soppy about how lovely life is down here. Early evening sees an enormous family-friendly crowd gather to watch bands on the stages at the Old Steine and Victoria Gardens, as fire-eaters, jugglers and a wild variety of street artists crank up the euphoria gauge before the fireworks welcome in the New Year.

SKATING

As autumn freezes over into the bleak mid-winter, Brighton gets its skates on and heads off to the Brighton Centre. Thanks to a brainwave by ex-skating champ and Lewes Crescent resident, Robin Cousins, the centre is now iced over every December until Holiday on Ice takes over in January, and a city full of mums, dads, wobbly six-year-olds and Wild Fruit transvestites groove to Kylie in a truly Brighton mood.

HOTELS

Alvia Hotel

36 Upper Rock Gardens, Kemp Town, Brighton BN2 1QF
T: 01273 682939
F: 01273 626287
www.alviahotel.co.uk
enquiries@alviahotel.co.uk
Rooms: 12

Notable because of the friendly owners and the stylish but simple décor, The Alvia is one of the many guest houses in Kemp Town which are close to the main action. There's Internet access for business travellers, and champagne and chocolates for the romantic weekenders, with options on breakfast time (within reason). Prices range from £20 for a standard single to £150 for a family suite with patio. The four-poster double king size costs between £70 and £120 depending on season.

Blanch House

17 Atlingworth St, Kemp Town, Brighton BN2 1PL
T: 01273 603504 F: 01273 689813
www.blanchhouse.co.uk
info@blanchhouse.co.uk
Rooms: 12

Star of the Sunday Travel pages, and nominated for the sexiest hotel at The Juicy Awards, this is the hotel of hedonism. Sip complimentary champagne in a Victorian free standing bath in the Perrier Jouet suite (£250 including free bottle of PJ), dream of far away lands in the Morocco (£150) or lie back in the India room (£125). Each room is en-suite with Trevi power showers and Molton Brown toiletries. The rooms also include: hand-made Belgian chocolates, Fogarty goose and duck down duvets and pillows, Reylon beds, hairdryers, telephones, Blanch House mineral water and coffee and tea making facilities. All rooms have sound systems and video televisions. On-site reflexology and late breakfasts for night birds (for an extra tenner), sumptuous restaurant and the coolest bar in town all add up to a treat of treats. Co-owner Chris Edwards is a legendary cocktail meister (The Groucho, The Pharmacy, The Jazz Café, The Atlantic...) and if he can't sort you out, call A&E. The stair carpets may be a bit shabby, some of the rooms may be on the small side and the ambience can be charmingly chaotic, but this is an original and genuinely Bohemian refuge from the corporate nightmare of hotel-land. There are plans afoot for a Blanch House in Granada. Rates: £125 to £250.

Brighton Pavilions

7 Charlotte St, Kemp Town, Brighton BN2 1AG
T: 01273 621750
F: 01273 622477
www.brightonpavilions.com
sanchez-crespo@lineone.net
Rooms: 12
Closed from Jan 12th-Feb 9th

Phil and Ken have been here for five years and have designed all the gorgeous, individual rooms themselves. The Titanic Pavilion is inspired by the ill-fated ship and decorated in rich blue with a mahogany four poster, while The Garbo Pavilion is where Greta herself smiles from behind glass at the elegant Art Deco surrounds. Prices range from £45 for a single to £100 for a Luxury Double, which includes a bottle of bubbly, fluffy bathrobes, flowers and full room service. The hotel is strictly non-smoking and there is a very pleasant breakfast room with patio which is a suntrap in the summer.

Cavalaire Hotel

34 Upper Rock Gardens, Brighton BN2 1QF
T: 01273 696899
F: 01273 600504
www.cavalaire.co.uk
cavalaire.hotel@virgin.net
Rooms: 11

The Cavalaire has always been one of Juicy's favourites, and the very camp and bubbly, Derek Jermey who took over last year, has kept it modern and ready for fun. It's still a non-smoking establishment, and all the rooms have en suite facilities. Breakfast is inclusive and prices range from £30 and £145 for a room with four beds.

Colson House

17 Upper Rock Gardens, Kemp Town, Brighton BN2 12E
T: 01273 694922

partner. But the single rooms are just as gorgeous, and with a pledge on the front door to offer you an unforgettable 'breakfast experience' this really is a treat. Prices range from £45 for a single to £140 for the super deluxe including breakfast.

Drakes

43-44 Marine Parade, Brighton
BN2 1PE. T: 01273 696934
www.drakesofbrighton.com
info@drakesofbrighton.com
Rooms: 20

New boutique hotel on the Kemp Town seafront, with a restaurant run by the people behind The Gingerman. It wasn't open as we went to press so let us know what you think online at www.juicymapminder.co.uk

Genevieve Hotel

18 Madeira Place, Brighton
BN2 1TN. T: 01273 681653
www.genevievehotel.co.uk
info@genevievehotel.co.uk
Rooms: 11

Big beds are the hallmark of the recently refurbished Regency Grade II listed Genevieve, namesake of one of Brighton's most romantic films, with luxury four-poster beds and a super king-size bed from £80. The hotel is now non-smoking and continental and veggie breakfasts are available. Rates: Singles from £45, doubles £55-£95 for a luxury four-poster room.

www.colsonhouse.com
info@colsonhouse.com
Rooms: 8

Re-made and re-modelled, one of the nicest, hotels in town. Clean, airy, spacious, and perfectly co-ordinated. This modern, gay-friendly hotel offers a great location near to the sea with welcoming young proprietors. Rates: £60 including breakfast.

Dove Hotel

18 Regency Square, Brighton
BN1 2FG. T: 01273 779222
F: 01273 746912

www.thedovehotel.co.uk
dovehotel@dovehotel.free-online.co.uk
Rooms: 9

The Dove has recently been taken over by new owners who have big plans to improve things. They really needn't do too much; the rooms are simply but beautifully decorated, and the whole place has an air of elegant, friendly charm. The super deluxe room is truly stunning with a kind of bed that could tear you away from all the sights that Brighton has to offer – if shared with the right

The Grand

Kings Rd, Brighton BN1 2FW
T: 01273 224300 F: 01273
224321
www.grandbrighton.co.uk
reservations@grandbrighton.
co.uk
Jan-Dec, 24 hours a day. After
9:00pm lounge only open to
residents. Rooms: 200

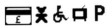

Every film or TV series that is worth
watching has a chase scene, a
balcony-dangling scene or just a bus
going past the front of the building'
scene that shows The Grand. It is
an impressively ornate building
which has housed more presidents
than The White House, more Prime
Ministers than Number 10, and more
celebrities than The Priory, but that's
made it a bit of a fat cat over the
years. It may be undergoing a facelift
at the moment, but while the rest of
Brighton has been sourcing antique
four posters, Oriental and Moroccan
bric a brac and using Brighton's best
new media brains to revamp their
websites, The Grand's still charging
a fortune for rather grotty non-sea
view rooms. Ooh, the number of
people who complain to us about
this place. Still, look on the bright
side; it's got on-site car parking,
baby-sitting facilities, and they'll
allow your dog in – as long as it's
small. They'll charge you though.

Granville Hotel

124 Kings Rd, Seafront,
Brighton BN1 2FA
T: 01273 326302
F: 01273 728294
www.granvillehotel.co.uk
granville@brighton.co.uk
Mon-Sun: 7.30am-10.30pm
Rooms: 24

A runner up in the Juicy Award
for hotel of the year in 2000, The
Granville is quality. This is smaller
than many of the seafront hotels
but easily as elegant and indulgent
for those who stay here. Each of
the rooms is individual and if you
really feel like treating yourself
why not stay in their Grand double
room and relax on the antique four-
poster bed? The organic restaurant
specialises in vegetarian dishes.
Rates: Doubles are £100 (with £125
for sea view), to £185 for the top
superior. Animal friendly.

Hilton Metropole

106-101 Kings Rd, Brighton BN1
2FU. T: 01273 775432
F: 01273 207764
www.brightonmet.hilton.com
Rooms: 334

Any hotel sitting next to The Grand
is going to be on a hiding to nothing,
but if you don't want to stay in a
Boutique hotels, do yourself a favour
and book this one instead. For a big
corporate hotel, the Metropole ticks
the boxes. There are 334 rooms (109
suites, 143 executive, 181 standard)
and three bar/restaurants, a covered
conservatory looking over the
Channel and a nightclub downstairs
for those with the stamina and
stilettos required. Of course it
lacks the character of the smaller
boutiques and guesthouses, but who
needs character when you have a
sauna, steam room, spa and on-site
beauty consultant? Prices vary greatly
and deals are always available. Rates:
Leisure rates starts at £168 for a non-
sea facing double, £218 for a 'superior'
double and £ 268 for a suite. Sea
facing rooms are between £30 and
£50 extra. Animal friendly.

Hilton West Pier

Kings Rd, Brighton BN1 2JF
T: 01273 329744
F: 01273 220757
www.hilton.com
custserv@worldres.com
Rooms: 131

Stand on the balcony and get a
grandstand view as the world's
only Grade 1 listed pier slides not
so elegantly into the sea. Take bets
with your partner whether it'll be
there in the morning. Oh, the fun
you can have with the West Pier. The
Hilton West Pier is the corporate
twin of Brighton favourite, The
Metropole, but while other chain
hotels in town will insist on inflicting
their appalling taste on their guests,
the Hilton's more subdued style is
much appreciated. The ylang ylang
body lotion and lavender-scented
'relaxing water' is another nice
touch, displaying an understanding
of what a night in a hotel should all
be about. The balconies overlooking
the English Channel could do with
a lick of paint though and the

much-hyped Hilton health club is a rain soaked dash down the road to the Metropole. Rates: Double £148, Double with sea view £178, superior double £198, suite £248. Prices come down according to demand and season. Animal friendly.

Hotel du Vin

Ship St, The Lanes, Brighton
BN1 1AD. T: 01273 718588
F: 01273 718599
www.hotelduvin.com
reception@brighton.
hotelduvin.com
Rooms: 33 rooms and 3 loft suites

If the UK is worthy of becoming a major tourist destination, it's largely because of the growth of small hip hotel chains like Hotel du Vin. Chic but not cheap, friendly but formal, it fills Brighton's need for somewhere to put our visiting pop stars and prime ministers without losing our style. Our room, sponsored by Domaine de Travaillon and stacked with bathroom goodies, opened out onto a rooftop quadrangle that, come the summer, surely is the sexiest place to have breakfast in town. The two-storey bathroom with Victorian bathtub, and walk-in monsoon shower up the tiled, windy stairs, is typical of the design features that mark this chain out, even if it's the twin tubs and telescope overlooking the English Channel of the Cristal Suite (£295 weeknights, £350 weekends) that get the attention of the travel editors. For the likes of you and me, a weeknight with your true love under a sumptuously white Egyptian cotton duvet, need only cost £129. Rates: From £119 to £350 for the full treatment. Breakfast is extra £9.50 for continental and £13.50 for full English.

Maison Mascara

33 Montpelier Rd, Brighton
BN1 2LQ. T: 01273 385959
www.mamaison-brighton.co.uk
info@mamaison-brighton.co.uk
Mon-Sun: 9.30am-10.30pm
Rooms: 8

As if Pascal from La Fourchette wasn't busy enough with his newly relocated flagship restaurant and his new North African restaurant, Mascara, he's now opened a small hotel too. Minimal and comfortable, stylish and so central, it's a treat, with prices ranging from £80-£130.

Montpellier Hall

Montpelier Terrace,
Montpelier, Brighton BN1 3DF
T: 01273 203599
Rooms: 9

A lovely find. If you're looking for something special, something that's both traditional and unique, where the staff are dressed in colonial livery with red tarbouches, this is it. Dating from 1846, Montpellier Hall is the last late Regency Italianate villa remaining in Brighton and Hove. The Regency building is one of Brighton's most historic, and the dining room and drawing room are suitably crammed with a mixture of ornamental antiques and gasoliers that give it a sense of grandeur. There is a spectacular walled garden with a pond and exotic plants where they host barbecues in the summer (there's room for a marquee holding 150 people) and seven parking spaces. Rates: from £85 double, but vary according to time and season. Animal friendly

Neo Hotel

19 Oriental Place, Brighton
BN1 2LL.
T: 01273 711104 F: 01273 711105
www.neohotel.com
info@neohotel.com
Rooms: 11

This new hotel is a welcome addition to the growing number of Brighton's boutique hotels. The bedrooms in this Grade II listed townhouse are all individually designed by Steph Harding, and details like hand-painted wall paper, designer bathrooms and the silk kimonos should teach the more complacent hoteliers a thing or two. Rooms are good value at around £85, and the breakfast is worth getting out of bed for. The only downside is the lack of smellies in the rooms, the rather noisy Expelair and the two-mattress beds – not what you need when you've booked a night of passion with your true love. But we'll let them off; it was probably just teething problems. You can rent out the whole hotel for 20 friends or colleagues for £1000 and they'll organise a private dining experience for you from around £25 per head.

New Steine Hotel

12a New Steine, Kemp Town,
Brighton BN2 1PB
T: 01273 681546 F: 01273 679118
www.newsteinehotel.com
reservation@newsteinehotel.
com
Rooms: 11

Comfortable and friendly, central and proper. Hervé, Georges and Stephane earned their four AA diamonds for their friendly service and mix of modern and what they sweetly describe as 'quaintly

comfortable English style' bedrooms. Dinner is French and open to the public (but booking is mandatory), and there's an Internet kiosk too. Breakfasts are English, vegetarian, vegan or continental. Rates: Single £25- £35, twin or double £45- £95. Animal friendly.

Hotel Nineteen

19 Broad St, Kemp Town,
Brighton BN2 1TJ
T: 01273 675529 F: 675531
www.hotelnineteen.co.uk
info@hotelnineteen.co.uk
Rooms: 8

Minimalist chic off the seafront with soothing Zen white walls, vast beds – three of which are on plinths of blue glass bricks – and local art and architectural flower displays making the place a feast for the senses. Another of Kemp Town's cool boutique hotels, which has added to the neighbourhood's reinvention over the last couple of years. All rooms are en-suite and feature original contemporary works by local artists. A television, video and hi-fi are provided. Sunday morning breakfasts are a complete treat as you help yourselves to chilled complimentary champagne. In the summer, you can take your bucks fizz and breakfast in the privacy of the stunning walled garden. As with an increasing number of boutique hotels, pampering treats are on offer here from massage to eyebrow shaping. Rates: Doubles are £95 to £135.

The Old Ship Hotel

Kings Rd, Brighton BN1 1NR
T: 01273 329001 F: 01273 820718
www.paramount-hotels.
co.uk/oldship
oldshipreservations@
paramount-hotels.co.uk
Rooms: 152

Dating back to 1559 and claiming to be the oldest hotel in Brighton, the four-star Old Ship should be one of the most impressive of the big sea front hotels. Recently subject to a £3million re-fit, it's more stylish these days (if you like vast expanses of deep red and dark wood finishes) and comfortable. The rooms are en suite bedrooms and most have sea views. The size means there isn't so much of the personal touch, but the staff are friendly and efficient. Rates: £158 for a standard double, £188 with sea view, suite £280. Animal friendly.

The Oriental

9 Oriental Place, Brighton BN1 2LJ. T: 01273 205050
F: 01273 821096
www.orientalhotel.co.uk
info@orientalhotel.co.uk
Rooms: 9

One of Brighton's original boutique hotels and winner of the first Juicy Award for Best Hotel. With its individually designed rooms, ornate furnishings and moody lighting, the Oriental is one of the most popular places for Brighton's creative and artistic types to hang

out. Two minutes from the sea, this small, friendly hotel is immaculately decorated with wooden floors and dark blue velvet. The front room looks like many of the cooler cafes in town and the bedrooms are small yet bright and airy and each are individually decorated. The double rooms are en-suite, and in the summer you can sit out on the balconies on the front bedrooms. Rates: Singles from £35, doubles from £60 and there's a twin bunk bed room for £100. And they are, they'd like you to know, animal friendly.

Paskins Town House

19 Charlotte St, Kemp Town, Brighton BN2 1AG
T: 01273 601203 F: 01273 621973. www.paskins.com
welcome@paskins.co.uk
Rooms: 19

Farm-fresh organic traditional and veggie breakfasts, fluffy towels, fresh flowers and four poster beds make Paskins one of the most famous town houses (built around 1810) in Brighton. Way better value than most of the more famous hotels, all the rooms are spacious and tastefully decorated, including their four-poster bedrooms, and they even use environmentally friendly products to clean them. A very nice, unpretentious hotel with the kind of genuine welcome and service that you rarely find these days. Rates: Singles from £30, Doubles from £35 to a luxury double with a four-poster for £75. Animal friendly.

Pelirocco

10 Regency Square, Brighton BN1 2FG. T: 01273 327055
F: 01273 733845
www.hotelpelirocco.co.uk
info@hotelpelirocco.co.uk
Rooms: 19

Winner of The Sexiest Hotel Award at last year's Juicy Awards. If you're looking for something a little bit different, a little bit rock'n'roll, you've found your bed. With 19 individually styled and decorated rooms, there's a theme for everyone, sponsored by the likes of PS2, Smint and Absolut Vodka, and with inspiration from artists and fashion labels, it is the hotel to stay in. The O2 suite with circular white bed surrounded by organza drapes and overhead mirror is an inspired addition (even if it's almost fairground quality; either that or we ate too much at The Epicurean beforehand). And the top to toe tiled bathroom with twin monsoon heads and 42" plasma screen to check your emails, proves that at £185 during the week and £235 at weekends (min two night stay), you can have luxury and imagination. New developments have seen the arrival of the Nookii Room. Housing a strip show sign and draped in black satin this is a grown up room for the more adventurous of couples. Prices range from £50 for the single to £130 for the Cissy Mo's Magic Garden, a double room for three people. If you've got to ask, try the Metropole.

Penny Lanes Hotel

11 Charlotte St, Kemp Town,
Brighton BN2 1AG
T: 01273 603197
F: 01273 689408
www.pennylanes.co.uk
welcome@pennylanes.co.uk
Mon-Fri: 8am-10pm, Sat-Sun: 9am-10pm. Closed for Christmas week.
Rooms: 12

Romantic, Victorian and specialising in comfort, Penny Lanes offers four posters, shaggy rugs and a sumptuous Eggs Benedict for breakfast. Vegans, vegetarians and carnivores come back for more from this tasteful little seaside guesthouse. Rates: Single £35, Doubles £79, Superior four-poster £99. Animal friendly.

Premier Lodge

144 North St, Brighton BN1 1RE
T: 0870 990 6340
F: 0870 9906341
www.premierlodge.co.uk
brighton.premierlodge@snr.co.uk
Rooms: 160

The ultimate in functional city centre hotels. Frills? No. Extras? No. Dancing girls who wake you up with a smile and a...? No. A hotel with beds in the centre of town at a price you can't argue with? That's about the size of it. Rates: £56 per room per night. There are 160 rooms that are due to be re-furbished in the next six months. There's also a meeting room available for conferences and seats 70. Animal friendly.

Prince Regent

29 Regency Square, Brighton
BN1 2FH
T: 01273 329962 F: 01273 148162
www.princeregent.com
Rooms: 20

Standing at the top of Regency Square, this has all the grandeur and elegance of the larger traditional hotels, but wrapped up in a smaller package, with friendly and personal service. The halls and rooms are draped with paintings, there are antiques everywhere you look and the carpets are a deep luxurious red. If you're after a romantic trip back in time where you can sit back and pretend you're Royalty, book the grand balcony room. For £150 you get en-suite, a magnificent antique

ornate fashion, and the one careful lady owner is herself a vegetarian, so all breakfast tastes are catered for. There are conference/meeting room facilities for up to 20 people and a licensed bar. Singles £50 to £60, doubles/twins £80 to £95. The Regency Suite (a large double suite with balcony and views) £110. Animal friendly.

Royal Pavilion Town House
12a Regency Square, Brighton BN1 2FG
T: 01273 722123 F: 01273 722293
www.rpthotel.co.uk
info@rpthotel.co.uk
Rooms: 8

With each of the rooms individually designed and drawing their inspiration from the Pavilion, The RPTH has the feel of a grand old hotel in the body of a Brighton town house From the exterior, it blends easily into the rest of the Grade 1 listed buildings of Regency Square. Four-poster beds are the centrepieces in all rooms, with an impressive bathroom consisting of a huge double bath and Monsoon shower. Oriental decor and furnishings feature throughout adding to the unique atmosphere of the hotel where the only thing that is English is the breakfast (full and delicious). At £170 – £200 a night it's expensive, but it's gorgeous enough to forget the cost. There are plans to open a similarly style restaurant opening out into Preston Street, with a Regency bar underneath.

four-poster bed, and a bay window and balcony with incredible views of the square, the sea and the West Pier. Seven of the 20 bedrooms enjoy an unobstructed sea view. If you want relaxing decadence, there's a double with en-suite Jacuzzi for £125. Prices start at £85 and rise to £150.

The Regency
28 Regency Square, Brighton BN1 2FH. T: 01273 202690
F: 01273 220438
www.regencybrighton.co.uk
enquiries@regencybrighton.co.uk
Rooms: 14

If Joan Collins ran a guest house, this would be it. History falls off

the walls here. This Grade II listed Regency town house was built as a private dwelling in 1820 and was owned by Jane, Dowager Duchess of Marlborough, from 1870-1886. And she was the third wife of the Duke of Marlborough and a great Grandmother of Sir Winston Churchill, so there. Unashamedly exploiting Brighton's heritage, it retains much of its original interior. The jewel is the Regency Suite, an ostentatious, canopied four-poster room with all the trimmings - gold brocade, velvet tassels, heavy rococo drapes and a view of the Square and the West Pier. Although this room is the piece de resistance, there are other comfy doubles and singles available. The bar and lounge are decorated in similarly

Sea Spray

25 New Steine, Kemp Town,
Brighton BN2 1PD
T: 01273 680332
www.seaspraybrighton.co.uk
seaspray@brighton.co.uk
Rooms: 9

Very chic, completely renovated contemporary, friendly boutique hotel. The themed rooms include a Renaissance Room with balcony and sea view and The Boudoir, a very special suite with wrought iron four poster adorned with satin, velvet and feathers. The staff are friendly and the rooms are more spacious than some of the other boutique hotels around here. Breakfast is made to order, with vegetarian and vegan options cooked on demand. Prices have gone up as word has spread; a single is £35, but the Boudoir Suite is £120 based on two sharing, and breakfast is included. Animal friendly.

The Seattle Hotel

Marina, Brighton BN2 5WA
T: 01273 679799 F: 01273 619899
www.aliashotels.com
info@aliasseattle.com
Rooms: 71

With its leather bed-heads and monsoon showers, private decks and local modern art (as well as a rather bizarre taste in furniture), The Seattle has made the most of its waterfront position with half the bedrooms, the Black and White Bar and the seafood restaurant, Café Paradiso,

reaching out towards the boats. The effect is tranquil but groovy, making it the choice of younger business folk looking for something more. Rates: Weekend special £205 for two people including two nights, breakfasts and £40 to spend in the bar or restaurant. Prices rise to £245 (non sea facing) and £315 (sea facing) in the summer. Animal friendly.

Strawberry Fields

6-7 New Steine, Brighton BN2
1PB. T: 01273 681576 F: 01273
693397. www.strawberry-fields-hotel.com
strawberryfields@pavilion.co.uk
Closed Dec 25th
Rooms: 27

If it's good enough for the Minister of Tourism who chose to stay here during a conference, it's good enough for us. Overlooking a garden square right next to the sea front it is hard to fault the location of this hotel. Inside, although the décor is far too busy and leaning on the chintz side the rooms are comfortable with good facilities and the family who own it are friendly and efficient. Many rooms are en-suite with sea views and about the average price for this area of town but offer an exceptional service, especially for families, with reduced rates for children, a play area a baby listening service with NNEB qualified supervision and qualified child minders. Rooms are from £25 to £40. Animal friendly.

Sussex Arts Club

7 Ship St, Brighton BN1 1AD
T: 01273 727371
www.sussexarts.com
info@sussexarts.com
Rooms: 7

The Sussex is a members club and a useful watering hole if you want to escape the riff raff polluting the locals pubs and bars. There are exhibitions and shows and all that arty stuff, but in this chapter we're talking beds. And bang in the heart of The Lanes, the Sussex is on the money. It has five double bedrooms (£80), one single (£65) and the Mrs Simpson suite (£100) with its four-poster bed. A continental breakfast is included, it's child friendly, but don't even think of bringing an animal with you. The club is open till 11 from Mon-Wed and till 2am during the other days. It is closed on Sunday.

Thistle Hotel

Kings Rd, Brighton BN1 2GS
T: 01273 206700 F: 01273
820692
www.thistlehotels.com/brighton
Brighton@Thistle.co.uk
Rooms: 208

Large and faceless, the Thistle is in many ways the antithesis of the cute, individual hotel for which Brighton is known. But horses for courses and with the Brighton Centre next door, there's no shortage of

conference delegates queuing up to get in. And the lobby bar is a good place to have meetings if you need a central location. There are 208-air conditioned bedrooms with suites, a full leisure centre with swimming pool, sauna and gym. Rates: £85 for a standard double, £120 with sea view, suite £204. Prices in the summer rise to £169, £199 and £219 respectively.

The Twenty One Hotel

21 Charlotte St, Kemp Town,
Brighton BN2 1Ag
T: 01273 686450
hotel21@pavillion.co.uk
Rooms: 8

Personal service is the part of the passion behind The Twenty One where the rooms are lavishly decorated. There's a four-poster in The Victorian Room and a charming apartment downstairs with a huge double shower, his and hers sink and private patio which, in the summer is covered with blossoms. Rates: from £35 for a single to £115 for the Patio Room, breakfast is included and there's a mini-fridge in most rooms.

The White House Hotel

6 Bedford St, Brighton BN2
1AN. T: 01273 626266
www.whitehousebrighton.com
info@whitehousebrighton.com
Rooms: 9

Smart boutique hotel in the east end of Kemp Town which is not as sumptuous or stylish as its competitors in the St James's St end of the village, but it's so much quieter down this part of town. The rooms are modern and 'The French Room' (about as French as the Laura Ashley linen on the bed) is delightful, opening onto a small balcony over-looking a patio garden. Prices range from £115 for this room to £30 for a single with shower and depend greatly on the season. Breakfast is inclusive and there is a good choice including a veggie option.

Self-catering

Best of Brighton and Sussex Cottages

Windmill Lodge, Vicarage Lane, Rottingdean BN2 7HD
T: 01273 308779
www.bestofbrighton.co.uk
enquiries@bestofbrighton.co.uk
Rooms: 100 properties

This company lets and manages many properties in Brighton and the surrounding area and is continually adding to its list, so phoning for a brochure is recommended. There's a good selection of interesting properties and all are inspected by The English Tourism Council and given a Star grading. They've got a luxury three bedroom/two bathroom balcony penthouse above the Metropole Hotel with excellent views both in an easterly and westerly direction which sleeps 6/8 people (and costs between £625 a week for four people up to £1075 a week in the summer for up to six people), a town house in Kemp Town and a maisonette in Arundel Terrace, other cottages in villages further from Brighton, and a Tudor Manor House which sleeps 18 people... The list goes on. Prices include electricity, gas, linen and cleaning.

Brighton Holidays Flats

50 Kings Rd, Brighton BN3 5SE
T: 01273 260100
www.cronin-accommodation.co.uk

booking@brightonflats.co.uk
Rooms: 30 holiday apartments, 3 holiday houses

You can't get more Brighton than these 22 self-catering apartments, situated on the seafront in the heart of it all. They have all been recently refurbished and the larger flats have a panoramic view of Brighton's beach nightlife – so when you are sitting in your spacious lounge with a G&T you can watch your friend queuing for a nightclub. The flats are booked up very quickly in the summer so be warned! A price for a studio, which sleeps one to two, is £315; four-person apartments are £510 per week. (These prices are for high season).

Sheepcote Valley

East Brighton Park, Whitehawk, Brighton BN2 5TS
T: 01273 626546
www.caravanclub.co.uk
Open for caravans 24 hours a day Jan-Dec, open for tents from Apr-Oct. Rooms: 170 Caravan pitches, 100 tent pitches

Situated in East Brighton park at the far end of Kemp Town and set in a beautiful natural valley, Sheepcote has 170 pitches for caravans and 120 for tents. There are showers and laundry facilities on site and no night-time curfew. Animal friendly.

Wild and Wonderful

Bristol Mansions, 19-20 Sussex Square, Kemp Town, Brighton

BN2 5AA. T: 01273 734344
www.wildwonderful.co.uk
christine@wildwonderful.co.uk
Rooms: 2

Sometimes a hotel is just so faceless. Wild & Wonderful is a self-catering apartment in Sussex Square (said by The Independent to be the most desirable address in the UK), which allows you to imagine that Cate Blanchett and Steven Berkoff are your neighbours for the weekend. The idea is one you wish you'd had; buy a spare flat, do it up, fill it with eco-luxury products and rent it out to weekend, weekly or monthly visitors for a lot of money. After all, a budget of £250 for a winter weekend gives anyone the choice of Brighton's best hotels, so the inclusive hamper (including a nice bottle of wine), the freezer full of organic ready made meals, the roll top bath (with its complimentary toiletries and soft organic bath towels), and the Louis XV style Antique bed, complete with finest organic cotton bed linen, is a bargain at the same price. There's also an honesty bar of wine and beer (nice idea; won't last) and if you don't think that's enough to impress your love, ring to book a bouquet of flowers, a bottle of champagne, a box of champagne truffles and gorgeous luxurious hemp/silk bed linen for an extra £50. Prices go up to £320 for the weekend in high season, and you can stay longer for an extra fee. The apartment sleeps two, but can house an extra two on the sofa bed for an extra fee.

RESTAURANTS

AFRICAN

The Blue Man

142 Edward St, Kemp Town,
Brighton BN2 0JG
T: 01273 622885
Mon-Sat: 7pm-10.30pm.
Avg. Price: £25

This new little BYO restaurant is
packed to the gills with Kemp Town
types who love the informality,
lovely service and its North African
décor (though you can get your own
from Inspirations on Lewes Rd). The
starters are mouth watering and
taste just like the real thing, but
the tagines (and many of the meaty
mains) are overpriced at around £12
and about as North African as
my grandmother. Give it time
though; with Mascara and Couscous
House giving it a run for its money,
the lamb will be falling off the
bone and soaking up the prunes
before you know it.

Couscous House

10-11 Preston St, Brighton
BN1 2HN
T: 01273 323230
Avg. Price: £20

Good new North African restaurant
challenging the might of Mascara
(and the force of La Fourchette
chef/patron, Pascal Madjoudj
who owns Mascara). Also offering
belly dancing on a Friday and
Saturday night, it was highly
rated by our Tunisian reviewer.
Apparently the delicious lamb
tagine, cooked with caramelised
prunes, almonds and sesame seeds
(£12.95) is the best in town.

Mascara

101 Western Rd, Hove BN1
2AA. T: 01273 278185
www.mascara.brighton.com
Tue-Sat: 12pm-2.30pm, 7pm-
10.30pm, Sun: 7pm-10.30pm
Private room available
Avg. Price: £20

An Aladdin's cave of Algerian food
with low lighting, rugs suspended
from the ceiling and cushioned
benches, Bedouin style. The menu
offers the standard tagine, pastilla
and couscous, with Rechta Zohra, a
chicken with home made noodles,
cinnamon, chick peas, carrot and
turnip (£12) the only dish throwing
us in to No Man's Land. The food is
good; Pascal from La Fourchette is
the main man and has a pedigree, but
we've been spoilt by Moroccan chefs,
and Pascal is not behind the decks
here so we'll forgive the blandness
and look at the big picture. There are
not many places in Brighton where
the service is spot on, the ambience
perfect and the food just fine, and
where you'll pay around £25 per head
for the experience. Throw in the belly
dancing after 9.30pm on Friday and
Saturday, and you've got a winner.

AMERICAN

Blind Lemon Alley

41 Middle St, Brighton BN1 1AL
T: 01273 205151 F: 01273 202051
www.bluescompany.co.uk
boss@bluescompany.co.uk
Mon-Sun: 12pm-11pm

Avg. Price: £15-20

Nestled away in Middle Street you
might never notice this hobbit-like
restaurant but for the bright yellow
alleyway leading to its front door.
The staff are warm and welcoming,
and the menu has a strong Mexican
and North American influence. There
is a good range of vegetarian food,
and the Blind Lemon Burger was
voted the best burger in the UK by
The Independent this year. The picky
might call it cramped, while the
Bohemian would call it cosy, with the
feeling of one big dinner party rather
than a room full of separate dinners.
Late in the evening it all grows very
merry with absinth all round. Watch
your head on the way up.

Momma Cherri's Soul Food Shack

11 Little East St, The Lanes,
Brighton BN1 1HT
T: 01273 774545 F: 01273 272288
www.mommacherri.co.uk
mommacherri@hotmail.com
Mon/Tues/Thurs: 5pm-11pm, Fri:
6pm-12am; Sat: 11am-12am, Sun:
10.30am-8pm. Avg. Price: £10

Plates are big in the Deep South, so
leave your Atkins Diet at home and
while Goaty Phil spins some soul
music, let Momma Cherri serve you
up her New Orleans style stir fry of
prawns, chicken, spicy sausage, rice
and vegetables (£10). Vegetarians
can share the Veggie Combo: stuffed
eggplant, bell peppers with couscous,

vegetable lasagne and stir-fry seasoned vegetables (£28 for two). A basic kids menu includes chicken nuggets and fish fingers but with a Soul Food side order of corn on the cob. High chairs and baby changing are available.

ASIAN

Bali Brasserie
Kingsway Court First Avenue, Hove BN3 2LR
T: 01273 323810 F: 01273 324572
www.balibrasserie.co.uk
Mon-Thurs: 11.30am-2pm, 6pm-10.30pm, Fri-Sat: 11.30am-2pm, 6pm-11pm
Avg. Price: £10

Maximum kitsch. A bizarre eating experience in the ground floor of a block of flats in Hove with a Saturday night clientele stuck in the Seventies and foreign exchange students posing in Balinese saris. The Tropical Bar, all bamboo, mirrored mosaic tiles and pool table, is worth a visit in itself, but the food, while authentically Indonesian, lets the side down and is no better than OK. The three-course rice table at £15.95 is the most popular with a buffet main course, but a Mee Goreng and Tiger beer will still give you change from £10.

Jim Thompson's
Unit 1, The Terrace, Kemp Town, Brighton BN2 1PS
T: 01273 666920 F: 01273 666926
www.jimthompsons.com
jimthompsonsbrighton@nhguk.com
Mon-Sat: 12pm-11pm, Sun: 12pm-10.30pm. Avg. Price: £20

You really do take a trip through Asia without cutting any corners at this bar, restaurant and bazaar. The food is irritatingly erratic though; some days the Malay curry can be sublime, on others a vegetarian spring roll can squirt you in the eye and the tofu would be better used as a mattress. The menu is probably to blame - too much to choose from and not enough love in the kitchen. Prices from £15.95 per person for the vegetarian feast to £24.95 for hungry meat lovers and £5.95 gets you an Asian buffet at lunchtimes during the week. Kids can enjoy a £3.95 Bento box with starter, main, noodles and ice cream. Live music on Friday and Saturdays.

Krakatoa
7 Pool Valley, The Lanes, Brighton BN1 1NJ
T: 01273 719009
Mon-Sat: 6pm-11pm
Avg. Price: £25

Once upon a time, this was a Juicy favourite, with low tables and floor cushions encouraging you to take your shoes off, assume your best lotus position and idle the night away over a nasi goreng and a Tiger beer. These days, the service is stressed, and the three floors are overstretching a great idea. The menu still takes the best from the

Orient with Gado Gado and Sake an alternative to Tsing Tao. Sotong Goreng (Singaporean style deep fried squid in a herbed crispy batter served with chilli sambal) £4.90. Sake Yaki (Japanese style grilled salmon with a classic Japanese sauce on a bed of fresh spinach leaves) £8.50.

CHINESE

China Garden
88-91 Preston St, Brighton BN1 2HG. T: 01273 325124
Mon-Sun: 12pm-11pm
Avg. Price: £30

The most opulent Chinese restaurant in town, the bill may be as big as your stomach by the time you peel yourself away from your feast. But it's worth it; the dim sum melt in the mouth, and the duck is so good you'll never go anywhere else for it in Brighton again.

Emperor of China
Waterfront Building, Marina, Brighton BN2 5WA
T: 01273 686833/01273 686855
Mon-Thurs: 12pm-11.30pm, Fri-Sat: 12pm-12am, Sun: 12pm-11.30pm
Avg. Price: £25-30

New Chinese in the Marina that knocks the dim sum out of the nearby Pagoda, serving delicious and well-priced classics with the kind of smile not always found in such places. The dining room is huge but

looks out over the soulless concrete rather than the boats of The Marina. However, you'll always find Chinese folk tucking in, which is a sure sign that the food is the real thing.

Gars

19 Prince Albert St, The Lanes, Brighton BN1 4FU
T: 01273 620033 F: 01273 777887
Mon-Sun: 12pm-11pm
Avg. Price: £20

A fire in the kitchen last summer almost devastated this popular Chinese, but the repair work revealed a hidden high-ceilinged room. The new chef comes from Sapporo, Preston Street's theatrical Japanese, and the menu now offers almost as much Japanese as Chinese. The 'leave it to us' lunch menu promised much, but offered a gristly pork in our char siu, a plate of spare ribs we're not sure we asked for, no sign of the Tiger Beer, and yet a bill for the lot.

FISH

Bankers

116 Western Rd, Hove BN1 2AB
T: 01273 328267 F: 01273 777157
Mon-Sun: 11.30am-10pm
Avg. Price: £7

One of the best fish and chips shops. As much a restaurant as a takeaway, you've got the option to have your fish cooked in matzo meal (a light, non-greasy Jewish alternative to batter), which makes the difference.

Bardsley

22-23a Baker St, Brighton BN1 4JN. T: 01273 681256
www.bardsleys/fishandchips.co.uk
Tue-Sat: 10.30am-2pm, 4pm-8.30pm.
Avg. Price: £10 BYO

Repeatedly in the Top 50 UK seafood restaurants, the tables may be Formica, but the fish is line-caught (so no bruises) and fried in palm oil. Roy and the Bardsley family have been doing it for 30-odd years and don't seem in the least bit tired of their trade. They close early (8.30pm) and do takeaways.

Brighton Pier Fish and Chip Shop

Brighton Pier, Brighton BN1 1TW. T: 01273 609361
www.brightonpier.co.uk
Oct-Mar: Mon-Fri: 11.30am-5pm,
Sat-Sun: 11.30am-8pm, Apr-Sept:
Mon-Sun: 11.30am-10.30pm
Avg. Price: £6

The one eatery in this guide that – odds-on – everyone will go to. Come down for the weekend as a tourist and you'll end up there. Live here? Then have your friends visit and take them there, it's worth it.

Café Paradiso

The Waterfront, Marina, Brighton BN2 5WA
T: 01273 665444
www.aliashotels.com
Mon-Sun: 12pm-3pm, 7pm-10pm

Avg. Price: £30

With chandelier lighting by night and sunshine streaming in from the Waterfront by day, Café Paradiso's vast dining room and mouth watering menu is what the Marina has been waiting for. These days the confusion over cuisine has been resolved, with the new chef bringing his own catch of fresh fish in every day, and serving it straight from the wood fire with a selection of delicious side orders. The amuse bouche of oysters and delicate mushrooms is a lovely touch, and the service is a joy with knowledgeable, friendly waiters hitting just the right balance between attending to your every need, and keeping well out of the way.

Harry Ramsden

Marine Parade,
Brighton BN2 1TA. T: 01273 690691 F: 01273 605097
www.harryramsdens.co.uk
hrbrighton@aol.com
Mon-Sun: 12pm-9pm
Avg. Price: £7

The most famous fish and chip shop in the UK, Harry Ramsden's is a magnet for the tourists with all the old fried favourites and two menus for the under 8s and 8-12s. The chips are no longer cooked in the beef dripping Harry used to be famous for, and are now cooked in a vegetable oil product made specially to taste like beef dripping... And yes, we checked with the lab for any porkies.

Loch Fyne Restaurant and Oyster Bar

95-99 Western Rd, Brighton BN1 2LB. T: 01273 716160
F: 01273 716161
www.lochfyne.com
brighton@lochfyne.net
Sun-Thurs: 10am-10pm, Fri-Sat: 10am-10.30pm. Avg. Price: £30

Loch Fyne's two stained glass domes on the upper floor and sumptuous seafood bar promise lobsters, oysters and a night of decadence. These days, the smokers have won their battle with the management, and reclaimed the action zone in the domes, leaving the less animated non-smokers rather isolated downstairs. The food in this nationwide chain remains variable; the oysters on ice were plump and succulent, but the pea and clam chowder was little more than pea soup; the grilled dorade was sublime, but the sea bass with pesto (£12.95) proved to be an unfortunate combination, with the pesto sauce overpowering the delicate flavours of the fish. And the market priced lobster at £24.95 would put off all but the most avid lobster fan. An extra charge for vegetables when mains are between £10 and £15 each is an unwise move when the food is so inconsistent. The wine list was neither extensive nor particularly good value, the best bet may be the cheapest wine which was the house white at £10.85 and which was pleasant enough. Only the attentive and friendly service remains consistent.

The Regency

131 Kings Rd, Brighton BN1 2HH
T: 01273 325014 F: 01273 747028
www.theregencyrestaurant.co.uk
Mon-Sun: 8am-11pm
Avg. Price: £15

Once upon a time, The Regency was a typical seaside restaurant. The fish was fabulous, but the décor and the service was, shall we say, unreconstructed. When Loch Fyne moved in around the corner with its chain of fish restaurants around the country serving organic this and sustainable that, we thought they'd eat The Regency for breakfast. And, bless, what did it do? It got itself a facelift. The banquettes and enormous windows, posh graphics and a palatial extension haven't changed its spirit. There's not a Soil Association label to be seen and they haven't a clue about sustainable farming, but by using local fishermen and their little nets, they're less likely to decapitate or mutilate the millions of fish ejected from the vast nets of the trawlers because their faces don't fit. They probably didn't even notice their accolade this year in The Observer Food Monthly's Food Awards. The best fish in town.

FRENCH

Café Rouge

24 Albert St, The Lanes, Brighton BN1 1HF
T: 01273 774422 F: 01273 724524
www.caferouge.com
Mon-Sat: 9am-11pm, Sun: 10am-10pm. Avg. Price: £15

The food's not as good as it was, but a plate of moules and newspapers for non-rush hour types, areas for the smokers and a great stress-free attitude towards kids mean that we'll always find our way there sooner or later. Average for lunch is £10. A kid's menu for £3.95 includes main dish, drink and ice cream.

La Fourchette

105 Western Rd, Brighton BN1 2AA. T: 01273 722556 F: 01273 386710
www.lafourchette.co.uk
info@lafourchette.co.uk
Mon-Sat: 12pm-2.30pm, 7pm-10.30pm, Sun: 2pm-3.30pm
Avg. Price: £30-40

Haute cuisine from personality chef, Pascal Madjoudj who has moved this nationally acclaimed little corner of France in its new bigger home two doors down on Western Road. There's a two course menu for £20, £23 for three. At lunchtime, you can get a fabulous two courser for £7.50. For pudding, try the assiette de gourmet, the chef's selection of the best in the house. The service is erratic but properly Gallic.

New Steine Bistro @ New Steine Hotel

12a New Steine, Kemp Town, Brighton BN2 1PB

T: 01273 681546
Tues-Sat: 6.30pm-10pm
Avg. Price: £20

The welcome at Herve's hotel/bistro is one of the warmest in town, and an evening spent over a few escargots and a duck confit is more about the sum than the parts. The tables might not have tablecloths, the glasses might well have come from Asda, but the food is fab (braised lamb shank with cabbage mash, grilled shark steak and marinated peppers), the service genuine and a reminder that France is often nothing to do with all the stiffness and nonsense that the English are supposed to expect.

One Paston Place

1 Paston Place, Kemp Town,
Brighton BN2 1HA
T: 01273 606933
F: 01273 675686
www.onepastonplace.co.uk
info@onepastonplace.co.uk
Tues-Sat: 12.30pm-1.45pm, 7.30pm-9.30pm
Avg. Price: £40

One Paston Place has been one of Brighton's fine dining experiences since Michael Caine first opened its doors as Brighton's own Langans. Mark and Nicole Emmerson managed to please those who like a little flagellation and superiority from their Maitre' D, but happily for those of us for whom eating is a joy rather than a penance, their reign is no more. Francesco has big plans to bring Michelin quality Italian food to Kemp Town in the next year, with a bar downstairs and the restaurant moved upstairs. In the meantime though, the food is lighter than it was but still deliciously haute cuisine, with melt in the mouth pan-fried foie gras, pain brioche tartine and Banulus syrup (£12) and fillet and sweetbreads of Welsh Lamb with thyme infusion and rice sartu (£21). The bill will come to more than £100 for two, but the lunch menu is a steal at £16.50 for two courses and £19 for three.

A GOOD LUNCH

Browns
3 Duke St, The Lanes,
Brighton BN1 2GN
T: 01273 323501 F: 01273 327427
www.browns-restaurants.com
Mon-Thurs: 12pm-11pm, Fri-Sat:
12pm-11.30pm, Sun: 12pm-11pm
Private room available
Avg. Price: £20

The high ceilings and large glasses
of red wine are only part of the
reason that even on a mid-winter
Monday evening, Browns will always
be buzzing. The salmon blinis and
the steak with Béarnaise sauce, the
goats cheese tart with caramelised
onion and the sticky rice pudding are
always top value, properly priced and
served with a rare kind of smile.

The Dorset
28 North Rd, North Laine,
Brighton BN1 1YB
T: 01273 605423
F: 01273 682322
www.thedorset.co.uk
Mon-Sun: 9am-11pm
Avg. Price: £10

The best spot for lunch when
you're in the North Laine for people
watching, with tables out on
Gardner Street, but the food often
disappoints. For the size of the bill
and the affection lavished on this
Brighton institution, it owes it to
its loyal clientele and stop charging
for the mayonnaise your dried

out fishcakes need in order to be
palatable. Kids have their own menu
featuring such delights as moules
and pasta.

The Fish Bowl
74 East St, The Lanes, Brighton
BN1 1HQ. T: 01273 778600
www.zelnet.com
Mon-Sat: 11am-11pm, Sun: 12pm-
10.30pm. Avg. Price: £15

Nice little find at the seafront end
of East Street where the fish and
the music are mellow by day and
hopping at night (see Bars section).
A surprisingly easy place to get
great fusion food for kids while
gorging yourself on their tuna,
pepper and red onion wrap (£4.50),
seafood linguini pasta with squid
and mussels (£6.95). The kitchen
closes at 7.00pm and that's when
the music takes over.

Ha! Ha!
Pavilion Buildings, Brighton
BN1 1EE. T: 01273 737080
F: 01273 746850
www.hahaonline.co.uk
brighton@hahaonline.co.uk
Mon-Sat: 11am-11pm, Sun: 12pm-
10.30pm. Avg. Price: £10

First things first. If you've got a
child with you, don't bother. If
you're pregnant or thinking of
having a baby, don't bother. They
don't like children here. They say
they haven't got insurance for
kids rather than nursing any deep

pathological feelings, but what
are these mini devil-worshippers
supposed to do that's so dangerous?
Spill ketchup on the waiters' brown
leather aprons? Pull a bar stool
away from under an old lady?
Anyway. It's actually a good place.
Perfect location (bang opposite The
Pavilion), plenty of space, different
areas for drinking, all stripped pine
minimalism and spacious, canteen-
style area. And the crispy spiced
salmon on noodle cake with tzatziki
dressing (£8.30) or free range eggs
on a heap of skinny chips with Ha!
Ha! brown sauce (£5) goes down a
treat. Music provided by regular DJs
on Friday and Saturday nights.

No Name Restaurant
81 St James St, Kemp Town, Brighton
BN2 1PA
T: 01273 693216
enquiries@nonamebar.co.uk
Mon-Fri: 11am-11pm, Sat: 10am-11pm,
Sun: 10am-10pm
Avg. Price: £20

A lovely little restaurant with
friendly service and excellent
food that actually fills you up and
tastes good at the same time. The
interior's all chunky timber with, for
once, the right lighting level – low,
warm and ever-so romantic. There's
even a small bar attached for pre-
dinner drinks.

Real Eating Company
86 Western Rd, Hove BN3 1JB
T: 01273 221444
www.real-eating.co.uk

Mon-Fri: 9am-6pm, Sat: 9am-6pm, Sun: 10am-5pm. Avg. Price: £15

Finally Brighton and Hove can call itself a city. This brand new Food Emporium is the kind you'll find in New York or Melbourne, with two floors of the best food money can buy served in the deli, on a plate in the restaurant or given away as a promotion by one of Sussex's many food producers. Chef, Cass Titcombe has been poached from The Tin Drum, Hove (which spotted him first in the earliest and best incarnation of Blanch House). At weekends, it's heaving with foodies settling in for the day and tucking into an Eggs Benedict (£7) or an Arbroath Smokie (£8) and thinking of moving in.

Tootsies

15-18 Meeting House Lane, The Lanes, Brighton BN1 1HB
T: 01273 726777 F: 01273 735875
Mon-Sun: 10am-10.30pm
Avg. Price: £15

You might not associate Tootsies with a big weekend breakfast, but this is our juiciest find at this char grill restaurant. It's always quiet first thing, which is perfect when you want to relax with a paper and a big breakfast, and £4.50 gets you get char grilled sausage, bacon and tomato, eggs and mushrooms all day. The toast is now sold separately, but there's plenty of it, and the freshly squeezed orange juice and free refills of tea or coffee completes

one of the best breakfasts in town. The restaurant is particularly kiddy friendly too, with entertainment in an upstairs room every Friday in the school holidays between 5pm and 7pm offering a range of local children's entertainers while you concentrate on your Caesar Salad. They even have an organic kid's menu featuring sausage and mash and chicken and rice. And they'll heat your baby food.

The Terraces

Unit 8, Madeira Drive, Kemp Town, Brighton BN2 1TB
T: 01273 570526
F: 01273 545259
www.the-terraces.co.uk
sales@the-terraces.co.uk
Mon-Sat: 11am-11pm, Sun: 12pm-10.30pm. Private room available
Avg. Price: £22

The food tends to be char-grilled or salady – and pricey (a warm chicken salad for £8.95? Have they not been to Tescos?) But the point of coming here is the view and nothing but. The waves are wild in winter and will calm your soul in summer, and it's even a hotspot for those who want to surf the net and watch the tide roll by.

Tin Drum

43 St James's St, Kemp Town, Brighton BN2 1RG. T: 01273 624777. F: 01273 620060
10 Victoria Grove, Hove BN3 2LG. T: 01273 747755
F: 01273 777552

95 Dyke Rd, Seven Dials,
Brighton BN1 3JE. T: 01273
777575. F: 01273 230663
www.tindrum.co.uk
tindrum@tindrum.co.uk
Mon-Fri: 11am-11pm, Sat: 10.30am-
11pm, Sun: 10.30am-10.30pm
Avg. Price: £20-25

The Tin Drum is one of those places
you'll go for breakfast, lunch, dinner,
poetry readings, a business meeting
or to meet your mates for a drink, and
whatever you want from it, you tend
to get. It's kid and granny friendly, the
décor is tasteful, and the menu's good
enough to make it a night out. Try
the Italian vegetarian and cannelloni
bean casserole (£7.15) or the Pan-fried
Sirloin Steak with horseradish butter
and sauté potatoes (£10).

GREEK

Ipanema

121-123 Western Rd,
Hove BN3 1DP.
T: 01273 779474 F: 01273 779474
Mon-Sun: 11am-11pm
Avg. Price: £15

A bizarre idea for a restaurant, but
one that seems to work – Spanish
Tapas upstairs and authentic Greek
food downstairs. The music, the
décor, the waiters, everything in this
restaurant couldn't be more Greek, so
why they want to do Spanish Tapas
is a question. The mezze is highly
recommended if you want to have a
taste of different dishes.

HOME DELIVERY

Kudos Foods

The Food Shop,
Church Lane,
Ripe BN8 6AS
T: 01273 206662
www.kudosfoods.co.uk
orders@kudosfoods.co.uk
Mon-Thurs: 9.30am-3pm, Fri:
9.30am-6pm, Sat: 9.30am-3pm.
Avg. Price: £20

Delicious gourmet home delivery
service using the freshest local
produce. Book yourselves a dinner
for 8 and then pretend that you
are that domestic god/dess. Kudos
are very discreet. Prices start from
£2.95 for a chicken liver parfait to
rich chocolate torte for 12-16 people
at £15.95.

B.Right.On

56 Greenways,
Ovingdean BN2 7BL
T: 01273 705606
www.chillipepperpete.com
brightfoods@hotmail.com
Mon-Sun: 6pm-9pm
Avg. Price: £7

Chilli based vegan and vegetarian
gourmet treats to take home,
prepared by husband and wife
team Peter Seymour and Miranda
Pellew. Peter is a chilli expert so
most dishes tend to be spicy.
Gluten and wheat free dishes are
also available. The minimum order
is £15, and they'll deliver direct to
your door – for free. They also do
outside catering.

La Cucina

4a Montpelier Place,
Montpelier, Brighton BN1 1NH
T: 01273 202206
Mon-Fri: 4pm-12am, Sat-Sun: 12pm-
12am. Avg. Price: £7

If you can't be bothered to cook, La
Cucina delivers an Italian feast to
your door. Starters such as ciabatta
topped with marinated tomatoes,
red onions and basil come in at £2.25,
the anti pasti of meats, artichoke
hearts, sun dried and char grilled
vegetables is £6.50, and typical Italian
main courses such as lasagne and
pizzas are also around £6.50.

INDIAN

Ashoka

95-97 Church Rd, Hove BN3
2BA
T: 01273 734193 F: 01273 202112
www.ashoka-restaurant.co.uk
Mon-Sun: 12pm-3pm, 6pm-12am
Avg. Price: £20

It's got a reputation as the best Indian
in town and after a night there, it's
hard to disagree. In 1995 it was The
Daily Mirror's Indian Restaurant
of the Year. That's big. Maybe the
staff were a little too attentive, but
it's difficult to find fault. The food
was just right. Nothing fancy, just
right. It doesn't try to be flash or
fashionable or cool or anything really
other than what it is. Prices are also
what you might expect (Tandoori
chicken masala £7.45), there's also a

large vegetarian menu and the food matches its reputation. Listen; if it's good enough for Cliff Richard, whose pictures shaking hands with the ecstatic manager adorn the walls, it's good enough for us.

Bayleaf

104 Western Rd, Hove BN1 2AA
T: 01273 722280 T: 01273 773804
www.brighton/www.brighton\
bayleaf.co.uk
Sun-Fri: 12pm-3pm, 5.30pm-11.30pm,
Sat: 12pm to 12am
Private room available
Avg. Price: £15

Modern British Indian food without the flock wallpaper and sitar muzak.

No one's going to persuade us that cheddar and mozzarella can be used in Indian cuisine, but their more traditional food is better, and the Habitat crockery shows that at least they're trying to pitch a groovier crowd. All the food is cooked to order so allow a good lump of time for your meal. The menu changes regularly and vegetables and side dishes vary daily according to the mood of the chef. Even the raita and chutney served with the complimentary pappadoms are homemade. Try the takeaway too; if everyone else is too busy, chances are that your Korma will be delivered by the boss in his Mercedes and Indian livery. Averages £15-£18 per head.

Indian Summer

East St, The Lanes, Brighton
BN1 1HP. T: 01273 711001
www.indian-summer.org.uk
Mon: 6pm-10.30pm, Tue-Fri: 12pm-3pm, 6pm-10.30pm, Sat: 12pm-10.30pm, Sun: 12pm-10pm
Avg. Price: £22

5 Victoria Terrace, Hove BN3
2WB. T: 01273 711001/01273
773090
www.indian-summer.org.uk
Tue-Sat: 6pm-10.30pm, Sun: 6pm-10pm. Avg. Price: £22

Say bye-bye to Bajis at this tiny Indian dining room as you journey

through uncharted territories including such a head-scratcher as Utthapam (£4.60) a 'pizza' made from rice and lentils. The Murgh Makhani is not what you'd expect; this is chicken breast prepared in a fresh onion and melon seed sauce served with sweet potato mash and stuffed baby aubergines (£10.50). With starters all coming in under a fiver and no main costing more than £15, originality comes at an affordable price. You'll be guided through the intricacies of each culinary concoction by waiting staff that are attentive without being obtrusive. But... the spice and flavoursome taste that makes Indian food so popular has been lost on this eatery's quest for originality. What remains is a

blandness permeating through most of the offerings that inspires yet disappoints in equal measure. A case of style of substance? Even if many Juicy readers disagree, for us, sadly, it was. Add your own user review at www.juicymapminder.co.uk

Memories of India on the Waterfront

9b Waterfront, Marina BN2 5WA. T: 01273 600088 Fax: 01273 600655

Mon-Sun: 12pm-11.30pm

Avg. Price: £20

Really excellent modern Indian food and a touch of luxury in the Italian dominated Marina, with scenes from

Bollywood's finest beamed from wall mounted monitors around the restaurant. Even if the Marina is still empty most of the time, you can bet your life on a queue outside Memories on a Saturday night, with their vast dining room packed to the gills. They'll do takeaways but don't deliver.

ITALIAN

Al Duomo

7 Pavilion Buildings, Brighton BN1 1EE. T: 01273 326741 T: 01273 321856 F: 01273 749792 www.alduomo.co.uk info@alduomo.co.uk

Mon-Thurs: 12pm-2.30pm, 6pm-11pm, Fri-Sun: 12pm-11pm

was won, the door was open, and Brighton raced in and created the alfresco pleasure dome you see today. Worth a tip, wouldn't you say? A two-course menu with a choice of five pizzas and four pastas plus dessert comes in at £5.95.

Alfresco

26 Kings Road Arches,
Brighton BN1 2LN
T: 01273 206523 F: 01273 227793
www.alfrescobrighton.co.uk
Sun-Thurs: 12pm-9pm, Fri-Sat:
12pm-10pm. Private room
available. Avg. Price: £15

Slowly restaurateurs are finding there are people who like to eat something other than burgers on the beach, and Alfresco is now facing enough competition to make it pull up its socks. Not enough, but we like to give praise where praise is due. It's still not the place to go if you're in a hurry, and the food is still uninspired, but the portions are generous, and, unlike the old days, the waiters get the order right. It's still a place to go because it's easy and the view is the best in town. Any lip from the famously rude waiters, call Pascuale, a proper gent.

Ask

58 Ship St, The Lanes, Brighton
BN1 1DE
T: 01273 710030 F: 01273 723903
www.askcentral.co.uk
Mon-Thurs: 12pm-11pm, Fri-Sat:
12pm-11.30pm. Avg. Price: £15

Private room available
Avg. Price: £10

Recently reinvented but built on the foundations of being one of the Brighton's best loved Italians for eons, this is now the city centre's main Big Party venue. Italian service and big wood burning pizza oven provide its beating heart and the vast two floors of steel, glass and wood, with a sky lit mezzanine overlooking the ground floor and bar, have propelled it into wedding and hen-night land. Get married at the Pavilion and totter over to Al Duomo for the reception before retiring to the beach to watch a heavenly sunset, and you've got a marriage to remember.

Al Forno

36 East St, The Lanes, Brighton
BN1 1HL. T: 01273 324905
F: 01273 749762
www.alforno.co.uk
info@alforno.co.uk
May-Oct: Mon-Thurs: 12pm-3pm,
6pm-11pm, Fri-Sun: 12pm-11pm Nov
– Apr: Mon-Fri: 12pm-3pm, Sat-Sun:
12pm-11pm. Private room available
Avg. Price: £15

Nice, kid friendly Italian in the centre of town from the people behind Al Duomo. This is the older sister whose pizzas are legendary and who revolutionised The Lanes 14 years ago by applying for an alcohol licence for its outdoor area. Once the fight

Popular with business folk, ladies who lunch and tourists who don't know that they should be at Latin in the Lanes. The thin crust pizzas compare nicely to Pizza Express, but don't expect anything outstanding other than a courtyard garden and a separate non-smoking room.

Bella Napoli
Village Square, Marina, Brighton BN2 5WA
T: 01273 818577 F: 01273 818577
www.bellanapoli.co.uk
Mon-Thurs: 12pm-2.30pm, 6pm-11pm, Fri-Sun: 12pm-11pm
Avg. Price: £15

Packed with Italian families at the weekend, this Neapolitan family run business will twirl its pizzas, kiss your babies and entertain your little ones all day while you quaff your way through their wine list. Excellent (and genuine) Italian ice cream and the coffee is straight out of Naples. Live Italian music on Thursday and Sunday evenings.

The Brasserie
15d Village Square, Marina, Brighton BN2 5WA
T: 01273 818026
Mon-Sun: 12pm-3pm, 6.30pm-10.30pm. Avg. Price: £25

So huge are the portions that you could almost forgive them for charging so much for dinner. If anyone is ever that hungry, it could be a good deal but as the only posh Italian in the Marina (the only posh anything in the Marina – apart from the yachts) it does a roaring trade. On a beautiful day, the tables are shuffled out onto the waterfront. Expect to pay £25 per head for three courses.

Darcy's
49 Market St, The Lanes, Brighton BN1 1HH
T: 01273 325560 F: 01273 735424
Sun-Fri: 12pm-10.30pm, Sat: 12pm-11pm. Private room available
Avg. Price: £30

Popular little Italian in the heart of The Lanes, with the kind of welcome that tourists love, but enough substance to keep the locals coming back for more.

Donatello
1 Brighton Place, The Lanes, Brighton BN1 1HJ. T: 01273 775477 F: 01273 734001
www.donatello.co.uk donatellobrighton@compuserve.com
Mon-Sun: 11.30am-11.30pm
Private room available
Avg. Price: £15-20

Bright and breezy family of pizzerias with Italian largesse and small bills. The food and the waiters are unreconstructed Italians, so the service is friendly, children are welcome, and the pizzas are damn fine. The biggest of the brothers commands an impressive presence in the heart of The Lanes, with nooks, crannies, conservatories, lounge bars and enough space to seat a Sicilian extended family. They do a two-course menu for £7.95 and three courses for £9.95 (£10.95 on Saturday night). Under 12's can have smaller portions of any pizza or pasta for £3.00. They do gluten-free pasta and pride themselves on not using GM products.

Fat Leo
16-17 Market St, Brighton BN1 1HH. T: 01273 325135
F: 01273 734001
www.fatleo.co.uk donatellobrighton@compuserve.com
Mon-Sun: 12pm-10pm
Avg. Price: £10

New restaurant from the people behind Donatello, this is linear and minimalist. The beautiful glass blue bricks lighting up the bar give it a modern feel, but the Donatello pedigree means that this is old style Italian hospitality. The range of food didn't impress our Italian reviewer but the quality of the lasagne, cannelloni agli spinaci e ricotta, bistecca alla pizzaiola and pizza with a good parma ham reminded her of her mamma's kitchen. Two courses at £6.95 and three course at £8.95.

Latin in the Lane
10 Kings Rd, The Lanes, Brighton BN1 1NE. T: 01273 328672 F: 01273 321600
Sun-Thurs: 12pm-2.15pm, 6pm-11pm, Fri and Sat: 12pm-2.15pm, 6pm-11.30pm. Private room available. Avg. Price: £25-30

Can a restaurant like Latin in The Lanes ever be judged the best in the city? It's certainly the best Italian, the service is consistently top notch and the food is perfect. From the counter of fresh oysters that greets you as you walk in, to the Sardine al succo d'arancia (sardines cooked in orange juice) (£4.95), to the locally caught fresh fish, the menu is enormous. And if you don't want fish, well, that's

OK too. Ostrich in port wine with spinach in cream (£14.95). Chicken in brandy, cream and pink peppercorns (£9.95)? No, it probably won't ever get a Juicy Award while there are chefs pushing back the culinary boundaries, but for those of you who don't care about awards, it doesn't get much better than this.

Leonardo

55 Church Rd, Hove BN3 2BD
T: 01273 328888 F: 01273 777219

www.leonardo-restaurant.com
info@leonardo-restaurant.com
Sun-Thurs: 12pm-11pm, Fri-Sat:
12pm-11.30pm. Avg. Price: £20

A big favourite among Hoveites, this is a top Italian which uses a touch of Modern British presentation to mark it out from the other Italians along this stretch. Unlike most good-looking Italians, beauty here is more than skin deep and the Risotto alla Risacca di Mare (£7.50) is one of the best in the city. The special set menu of £7.95 for two courses is astonishingly good value and the service has been hauled up since the last review. The only problem is the lack of no-smoking areas; it doesn't matter how good the food is, when someone's puffing away behind you, it'll always taste foul.

Marocco's

Kings Esplanade, Hove BN3 2WA. T: 01273 203764
Mon-Sun: 10am-6pm
Avg. Price: £25

Renalto has been running this little Italian on Hove beach since the Mods and Rockers were here. Perhaps it's because he insists on importing the best ingredients from Italy, he's found it hard to retire, and handed it over to his son when local opinion forced him not to close up shop and head for the easy life. The perfect place for an ice cream after a stroll along the front.

Orsinos

141 Church Rd, Hove BN3 2AE
T: 01273 770999 F: 01273 778277
www.orsinorestaurant.com
Sun-Thurs: 11am-11pm, Fri-Sat: 11am-1pm. Avg. Price: £20

Recently refurbished, this big spacious Italian pizzeria is where the waiters tickle cute kids and sing to beautiful women and where the risotto marinara reminds you of every other

risotto marinara you've ever had in a big spacious Italian pizzeria where the waiters tickle cute kids and sing to beautiful women. Which is why it's always packed to the gills. There's a DJ and dancing at the weekend so you can work off your pasta.

Picasso

24 Ship St, The Lanes, Brighton BN1 1AF
T: 01273 321233 F: 01273 710196
Mon-Sun: 12pm-11pm
Avg. Price: £10

Another pizza place in The Lanes, this time from the people behind Waikika Moo Kau. Like its cousins in The Lanes and Kensington Garden, the plates are brimming with nice enough fare, but despite the added extras like Italian lessons piped into the loos, it hasn't got their character etched onto the walls or their smiley service.

Piccolos

56 Ship St, The Lanes, Brighton BN1 1AF. T: 01273 203701 F: 01273 820820
www.scoot.co.uk/piccola_restaurant-brighton
Mon-Sun: 11.30am-11.30pm
Avg. Price: £15

Extremely popular Italian for a Pizza restaurant which doesn't boast an Italian family ownership. Particularly child friendly with two floors for them to run around in. The pizzas are good too and they do take away.

Pieros

30 Spring St, Brightons BN1 3EF.
T: 01273 329426
Tues-Sat 6.30pm-10pm

Although Pieros is only just off the main Western Road thoroughfare, it is only the locals who ever discover it. This is probably because it is a tiny Italian restaurant in the ground floor of one of the terraced Georgian cottages which predominate locally – the dining room only seats 20! Run for over 30 years by Italian-Welsh couple Piero and Jenny, the menu belies the size of the place with an extensive repertoire likely to satisfy the most demanding of Italian food lovers. Particularly recommended are the Capriccio Italiano, an escalope of veal with ham and mozzarella served with a wine sauce (£11.35), and prices include the fresh vegetables. Pieros is unlikely to disappoint and delights as much for the intimate atmosphere as the food. It is so popular that you absolutely have to book ahead. £25.

Pinocchio

22 New Rd, Brighton BN1 1UF
T: 01273 677676 F: 01273 734001
www.pinocchiobrighton.co.uk
donatellobrighton@compuserve.com
Mon-Sat: 11.30am-11.30pm, Sun: 12pm-9.30pm. Private room available. Avg. Price: £20

Donatello's smaller sister, this is classic Italian fare and packed with pre and post theatre goers. On panto night at The Theatre Royal almost next door, the place is teaming with small, excited children tucking into their Spaghetti Bolognese and ice creams and not even realising that this is what childhoods are made of.

Pizza Express

107 Church Rd, Hove BN3 2AA
T: 01273 770093
Mon-Sat:11.30am-11pm, Sun:
11.30am-10pm
22 Prince Albert, North Laine,
Brighton BN1 1HF
T: 01273 323205
Mon-Sat: 11.30am-12pm, Sun: 12pm-
11.30pm
Waterfront, Marina, Brighton
BN2 5WA. T: 01273 689300
Mon-Sat: 11.30am-11pm, Mon-Sun:
11.30am-10pm . Avg. Price: £15

An institution. In the last few years, Pizza Express has repositioned itself and now sits head and shoulders above the other pizza chains. The staff are endlessly patient, and it's the place to take kids if you know they're going to throw their food at the wall. If you don't want to be surrounded by young families, don't go on a weekend lunchtime. By night, the lights dim, and the atmosphere is more chilled. Sitting out on the deck at the Marina on a beautiful summer's evening before nipping over to the UGC is a joy.

Zafferelli

31 New Rd, Brighton BN1 1UG
T: 01273 206662/01273 206702
F: 01273 772948

www.zafferelli.com
design@zafferelli.com
Mon-Thurs: 12pm-10.30pm, Fri-Sat:
12pm-11pm. Avg. Price: £20

Recently refurbished, but established since 1997, Zafferelli is a large, airy Italian in a perfect position in the centre of town off the main shopping drag and just by the Theatre Royal. Popularity with the theatre crowd aside, Zafferelli has placed itself in an odd position: More individual than the Express or Hut chains, it's not as family-friendly as somewhere like Donatello but it isn't as chic as some posh place you'd take your partner to impress them. The pale wooden floor, white walls and bland artwork make it appear clean but cold, efficient but lacking in warmth. The food was good though: the pizzas big (maybe too big, but better too big than too small) and reasonably priced. The pizzas range between £4.95 and 7.95, Salmone alla Griglia (that's grilled salmon to you) is £10.75 and Bistecca al Pepe (sirloin steak in green pepper sauce) is £13.95.

Zizzi

7 Prince Albert St, The Lanes,
Brighton BN1 1HE. T: 01273
323273
Sun-Wed: 10am-11pm, Thurs-Sat:
10am-11.30pm
Avg. Price: £20

Our Italian reviewer tells us that Zizzi is a nickname for a particular part of a man's anatomy, which is an odd

choice for such a stylish chain of city restaurants. More a place to get a quick bite than somewhere to get a true taste of Italy, Zizzi could never compete with the more authentic Al Forno, Al Duomo, Donatello or Fat Leo's – all of which share its neighbourhood.

JAPANESE

E Kagen

22-23 Sydney St, North Laine,
Brighton BN1 4EN
T: 01273 687068
www.white-dragon@orbix.
net.uk
Mon-Wed: 11.30am-6pm, Fri-Sat:
11.30am-3.30pm, 6.30pm-10pm
Avg. Price: £20

Formerly a basic but popular Chinese noodle bar, the food is now Japanese and not quite as cheap, but the feel is the same. Think noodle bar in Malaysia rather than chic sushi restaurant, but prepare for a similar sized bill. BYO.

Moshi Moshi

Opticon, Bartholomew Square,
The Lanes, Brighton BN1 1JS. T:
01273 719195
F: 01273 719196
www.moshimoshi.co.uk
brighton@moshimoshi.co.uk
Tue-Sat: 12pm-11pm
Avg. Price: £15

Fast, healthy and inexpensive, this is a real Juicy favourite and where you'll find us most days of the week. The sushi confounds any preconceptions of conveyor belt food, with salmon so fresh it melts in the mouth, and starts at £1.20 a dish. The a la carte menu is diligently explained by the Japanese waiters, but try the Kaiseki 12 courser (£22) for an interesting introduction to Japanese Haute Cuisine. On a sunny day, you can sit outside, and those who haven't spent a lazy Brighton afternoon over a few sakes and a couple of unagi sushi (grilled eel in teriyaki marinade) and prawn and mago maki, should get out more. Home delivery includes a free extra dish, and all conveyor best dishes are £1.50 on winter Sundays. Midnight Moshi is a members club, which is open late on Fridays and Saturdays to those who want an escape from the smokier options.

Oki Nami
208 Church Rd, Hove BN3 2DJ
T: 01273 773777
www.okinami.com
info@okinami.com
Mon: 6pm-10.30pm, Wed-Sat: 12pm-2.30pm, 6pm-10.30pm, Sun: 1pm-9.30pm. Avg. Price: £30

Stylish little Japanese which sits quietly at the Hove end of Western Road, doing very nicely thank you well before Hove filled up with sushi sucking Crouch End émigrés. Rather too stark for a two-hour evening, with absolutely nothing to look at other than your food, your partner and the straight lines of the benches and tables, it could do with the

fascinating focus of the sushi bar generally found in such places. They even provide a little origami to help pass the hours, but the food is fab: try the Tsunami set meal (£21.95 per head) to have your tongue tickled as the five courses of sushi and teriyaki build like the tidal wave it's named after.

Sapporo
38-40 Preston St, Brighton BN1 2HP. T: 01273 777880
F: 01273 734862
Mon-Fri: 5pm-11pm, Sat and Sun: 12pm-11pm. Avg. Price: £20

Not so long ago, this was a tame Japanese with so-so food in the street of so-so food, and apart from the extraordinarily over-the-top central sushi bar where you'll be entertained by the juggling of pepper pots and tossing of prawns, it still is. Taking tips from The Mongolian Brasserie and chefs from The 'let-me-entertain-you' Philippines, the owners have made sure that chicken teriyaki will never seem the same again. As the flames shoot and the crowd whoops, the dinners in the cheap seats vow to book the hot spot next time or go to Oki Nami for the real thing. Averages £15-£20 per head and try the teppanyaki Goma-Yaki (Chicken breast coated with sesame seed) £10.90.

LEBANESE

Kambis
107 Western Rd, Brighton BN1 2AA. T: 01273 327934

Mon-Sun: 11am-12am
Avg. Price: £20

Authentic Lebanese in the heart of Western Road which, to a less discerning eye, looks like the kind of kebab takeaway which might serve an inebriated clubbing crowd. Peek inside to find a genuinely Middle Eastern atmosphere with gentle and unassuming service and vegetarian and meat mezzes to make your mouth water. The fare is what you'd expect in towns where there's more of an Arabic connection than Brighton; even the signs on the loos are in Arabic. After dinner, ask to partake of the shisha, a kind of elegant version of a bong, and you're in for a truly Alice in Wonderland experience.

MEXICAN

Dig in the Ribs
47 Preston St,
Brighton BN1 2HP
T: 01273 325275 F: 01273 682322
www.digintheribs.co.uk
Mon-Sat: 12pm-11.30pm, Sun: 12pm-10.30pm. Avg. Price: £10

Tex Mex in the street of so-so food, populated with children before 7pm who come for the rhino shaped nuggets and pile of nachos, and pre-clubbers who come for the margheritas and, er, nachos. Shame; they should try the sizzling fajitas, or nick the sparkler ice cream from the kids. The salsa comes in vats rather

than anything looking like a tomato, but if you like your food fast and friendly, this could be your spiritual home.

El Mexicano

7 New Rd, Brighton BN1 1UF
T: 01273 727766 F: 01273 727898
www.elmexicano.co.uk
elmexicano@youtopia.co.uk
Mon-Thurs: 6pm-11pm, Fri: 11am-2.30pm, 6pm-11pm, Sat-Sun: 11am-11pm. Avg. Price: £20

One of the handful of genuine Mexican restaurants in the UK, El Mexicano doesn't do the Tex Mex

thing with its chimichangas. In fact it doesn't even do chimichangas. Instead, you'll get a bitter green tomato salsa which we think is delicious but which is probably an acquired taste, and a hot chilli salsa to spice up your own enchiladas (£7.95). Some of the dishes you may never have come across before: Mole (£9.95) is a chicken bathed in over 100 ingredients, including chillies, nuts and chocolate, Crema de frijoles (black bean soup, with cheese and strips of crispy fried tortillas £3.25), Picadillo (authentic Mexican chilli con carne with almonds, potato and raisins £7.75). The Margaritas and the Sols, the big party bookings and the Latino music are more of what you

might expect. Top service makes the night a friendly one. Bar Valentino upstairs is a cocktail bar, which is open until 2am.

Los Amigos

60 Church Rd, Hove BN3 2FP
T: 01273 778777 F: 01273 821462
Mon-Fri: 10.30am-3.30pm, 5.30pm-11pm, Sat-Sun: 10.30am-11pm
Avg Price: £15

Tex Mex joint where the idea is to fill up rather than feast your senses. The food is fine enough; the fajitas sizzle, and the enchiladas are exactly what it says on the tin. The service is friendly and attentive, the décor is sparse (and perhaps ironic) with fake cacti and large sombreros adorning the walls, but the ambience in this Hove high street restaurant is about as far removed as it gets from Mexico.

The Cactus Canteen

Brighton Square, The Lanes, Brighton BN1 1HD
T: 01273 725700
F: 01273 732820
Sun-Thurs: 12pm-10.30pm, Fri-Sat: 12pm-11.30pm. Avg. Price: £15-20

Big servings and kicking music have the weekend crowd thronging their way into these Tex Mex banquettes in the heart of the Lanes. 12oz steaks go for around £13.95 and there are plenty of veggie fajitas (£10.95), Quesadillas (£9.95), enchiladas (£9.95), Pollo a la Creole char-grilled chicken breast in homemade tangy Creole sauce (£9.95) to make the Brighton crowd happy. It's also a top choice for a kiddy friendly lunch.

Santa Fe

75-79 East St, The Lanes, Brighton BN1 1NF
T: 01273 823231 F: 01273 823235
www.santafe.co.uk
brightonsf@santafe.co.uk
Mon-Sat: 12pm-10.30pm, Sun: 12pm-10pm. Private room available.
Avg. Price: £25

Bright, modern, spacious and the kind of place you'd head to for a hen night or big party. The food is said to have been inspired by real New

Mexican cuisine that comes from the kitchens of Native Americans and Spanish pioneers, and there's plenty on the menu that you'll never have heard of; chipotle shrimp and corn cakes, or lime and green chile salmon for example. But there's enough of a nod to Modern European food to tempt you to try out the new flavours and the lime and chile dish is no more frightening than a char-grilled marinated Atlantic salmon fillet. The cocktail bar is a truly Latin experience. There's also a private room for hire. They offer a £3.50 kids menu including pasta and chicken goujons.

MODERN BRITISH

Barry at the Tureen

31 Upper North St, Brighton BN1 3FG. T: 01273 328939
Wed-Sat: 7pm-12am
Private room available
Avg. Price: £20

There are a few really intimate dining rooms in Brighton, but none as genuinely welcoming as Barry's. Queen of The Tureen, he's a self taught chef who cribs his dishes from The Evening Standard and buys his roast potatoes in a pre-prepared pack from Tescos ('well, why bother with all that par-boiling when Aunt Bessy's are just as good?'). Somehow he manages to bake the perfect cheese soufflé while settling his giggling table of eight, advising on wines and sizing up just how much chat his customers are up for. Three courses for £19.50 (£17 for two) is great value;

try the caramelised red onion and sun dried tomato tart followed by chicken breast, boned and wrapped in bacon with an apple and thyme stuffing, roasted and served with a red wine gravy and a frozen blackberry liqueur soufflé.

Blanch House Restaurant

17 Atlingworth St, Kemp Town, Brighton BN2 1PL
T: 01273 645755 F: 01273 689813
www.blanchhouse.co.uk
info@blanchhouse.co.uk
Tues: 7pm-10.30pm, Wed-Fri: 12pm-3pm, 7pm-10.30pm, Sat: 1pm-2.30pm, 7pm-10.30pm
Avg. Price: £50

Blanch House has probably managed to secure more column inches in its short life than the rest of Brighton's hotels and restaurants put together, and most of it is well deserved. The dining room is stunning in white leather, and the food a picture on a plate. The bar is one of the best places in town to stop for a late drink and the hotel is a triumph of imagination. The restaurant however has always fallen down on its rather sullen service, despite a number of staff changes, which when you're paying around £100 for two, leaves a bad taste in even the most well fed of mouths. The menu is simpler these days but it was never the food that was the problem.

Due South

139 Kings Rd Arches, Brighton BN1 2NA. T: 01273 821218

duesouthbrighton@yahoo.com

Private room available

Avg. Price: £25

Due South is one of the newest additions to the seafront's plethora of chaos and consumption. Just along from Gemini's, it offers a welcome alternative to the usual beach fodder of chips, burgers and candy floss in the form of freshly, locally produced, beautifully prepared cuisine. They specialise in locally caught fish, but there are plenty of vegetarian options as well as hefty carnivorous portions for the red meat lovers – our reviewer was particularly impressed by the rabbit kebabs, but then she's a country girl at heart. Sit indoors overlooking the sea, or bask in the sunshine and watch the world go by. Extras include a business breakfast, a snack and tapas menu in afternoon and takeaway and delivery will be available soon.

English's

29 East St, The Lanes, Brighton BN1 1HL. T: 01273 327980/ 01273 328645 F: 01273 329754

www.englishs.co.uk

info@english.co.uk

Mon-Sat: 12pm-10.15pm, Sun: 12.30pm-9.30pm. Avg. Price: £20

Brighton's oldest fish restaurant celebrates its antiquity with the walls of its Red Room almost whispering stories from the

Edwardian gay days. A favourite with Charlie Chaplin and Lawrence Olivier, it is housed in three fishermen's cottages dating back 400 years on the edge of the Lanes, and creaks with authenticity. Apparently, if kids finish all their food, they get a tour of the kitchen.

Epicurean

33 Western St, Brighton BN1 2PG. T: 01273 776618

www.epicurean-brighton.com

Tue-Sat: 12pm-2pm, 6.30pm-10pm

Avg. Price: £35-40

Bruno Pruvost comes with Michelin star from Rouen and culinary reputation from Woodheys in Manchester, and fills the gap between Hotel du Vin and The Gingerman. More intimate than HdV and more luxurious than The Gingerman with its blue leather chairs, Wedgewood cutlery and gold and blue carpet, the food gives both a run for their money. It may be Modern British, but remember that it's cooked by a very Gallic former Michelin Man; try the flower of thin home smoked king scallops marinated in hint of pistou and served with fresh plum tomato concasse (£7.60) followed by a glazed medley of Dover Sole fillet and baby spinach with fresh mussels veloute on fresh black ink squid tagliatelle (£18.90). Per head, it's about £35-£40 although food fans will be thrilled to hear that the lunchtime set menu (Tues-Sat) is £8.50 and £12.50 for three courses.

Freemasons

38-39 Western Rd, Hove BN3 1AF. T: 01273 732043

info@freemasonspub.co.uk

Mon: 12.30pm-6pm, Tue-Sun: 12.30pm-9pm. Private room available. Avg. Price: £20

Tanya and Darcy have left The Freemasons now, but as we went to press, the new owners were putting together a fine dining experience to rival theirs. The restaurant is upstairs in this listed building with original art deco features recently revealed to add to the atmosphere.

Fringe Bar

10 Kensington Gdns, North Laine, Brighton BN1 4AL T: 01273 623683

Mon: 6.30pm-10pm, Tue-Thurs: 12pm-3pm, 6.30pm-10pm, Fri, Sat and Sun: 12pm-5pm, 6.30pm-10pm

Avg. Price: £25

Sourcing local produce and building its reputation on freshness, The Fringe is now one of the best restaurants in the North Laine. It's not just hot on its menu, cool on its music and ambience but one of the few examples of great service in the city, with waiters informed and interested in the food they serve. Try the duck breast with rissole potatoes and raspberry jus at £10.25 with classic crème brulee and seasonal berries (£3.95) to follow.

Gingerman

21a Norfolk Square, Hove BN1
2PD. T: 01273 326688 F: 01273
326688
Tues-Sat: 12.30pm-2pm, 7pm-10pm.
Avg. Price: £35

Tucked away between Western
Road and the sea is The Gingerman,
one of Brighton's gourmet treats
– particularly for meat fans. Stylishly
simpler than Hotel du Vin with
slightly more space than L'Epicurean,
and attaining Brighton's Holy Grail
– consistency in both quality of
food and service, it's one of the
city's favourite restaurants. It's still
dominated by fat cats, despite the
efforts of the informal waitresses,
and is always booked up weeks in
advance. If you're looking for the
place to take your love, ask for the
table to the left of the door and
close the luxuriously thick curtain to
keep the world out while you tuck
into your Potato and Roasted Garlic
Soup with Poached Egg and Croutons
followed by Roasted Squab Pigeon
with Truffled Celeriac and Aged Port
Reduction. The themed assiettes
for dessert change according to the
season, and to Ben's current penchant
but cannot be missed. Two courses
are £22 and three, £25.

Havana

32 Duke St, The Lanes,
Brighton BN1 1AG
T: 01273 773388 F: 01273 748923
www.havana.uk.com
Mon-Thurs: 10.30am-10.30pm, Fri-
Sat: 10.30am-11pm, Sun: 10.30am-

10pm. Avg. Price: £25-30

Havana is turning into one of
Brighton's consistently good
restaurants from what was once a
parochial pretender. A place you can
really dress up for, as you'd expect,
there's an air of colonial Spain about
it: loured shutters, huge overhead
fans and a rather grand balcony
overlooking the central dining
area. The food is fancy; steamed
pink bream stuffed with a salmon
mousse, spinach and coral dust,
served on pureed and glazed fennel
with a crispy potato and pied blue
mushrooms, confit shallots with a
red wine sauce at £17.95 for example.
There are cheaper options of course,
but it's hard to leave Havana with
enough cash for a cigar.

Hotel du Vin

Ship St, The Lanes, Brighton
BN1 1AD. T: 01273 718588
F: 01273 718599
www.hotelduvin.com
info@brightonhotelduvin.com
Mon-Sun: 6.30pm-10pm. Private
room available. Avg. Price: £40

The most important recent addition
to the gastro-scene in Brighton,
the food is simply perfect, and the
service is as French as it gets. With
no second sittings or stressed service
to hurry you through your meal,
the gravadlax with fennel ceviche
and sweet mustard starter (£6.50)
followed by free range Guinea fowl
with crisp polenta, fondant leek and

salsa verde (£14.50) hits the balance
so hard to find in fine dining; too
heavy and you wish you hadn't
started, and too light and you're
raiding the nuts in the mini bar by
midnight. Corinne, the wonderful
sommelier who migrated from
Hotel du Vin in Birmingham, is still
confounding the image of the snobby
French wine buff with her practical
and effortless matching of wine to
food. At around £40 per head all in,
it's not cheap but boy, is it worth it.
There's a jazz band on Saturday night.

La Marinade

77 St George's Rd, Kemp Town,
Brighton BN1 1EF
T: 01273 600992 F: 01273
600922
www.lamarinade.co.uk
info@lamarinade.co.uk
Tue-Wed: 6pm-12am, Thurs-Sat:
12pm-3pm, 6pm-12am. Avg. Price:
£30-40

Quality European cuisine where cut
glass voices ("Why would anyone
stay outside Venice?") debate the
choice of wine ("perhaps the Krug
'89"). Don't be surprised then if a
meal at this little restaurant in East
Kemp Town, with its pleasantly
understated French service is likely
to set you back £70.00 for two; try
the roasted milk-fed Pyrenean lamb,
the guinea fowl supreme stuffed
with foie gras or the fillet of sea
bass spread with aubergine caviar
followed by banana and sesame
flambé, and see if you can still fit
through the door. If you can't, your

wallet certainly can. Despite the French feel, the Chef/Patron is as English as Shoreditch and fancies himself as a bit of a Marco Pierre White. He's passionate about his food and if anyone dares to ask for extra seasoning, they're likely to be out on their ear.

Peers

52 Lansdowne Place, Hove
BN3 1FG. T: 01273 775565
www.peersrestaurant.co.uk
enquiry@peersrestaurant.co.uk
Mon-Sun: 10.30am-10pm
Avg. Price: £25

Anyone who has been to Peers, the

new gourmet restaurant on Western Rd, might notice that it all looks a little familiar. Peers is either a homage to the glories of Seven Dials or a cheeky rip off, in décor at least. The food is hard to fault; the pan-fried fillets of brill on a bed of wilted spinach and woodland mushrooms with a cider and saffron mussel sauce followed by mille feuille of champagne marinated strawberries and creme patisserie with spiced berry compote was sublime, but somehow where the idea comes from a lottery winner's business plan rather than the love of a hot stove, you can even smell it on the napkins. Two courses for £18.50, three for £22.95.

Prompt Corner

36 Montpelier Rd,
Brighton BN1 3BA. T: 01273
737624/01273 748911
www.promptcorner.com
alan@promptcorner.freeserve.
co.uk
Mon-Sun: 6pm-11.30pm
Private room available
Avg. Price: £40

Prompt Corner is a Brighton institution with a theatrically themed menu reminding us that it was set up by a thespian back in 1948, and the wall-to-wall movie and theatrical memorabilia adding to the intimate atmosphere. The menu maintains

Yabba Jabba Beefy Tea

by Terre a Terre

the theatrical theme; the appetisers compose Act 1 – go for the divine crab cakes before moving on to Act 2 and the Sole Florentine – a delicate dish that tickles the taste buds. Act 3? The Beef Wellington is classically prepared and hard to fault. The wine list has a good selection, and is knowledgeably described and competitively priced. And as this is classical theatre, don't expect anything from the waiters other than unobtrusive service and attention to detail; comedy waiters belong to a very different experience. Expect damage of £50 for two to include delicious desserts and wine for two. Booking recommended.

Quentin's

42 Western Rd, Hove BN3 1JD
T: 01273 822734 F: 01273 822734
www.quentinsrestaurant.co.uk
Tue-Fri: 12pm-2.30pm, 7pm-11pm,
Sat: 7pm-11pm, Sun: 12pm-5pm
Avg. Price: £30

Possibly the most bizarre of Brighton and Hove's fine dining offerings, there are dishes you really, really won't find anywhere else. Go on – tell me where else you'll get a crocodile steak in coconut and lime, sautéed red rice with a red onion and chilli jam (£6.95) followed by Venison haunch faggots, garlic pomme purée, steamed courgettes and carrots with a chocolate and red wine jus (£17.95)? The weeny inter-courses pad the whole evening out to a minimum of a two and a half hour gastro-fest and happily, there's no second sittings,

so you can lounge there all night listening to Boyzone and popping down to the ladies (again) to check just how pornographic those pictures on the wall really are. Not a place to take the kids for lunch, unless you can explain why the bull dyke with exposed breasts in the nice painting next to the loo has bits that look just like daddy's...

QUOD

160-161 North St, The Lanes,
Brighton BN1 1EZ
T: 01273 202070 F: 01273 731001
www.quod.co.uk
quodbright@quod.co.uk
Mon-Sat: 10.30am-11pm, Sun:
10.30am-10.30pm
Private room available
Avg. Price: £30

You can always spot a success story in Brighton by the way the walls swell on a midweek evening. In most restaurants, you'll probably catch the waiters doing their toenails on a wintry Wednesday evening, but Quod packs them all week long into its Tuscan interiors. The earthy menu which ranges from Steaks (£17.95) and lamb shanks (£10.95) to pizzas (£7.95) and pastas (£8.95) mean that it's great for both business lunches and romantic dinners, and on Sundays, children eat free. (They also do a two course Express Lunch for £5 Mon-Sat). Artwork by some of the UK's most interesting new artists accompany the restaurant/bar next door in QUODArt.

Saucy

8 Church Rd, Hove BN3 2FL
T: 01273 324080 Fax: 01273 732116
Mon-Fri: 12pm-2pm, 6pm-10pm,
Sat: 12pm-11pm, Sun: 12pm-3pm
Avg. Price: £30

Mention eating out in Hove to your friends and the chances are they'll mention Saucy. The food is certainly fabulous – Cashel blue cheese and chive tartlet with asparagus sauce £4.50 and Pan-fried calves liver and bacon with thyme potato gratin and a rich balsamic jus were particularly delicious and well presented and there are plenty of specials, sides and extras to choose from plus a mouth-watering cocktail list. It's just the lack of atmosphere that leaves you wanting. OK, so it's meant to be bright and modern (orange is the new black) but it can feel a little bit soulless and clattery – which is not conducive to romantic types. On the plus side, if you've got kids, this is a much-needed stop-off on your day out. Forget chicken nuggets – your tweenies will be treated to the likes of bangers and mash and bubble and squeak with poached egg. They also do a business lunch – £8.95 for two courses.

Seven Dials

Buckingham Place, Seven Dials,
Brighton BN1 3TD
T: 01273 885555 F: 01273 888911
www.sevendialsrestaurant.co.uk
sam@sevendialsrestaurant.co.uk
Oct-Apr: Tues-Sat: 12pm-3pm;

7pm-10.30pm; Sun 12.30pm-
9.30pm. May-Sept: Tues-Sat:
10.30am-10.30pm; Sun: 12.30pm-
9.30pm. Private room available
Avg. Price: £30

Winner of a Juicy Award for Best
Restaurant in 2002, Seven Dials is
the dream of chef Sam Metcalfe,
whose pedigree is proper job (Chez
Nico, The Terrace, Pied a Terre). The
service is inconsistent, but the food
is often some of Brighton's finest. Try
the private dining room downstairs
for a birthday or business splash. A
la carte, two courses £20 or three
courses £25. On Sunday they do a

mini roast for the kids. The Terrace
outside is beautifully designed and
takes your mind away from the
fact that it's situated off a major
roundabout. Last orders on terrace
9.30pm.

Tables 88 at Dadu

124 Kings Rd, Brighton BN1 2FA
T: 01273 722525 F: 01273 728294
www.dadurestaurant.co.uk
Mon-Sun: 12pm-2pm and 6.30pm-
10pm. Private room available
Avg. Price: £25

This seafront restaurant has changed
hands recently (the Dadu part of the

name will eventually be dropped)
but it still seems to be suffering
from an identity crisis. As the maitre
d' confessed, the new menu has
been designed to include a bit of
everything. The décor is stylish
enough - minimal yet warm - and
there's a funky little cocktail area
but the food remains inconsistent.
The crab cakes with chilli sauce were
excellent for £4.50 as was the fillet of
beef in mushrooms for £12.95, but the
tempura prawns came with a very
bland sesame dip and the side salad
was lacking in va va voom. Service
was warm and friendly though, and
there's a DJ in the cocktail bar on
Friday and Saturday nights.

The Bay @ The Rendezvous Casino

Marina Villlage, Marina, Brighton BN2 5UQ
T: 01273 605602
www.lciclubs.com
Mon-Sat: 7pm-11pm, Sun: 1pm-3pm, 7pm-11pm. Private room available.
Avg. Price: £30

Haute Cuisine at Brighton's best casino. The Bay is a small restaurant with a choice of three menus at £25, £28 and £30, and £45 in the private dining room. The menu is Modern British; fillet of Aberdeen Angus topped with spinach and Roquefort Mousse, roasted and served with pomme fondant and a Madeira jus; steamed fillet of black bream served on shredded ginger and spring onion with light fish bouillon. The clientele is property tycoons and their molls out for a night of Black Jack. Jeans are not allowed

The Eagle Bar and Bakery

125 Gloucester Rd, North Laine, Brighton BN1 4AF
T: 01273 607765 F: 01273 626754
Mon-Sat: 11am-11pm, Sun: 12pm-10.30pm. Avg. Price: £15

Chic, arty, vegan bakery from the boys behind the Hop Poles. The menu is mouth-wateringly fusion (Thai Chicken Breast on a wild mushroom risotto (£7.50), Goats Cheese and Red Onion Tartlet (£6.95) with a side order of honey roast

squash on a bed of roquette (£2.95), while the interiors are earthy metals and solid wood.

The Strand

6 Little East St, The Lanes, Brighton BN1 1HT
T: 01273 747096 F: 01273 747096
Fri-Sat: 12pm-10.30pm, Mon: 6pm-10pm, Tue-Thurs: 12pm-10pm
Avg. Price: £20

Tucked behind Bartholomew's away from the traffic of The Lanes' tourists, The Strand is one of Brighton's more interesting restaurants. The waiters are trendy, friendly and everything is home made. Try the pan-fried locally (Newhaven) caught scallops with vegetarian haggis and tomato chutney (£4.75) followed by confit duck on sweet potato, caramelised red onion and soft herb cake with a kummel (caraway) sauce (£15.75).

Coriander

5 Hove Manor, Hove St, Hove BN3 2DF. T: 01273 730850
www.sussex2do.com/corianderrestaurant
Tue-Sun: 12pm-10.30pm
Avg. Price: £30

Coriander ticks all the right boxes; exotic ambience (welcome to the Kasbah), plenty of space between tables so you're not sharing your intimates with the couple next door, friendly and knowledgeable staff who actually seem to enjoy what they do and, of course, the

exquisite Moroccan/Latin-American food which is prepared with much loving care by chef David Smales, using 90% organics. The grilled aubergine, feta cheese and nut burger for £12.50 was a real treat, as was the Cape Malay seafood curry at £16. Expect to wait a while for your food but then that gives you plenty of time to sit back and soak up the atmosphere. If you're a large party, they'll do a four course North African banquet for £20-25 per person, what better occasion to make like a native and partake in a shisha waterpipe (apple, strawberry, melon, mint or cherry tobacco) at £4 a round.

Niche

42 Waterloo St, Hove BN3 1AY
T: 01273 733733
www.nichebrighton.co.uk
Tue-Sat: 11am-4pm, 7.30pm-2am, Sun: 12pm-4pm. Private room available. Avg. Price: £25

Formerly Fruit de Mer, this tiny kitsch dining room, with feather boas adorning the mirrors in the loos, Sybil Fawlty impersonating hostess, private room upstairs and bar and karaoke machine in the cellar bar, is hen night or birthday party heaven. The food is similar to (although not as good as) the Fruit de Mer fusion menu at £16 for two courses on weeknights and £19 at the weekend, with appetisers to whet your whistle while you order, and citrus palate fresheners between courses.

The Coach House

59 Middle St, Brighton BN1 1AL
T: 01273 719000 F: 01273
700909
www.coachhousebrighton.
com coachhousebar@aol.com
Mon-Sun: 12pm-11pm
Private room available
Avg. Price: £25

Favourite among the mass of new
media types who work at the Media
Centre surrounding it, The Coach
House is warm and inviting with
great service, a two hour happy hour,
excellent cocktails, a suntrap of a
courtyard for the summer and a large
fire roaring through the winter. Food
is a fusion of international flavours
with pan-fried duck breast with
sweet potato mash, honey, orange
and fig sauce, fish tagine (both at
£10.95) and home made falafel and
tabouleh (£7.95) sitting happily on the
same menu.

SEA FRONT FOOD

The Beach

Kings Rd Arches,
Brighton BN1 1NB
T: 01273 722272
F: 01273 722272
Mar-Oct: 11am-11pm
Avg. Price: £10

With a sun terrace and the only food
on the beach after El Taco Way has
packed its bags at 8pm, how
could it fail? The pizzas are all
right, and the lager is suitably
cold, but this is simply somewhere
to fill your boots when you
can't be bothered to cross the
road. Service is friendly enough,
with students doing the honours.
Pizzas are around £5.

The Boardwalk

250a Kings Rd Arches,
Brighton BN1 1HP
T: 01273 746067
Mon-Sun: 11am-11pm
Avg. Price: £15

If location was everything, we'd all
be living at The Boardwalk. This

much-needed eatery sits just to the west of Brighton Pier and has a decked terrace leading out onto the beach. Inside, the two tiers are always packed on a sunny day, although the service is typical of Brighton's beachside cafes. The

various managers have tried various menus, and once upon a time, you could even get calves liver while you watched the sun set. These days, it concentrates on light meals and coffees, but the food is not the reason you're here.

TAPAS

Casa Don Carlos
5 Union St, The Lanes, Brighton BN1 1HA
T: 01273 327177
Mon-Fri: 12pm-3pm, 6pm-11pm,

Spanish service to a backbeat of Ricky Martin and the Gypsy Kings. The food is fab and inexpensive - marinated anchovies and prawns with garlic mayonnaise (both £3.95), patatas bravas (£2.95), calamares (£4.25) - which means the place is always packed. Book if only to check that there's no Sangria-swigging birthday party in that night.

Dali

87-89 Dyke Rd, Seven Dials, Brighton BN1 3JE
Mon-Sun: 10am-11pm

As we went to press, Seven Dials was about to get another interesting restaurant – bang next to The Tin Drum. Serving all day tapas, churros, drinks and coffee, the setting is promised as a surreal homage to the great man himself. There will also be an extensive Catalan menu in the evenings, and plans are for a surprising outdoor area at the back.

La Tasca

165 North St, Brighton BN1 1EA
T: 01273 737342
www.latasca.co.uk
Mon-Sat: 12pm-11pm, Sun: 12pm-10.30pm. Avg. Price: £15

Mixed opinions on this large Tapas house on the High Street; it's loved by regulars, and snootily dismissed by those who will go the distance

for a good patatas bravas. By night the atmosphere does get better with Spanish music forcing you into a more Mediterranean mood, but this is probably one for large groups who are more up for the crack than the croquettes.

Joogleberry Playhouse

14-17 Manchester St, Kemp Town, Brighton BN2 1TF
T: 01273 625619
F: 01273 687171
www.joogleberry.com
info@joogleberry.com
Mon-Sat: 12pm-1pm, Sun: 12pm-12pm.. Avg. Price: £15

Another of the comedy clubs which feeds its public before the belly laughs on offer, Joogleberry does it with panache. Beautifully presented and served with a smile, the honeyed Joogleberry chicken wings are a must, and the won ton are almost as good as China Garden's.

Komedia Kitchen

Gardner St,
North Laine,
Brighton BN8 6AS
T: 01273 647100
Mon-Sat: 12pm-11pm, Sun: 1pm-10.30pm. Avg. Price: £10

Mainly for Komedia comedy goers, the food is good enough to make a special trip for. Paul from The Eagle pub is behind the menu, which ranges from Spanish tapas to Lebanese nibbles.

Sat-Sun: 12pm-11pm. Avg. Price: £15

Shaking off the competition from newcomer La Tasca in North Street, Carlos and Ramon take turns to provide the unrelentingly authentic

Lucy's

26 Kings Rd, Hove BN1 2LN
T: 01273 220222
Mon-Fri: 10am-5pm, Sat-Sun: 9am-
5pm. Avg. Price: £15

If you've got sunshine and kids, this is perfect for a late breakfast or long lunch. Cast in the shadow of the West Pier, it's next to the children's playground and you can sit there and eat and chat and drink while your little angels throw themselves around the climbing frames, safe and in view, but still out of the way. At weekends from Easter until autumn they'll stay open to 8 or 9pm if the demand is there. The tapas in the evenings for around £4 a plate means that you can watch the sun set over a Sangria for under a tenner

THAI

Aumthong Thai

60 Western Rd, Hove BN3 1JD
T: 01273 773922/01273 329183
31 Kings Rd, Brighton BN1 1NR
T: 01273 777256/01273 771110
www.aumthong.com
Mon: 6pm-11pm, Tues-Sat: 12pm-
2.30pm, 6pm-11pm, Sun: 12pm-
2.30pm, 6pm-10pm. Avg. Price: £10

Once this was always packed and one of the most popular Thai restaurants in town, but popularity is not always a good thing, and the expansion into Kings Road has left both restaurants lacking in the Zen-like tranquillity once associated with this restaurant.

The King and I

2 Ship St, The Lanes, Brighton BN1 1AD. T: 01273 773390
Mon-Sun: 12pm-3pm and 6pm-11pm

Highly commended by the King of Thailand for providing some of the best Thai food in England. The King and I is Tucked away at the end of Ship St, it is small and beautifully furnished in dark wood with murals on the walls. Service is unobtrusive and the food is well presented and authentic.

Mai Ped Ped Ped

11 Market St, Brighton BN1 1HH
T: 01273 777240
www.maipedpedped.com
maipedpedped@aol.com
Mon-Fri: 11.30am-4.30pm, 5.30pm-11pm, Sat: 11.30am-11p, Sun:
11.30am-10pm. Avg. Price: £15

Popular Thai on two floors serving delightful dishes such as Hiccup Duck and Misty Violet (aubergines). The menu, written in erratic English by the owners, is just as charming, and the service is purely Thai. The only problem is the building; it's freezing in winter. and it has the kind of acoustics that means that you can't hear yourselves think when there's a party of more than four. But it's not enough to put off its loyal clientele who come back again and again for the consistently great and well-priced food and beautiful service.

Sawadee

87 St James Street, Kemp Town, Brighton BN2 1TP
T: 01273 624233
www.sawadee.thai@virgin.net
Mon-Sun: 12pm-3pm; 5pm-11pm
Avg. Price: 15-20

Gentle Thai restaurant in the heart of Kemp Town where the mussels are steamed in lemon grass, sweet basil and chilli (£8.50), the grilled sea bass wrapped in banana leaves with Thai chillies, lime leaves, sweet basil and galangal (£11.50) and spare ribs soaked in honey and garlic (£7.95). The service and food is erratic, but when it's good, it's very good.

Thai Connection

14 Blatchington Rd, Hove BN3 3YN. T: 01273 205009

Split level Thai restaurant serving some of the best Thai food in the city. The menu and the surroundings are what we've come to expect, but the quality of the food and the value of the package has had Hove chattering about it to anyone who'll listen.

VEGETARIAN

Food for Friends

17-18 Prince Albert St, The Lanes, Brighton BN1 1HF
T: 01273 202310 F: 01273 775841
www.foodforfriends.com
simonhope@hotmail.com
Mon-Sun: 11.30am-10pm

Avg. Price: £15

This once bastion of old style vegetarianism has hit the new Millennium with table service and smiles and a menu that catapults it way into the foodie stratosphere. The menu changes regularly but always looks to the globe for its inspiration; its platter of Asian inspired crunchiness will still feed a bus load of vegans and still allow them to do their weekly shop at Infinity. The communal newspapers may have gone but the empathy is still free. An after work extended happy hour offers global tapas and 2 cocktails for the price of 1 until 7pm.

Gardenia

2 St James St, Kemp Town,
Brighton BN2 1RE
T: 01273 686273
Mon-Thurs: 10am-8pm, Fri-Sun:
10am-10pm. Avg. Price: £10

Vegetarian café style restaurant bang in Kemp Town's main street where everything is home baked, fresh and organic vegetarian and vegan. Fans report the best 'meaty' veg sausages ever, with a big choice on pies, tarts, cakes and outrageous 'creamy' vegan desserts. It's all home made with love, which stands for something in this hippy heart of Boho Brighton.

Terre A Terre

71 East Street, The Lanes,
Brighton BN1 1HQ
T: 01273 729051 F: 01273 327561
www.terreaterre.co.uk
mail@terreaterre.co.uk
Oct-Mar: Tues: 6pm-10.30pm,
Wed-Sun: 12pm-10.30pm, Apr-Sep:
Mon: 6pm-10.30pm, Tues-Sun:
12pm-10.30pm. Avg. Price: £20-30

Juicy Restaurant of the Year at the Juicy Awards in 2000, and still getting better all the time, the likes of the Mustard Seed Muffin, deep fried & served with tamarind jelly and minted coconut lime are distracting the carnivores from the fact that there's no meat on the menu, but they're also attracting the attention of the national newspapers and a worldwide fan base. A fairy lit decked patio has opened up the once dark interiors, and the enlightened service, although sometimes too slow, is still the best and friendliest in the city. Expect to pay between £20 and £30 per head with wine. If you're booking for a weekend, call a week in advance to ensure a table. Kids can eat from main menu or there are such delights as eggie bread and macaroni cheese.

Trogs

24 George St, Kemp Town,
Brighton BN2 1RH
T: 01273 687821 F: 01273 278294
www.trogsrestaurant.com
info@trogsrestaurant.com
Mon-Tue: 11am-4pm, Wed-Sat:
7pm-10pm, Sun: 10am-6pm
Avg. Price: £20

Trogs used to be on the seafront but it's now moved inland taking with it the same excellent chef preparing imaginative organic vegetarian food. On entry, you feel like you're in your local café (the upstairs does a traditional veggie menu) but down the iron wrought spiral staircase and they've gone for a souk vibe with bright cushions, ornate lanterns and mosaic tables. The menu, which changes every month, has a bit of everything; Sushi, South American, Italian... It's very inventive, but when you're paying £13.50 for a main, you expect sharper presentation and more comfortable seating.

CAFES

Bagelman

7 Bond Street, North Laine,
Brighton BN1 1RD
T: 01273 387171
www.bagelman.co.uk
Mon-Sat: 8am-5pm,
Sun: 10am-4pm

The Bagelman does exactly what
you want done to your bagels with
the freshest ingredients – and he
doesn't charge a fortune. There's no

need to stray from smoked salmon
and cream cheese (the lox deluxe)
and many people don't but if you
do, two popular choices are the ATM
(avocado, tomato and mozzarella
with basil) and the Funky Tuna (tuna,
avocado, lemon juice, olives). With
a new bigger, better bakery behind
the shop, world domination awaits.
For Bagelman obsessives there is a
reward card system – buy 10 get 1
free. Good for those of us who think
you can't have too many bagels.

Big Fish Café

Hove Lagoon, Hove BN3 4LX
T: 01273 770400
Mon-Sun: 9am-late

A parent's dream of café, with big
tables, hot comfort food and a
playground outside, Big Fish will be
packed by the summer as news of
its arrival spreads through Hove and
beyond, especially as it now has a
licence. They even allow dogs on a

lead. But take the papers; the food takes about as long to arrive as the Sunday train from Victoria.

Billie's
34 Hampton Place, Montpelier, Brighton BN1 3DD
T: 01273 774386
Mon-Fri: 8.30am-4.30pm, Sat-Sun 9am-5pm

The place for all-day breakfast. There's no chance that a normal person will ever finish one of the enormous hashes – but the effort is worth it. They come in a variety from farmhouse (eggs, bacon – the works on top of a hash) to Ranchero (salsa, guacamole and sour cream on top of your hash). At the weekend, you'll be lucky to get in, and if you've got a buggy or a wheelchair, forget it.

The Boardwalk
250 Kings Rd Arches, Brighton BN1 1HD   T: 01273 746067
Fri-Sat: 11am-10pm, the rest of the week is weather dependant

The perfect location if the sun is shining or the waves are crashing, with a decked patio and two tiered interior. The food is so, but who cares when the view is so fab?

Cafe 22
129 St James's St, Kemp Town, Brighton BN2 1TH
T: 01273 626682
Mon-Fri: 9am-6pm, Sun: 12pm-5pm
Once upon a time, Freddie's Scene

22 was the place to find out anything about gay and lesbian Brighton and Hove. Now under new management, the focus is still on the cafe, but also on the sex toys and art. Hang out at lunch and Saturday afternoons, and you'll find your way to the heart of the gay community.

Café Motu
6 Trafalgar St, North Laine, Brighton BN1 4EQ
T: 01273 709655
Mon-Fri: 9am-4pm, Sat-Sun: 9am-5pm

If you can tell the quality of a place by how busy it is, Motu is top notch. The solid looking wooden interior is matched by the solid looking English breakfasts. There's ciabatta if you're feeling a bit adventurous, but no croissants on Saturdays.

Café One Ten
109c Dyke Rd, Seven Dials, Brighton BN1 3JE
T: 01273 737310
Mon-Sat: 8.30am-4.30pm

Right on Seven Dials, this little cafe manages to pull off the trick of being small, stylish and comfortable. There are comfy sofas and local art, homemade (and some vegan) cakes and Fair Trade coffee.

Cake
59 Blatchington Rd, Hove BN3 3YJ
T: 01273 203204

Mon-Sat: 9am-5.30pm, Sun: 10am-7pm

Nice cross between a cosy caff and a chic café with home made cakes and proper coffee, full English breakfasts, with vegetarian options (try the tarragon mushrooms) and comfort food galore. This being Hove, the coffees include soyaccinos and other non-dairy drinks.

Capers
27 Gardner St, North Laine, Brighton BN1 1UP
T: 01273 675550
Tues-Sat: 9am-5.30, Sun: 10am-3pm

Sitting in the middle of The North Laine, Capers serves good old-fashioned food properly, and the smiley, chatty service makes you feel glad you chose the place. The sausage and mash is made from locally-produced pork and sage and smothered with thick onion gravy. The baguettes are full of chicken and things and there's a top banoffee pie. They do a good breakfast, too.

Chalet Café
Preston Park, Preston Park, Brighton BN1 6HN
T: 01273 503477
10am-5pm in winter, 10am-6pm in summer

Ah the joys of playing in Preston Park on a sunny Sunday afternoon,

hiring one of those mad bicycles made for five, and then scoffing some homemade cakes and a hot chocolate at the Chalet Café. They even sell vegetarian sausages. Perfect.

Coffee Republic

16 Prince Albert St, North Laine, Brighton BN1 1HF
T: 01273 727726
39 Bond St, North Laine, Brighton BN1 1RD
T: 01273 723912
157 Church Rd, Hove BN3 2AD
T: 01273 749191
Mon-Fri: 7.30am-6pm, Sat: 9am-6pm, Sun: 10am-5pm

It may be a chain, but the coffee's great, the sofas smart and comfy. When the Hove branch opened, it helped turn a parochial neighbourhood to chic shopping area.

Conberts

16 Sydney St, North Laine, Brighton BN1 4EN
T: 01273 625222
conberts@btopenworld.com
Mon-Sat: 10am-6pm,
Sun: 12am-4pm

Here's a nice idea – shop for jewellery and have a cup of coffee and a cake while you decide what

to buy. This shop offers handmade pieces of jewellery at good prices but what makes it different to the many shops of this kind in The North Laine is that you can relax and people-watch over a cuppa after you've made that essential purchase.

Costa Coffee

32 Bond St, North Laine, Brighton BN1 1RD
T: 01273 772024
Mon-Sat: 7am-7pm,
Sun: 9am-6pm

2 Dyke Rd, Brighton BN1 3FE
T: 01273 725124

Mon-Sat: 7.30am-8pm,
Sun: 8am-7pm

42 Market St, Brighton BN1
1HH. T: 01273 329575
Mon-Sat: 7.30am-6.30pm, Sun
9am-6.30pm

Comfy chairs and a vast array
of coffees and teas mean that
this is where most of Brighton's
freelancers, shoppers and ladies
who lunch tend to meet.

The Curve Bar@Komedia
45 Gardner St, North Laine,
Brighton BN1 1UN
T: 01273 603031

Attached to the Komedia Theatre,
this bright spacious bistro is the
obvious place to have a coffee or
a meal after a show, with a mosaic
entrance, stainless steel bar, soft
moving light show and mezzanine
internet cafe. The location is
perfect, and when the sun shines
and they open the glass-fronted
doors, there's no better place to
watch the world go by.

The Dumb Waiter
28 Sydney St, North Laine,
Brighton BN1 4EP
T: 01273 602526
Mon-Sat: 9am-6pm, Sun: 10am-
3.30pm

Eatery with all day breakfasts,

veggie burgers, sandwiches and
baguettes all for around £3.

The End of the Lanes
53 Meeting House Lane, The
Lanes, Brighton BN1 1HB
T: 01273 729728
Mon-Sun: 8am-6pm

The French influence in this cosy
little cafe is in the continental
pastries and a delicious selection
of home made cakes. There are
over 100 different types of hot
chocolate, shakes and ice teas, and
just to confuse you even more,
the menu is in French. But when
your cocoa is adorned with multi-
coloured marshmallow stars and
served by a man with a gorgeous
French accent, who cares?

Frank In Steine
Old Steine, Brighton BN1 1JY
T: 01273 674742
Mon-Fri: 9am-4pm, Sat-Sun:
10am-4pm

Right in the middle of the
Old Steine, this is what you
might call a convenient place.
Convenient. Get it? Oh never
mind. Frank In Steine is a converted
toilet. They claim that the coffee's
the best in Brighton and while
that might be pushing it a bit,
it's not bad. What it does do
best is offer a place to watch
the world go by on a sunny day,
and kiddie's bikes and toys to
keep the littlies occupied.

Infinity Café
50 Gardner St, North Laine,
Brighton BN1 1UN
T: 01273 670743
Mon-Sat: 10am-5pm

Small but popular café, a workers'
co-op that offers fans of the organic
food store (around the corner in
North Road) somewhere to go. The
food is, as you'd expect, organic, the
salads crunchy and wholesome. The
coffee is delicious (and, of course,
fair trade) but it is small and at
lunchtime you'd probably do well to
get a takeaway.

Inside Out
95 Gloucester Rd, North
Laine, Brighton BN1 4AP
T: 01273 692912
Mon-Sat: 8am-6pm, Sun: 9am-5pm

Just the place to sit out on the
wooden deck and watch the world
go by over a fresh juice, smoothie,
speciality tea or good old coffee.
The food's good too, and comes on
big plates. Homemade dips (£4.25),
grilled halloumi salad with lemon
couscous and minted tapenade
(£5.95). We particularly liked the
comedy one-way mirror in the loo;
apparently people come from far
and wide to challenge their fears of
being watched while they wee.

Kai Organic Café
52 Gardner St, North Laine,
Brighton BN1 1UN
T: 01273 684921

kaiorganic@btinternet.com
Mon-Sat: 9am-5pm, Sun: 9am-5pm

Kai, it seems, is Maori for 'real food' and, fittingly, absolutely everything here is organic. The service is friendly and images by local photographers and artists provide something to gaze at while you sip your lunchtime soup. Why these organic health cafes don't offer a wheat free breakfast with so many Brightonians bulging at the very thought of a slice of toast, is beyond us.

Kensington's Café
1 Kensington Gdns, North Laine, Brighton BN1 4AL
T: 01273 570963
Mon-Sat: 9.30am-5.30, Sun: 10am-5.30pm

Possibly the best thing here is the small balcony where you can watch the bustle of the street from a safe distance while tucking into a steaming jacket. They sell alcohol, but only with food and for those who love their caffeine there is a coffee loyalty card.

Mac's Café
30 Arundel Rd, Kemp Town, Brighton BN2 5TD
T: 01273 692621
Mon-Sun: From before dawn-3pm

To call Mac's a 'greasy spoon' is like saying The Grand Hotel is a B&B. As greasy spoons go, it's a Roller.

Listen, you know how you can always tell the best caffs because they're the ones the cabbies go to? Well Mac's is a bit like that. The best fry-up breakfast shop in town, it opens at some ungodly hour and is always but always busy. A proper institution.

The Mad Hatter
35 Montpelier Rd, Hove BN1 3BA. T: 01273 722279
www.themadhattercafe.co.uk
Mon-Sat: 8am-8pm, Sun: 10am-7pm

Relaxed and stylish hippy hangout which throws Indian rugs and Moroccan cushions on the pavement outside in the summer, shows films upstairs once a month and plays music once a week.

The Market Diner
19 Circus St, Old Steine, Brighton. T: 01273 608273
One of the few properly legendary places in town. Open all night, The Market Diner is one of those statutory post-club places where everything looks better than it probably is, largely on account of the fact that everyone's pupils are just that little bit skewed.

Marrocco's Ice Cream Parlour
8 Kings Esplanade, Hove BN3 2WA. T: 01273 735098
Open in the summer

Real Italian ice cream served by

people who have been doing it and loving it for years and years. (see Restaurant chapter).

The Meeting Place
Kings Rd, Hove BN3 1HP
T: 01273 206417
meetingplacecafe@fsdial.co.uk
Mon-Sun: 7am-sunset

Right on the seafront (opposite Brunswick Square) and open all year, this is a top place to meet friends thanks to the bright yellow wind barriers. There's an outside heater lamp and great toasted sandwiches, so you can eat out in the middle of winter – though why you'd want to...

The Mock Turtle
4 Pool Valley, The Lanes, Brighton BN1 1NJ
T: 01273 327380
Tues-Sat: 10am-6pm

Tea, egg and cress sandwiches and the best home made cakes in Brighton, as well as locally produced sausages and homemade soups. Your mother and aunty will love this place.

Mooch
Kensington Gdns, North Laine, Brighton BN1 4AL
T: 01273 693510
Mon-Sat: 8am-5pm, Sun: 10am-4pm

Buy your hand-made toys while

stopping for a spot of lunch in this innovative little café. Service tends to be slow while they get their heads round which hat they're wearing, but the food is earthy and home-cooked. Not a place for a rushed lunch.

Nia Café
87-88 Trafalgar St, North Laine, Brighton BN1 4EB
T: 01273 671371
Mon-Sat: 9am-6pm, Sun: 9am-6pm

Ideally placed at the far end of the North Laine drag, Nia is one of the nicest cafés in the area, but because of that it's often difficult to get in. The décor is wooden and solid and straightforward and the service friendly. The menu is varied with drinks, cakes, light meals, main meals and breakfasts (Oak Smoked Kippers with Rye Bread and Lemon at £4.95). They also do sarnies – baguette, bagel, ciabatta or panini – with fillings including salami, smoked salmon and feta. Try the Welsh rarebit for £4.50 or the Fish Cakes with caper and coriander salsa for £6.50. The specials tend to be more vegetarian but Sausage and Mash is always on at £6.50.

Off Beat Café
37 Sydney St, North Laine, Brighton BN1 4EP
T: 01273 604206
Mon-Fri: 10am-6pm, Sun: 11am-5pm

Nice, simple 50's-style café with little in the way of pretension, but

what it lacks in chrome extras it makes up in attitude. They also do a nice line in toasted sarnies on Italian bread.

Pavilion Garden Café
Royal Pavilion Gdns, Brighton BN2 5PB
T: 01273 674084
Open in the summer

Summertime and the living is easy. Birds are singing and... So the birds are pigeons. They're all God's creatures and they're as entitled as anyone to nick your scones. Anyway, if it wasn't them it'd only be those winged gangsters we call gulls. When the sun's shining and you're sitting here and the kids are running around... Well, it doesn't get a whole lot better.

The Pavilion Tea House
Hove Park, Hove BN3 7BF
T: 01273 727003/07776 161547
Mon-Sun: 10am-dusk

Family run café with great hot chocolate, coffee and homemade cakes in the middle of one of the city's loveliest parks. It's particularly child friendly, with kids bikes and trikes knocking about the garden ready to be trashed. They also cater for children's parties as well as Grown Up's Tea Parties for mums and dads, aunts, uncles and grandparents, with traditional English tea and cakes served on their best china tea set.

Philippe De France
69 East St, The Lanes, Brighton BN1 1HQ
T: 01273 220691
Mon and Tues: 8.30am-8pm,
Wed-Sun: 8.30am-10.30pm

The decor is minimal, the ambience urban and the menu mouth-watering. There's a huge range of tantalising delicacies – patisseries, coffees, homemade chocolates, ice cream and savoury snacks. Try the Croute Provencal (French bread, tomatoes, garlic, olive oil, black olive tapenade, anchovies and melted goat's cheese, £5.95), the Saucisse de Toulouse grillee au jus (Grilled Toulouse sausage with onion jus and mashed potatoes, £7.00) or the Tarte Nicoise (tuna, onion, black olives and tomato tart, £4.95).

Puccinos
1 Bartholomew's, The Lanes, Brighton BN1 1HG
T: 01273 204656
35 George St, Hove BN3 3YB
T: 01273 730437
Mon-Sat: 8am-6pm, Sun: 9am-6pm

Comfortable, friendly café in the Lanes which teems with breast feeding mothers and young children in the upstairs lounge by day, and chills into a feet-up, sofa seated bar by night. In the summer the windows disappear (as long as the rain stays away), lending a laid back, watch-the-world kind of feel as you scoff their fine cakes. The comfy sofas by the window make you almost feel as though you're in an episode of Friends. Brighton café life at its most friendly.

Pulp
31 Bond St, North Laine,
Brighton BN1 1RD
T: 01273 735040
Mon-Sat: 10am-11pm,
Sun: 11am-9pm

Fair trade coffee, organic falafel, homous, roasted vegetable ciabattas, alfalfa, and everything for lover of wholesome food.

Pulp Kitchen
Bond St, North Laine,
Brighton BN1 9RD
T: 01273 735040

Soya smoothies and spirulina and juices designed to make you feel good at this new café with vegan, dairy and wheat free options.

Queen's Perk
91 Queen's Park rd, Queen's Park, Brighton BN2 0GJ
T: 07973 429768
www.queensperk.com
Mon: 9am-4pm, Tues-Fri: 9am-5.30pm, Sat: 10am-4pm

Fair trade, organic, wheat free and vegan friendly and designed for parents with young kids by a young mum, it doesn't get more

Brighton than this' They even sell second hand clothes for kids and have messy play on Tuesdays and Thursdays.

Redeli
59d Ship St, The Lanes,
Brighton BN1 1AE
T: 01273 748222
www.redeli.com
Mon-Fri: 8.30am-5.30pm, Sun: 10am-4pm

Tiny little café in The Lanes where the emphasis is on health (although nobody will convince us that those cheesecakes are good for your heart). Friendly and accommodating, they'll listen to your tales of allergies and intolerances and serve you a feast. They'll even deliver your business lunches at no extra charge.

Redroaster
1d St James's St, Kemp Town,
Brighton BN2 1RE
T: 01273 686668
mail@redroaster.co.uk
Mon-Fri: 7.30am-7pm, Sat: 8am-7pm, Sun: 9am-6pm

Buzzy, European style coffee house with high ceilings and lovely big leather seats to really stretch out, and pavement tables where you can watch the bizarre world of Kemp Town go about its business. The coffee is as fresh as it gets, and a honey roasted aubergine, courgettes and black olive tapenade panini followed by a sweet banana

smoothie will make you smile for the rest of the day.

Sanctuary Café
51 Brunswick St East, Hove
BN3 1AU T: 01273 770002
Mon-Sun: 9am-11pm

Classic vegetarian food with global twists, late night coffee and cake on the ground and upper floors, music, poetry readings, cult films in the Beatnik basement, and sunny lunches out of windowless windows. The look is sculpted Boho with exhibitions from local (and sometimes cutting edge) artists. And if you want to pick up a flyer about underground yoga classes for vegetarians, there's no finer place.

Shake Away
8 Bond St, The Lanes,
Brighton BN1 1RD
T: 01273 711179/01273 711179
www.shakeaway.com
Mon-Sat: 9am-6pm, Sun: 10.30-4.30pm

A trillion different flavours of milk shakes, with sweeties and chocolate bars thrown into the mix.

Stanmer Tea Rooms
Stanmer Park, Stanmer Village,
Brighton BN1 9PZ
T: 01273 604041
Mon-Sun: 9am-5.30pm

New owners David and Lyn have

replaced the sullen owners of the past, and with 23 years in the business, they know that after a romp in the woods or a toddle around the duck pond, we want steaming hot soup, hot chocolate, chips'n'cheese or a plate full of home made cake. The restaurant seats 25 and can be hired out for special occasions.

Starbucks
201 Western Rd, Brighton BN1 2BA T: 01273 324097
Mon-Fri: 7am-7pm, Sat: 7.30am-7.30pm, Sun 8am-7pm

18-19 Market St, The Lanes, Brighton BN1 1HH
T: 01273 328157/01273 724526
Mon-Fri: 7.30am-6.30pm, Sat: 8am-7pm, Sun: 8am-6.30pm

Sainsbury's Lewes Rd, Brighton BN2 3QA. T: 01273 695171
Mon-Fri: 8am-6.30pm, Sun: 10am-4pm

Borders Books, Churchill Sq, Brighton BN1 2TB
T: 01273 220435
Mon-Sat: 9am-8pm, Sun: 11am-4pm

The normal Starbucks charm, and if you're out and about Sunday morning, this is the only place which is open for a posh – and Fair Trade – coffee. They're always busy,

and you'll be lucky to get a comfy chair. The café in The Lanes is the most relaxed and gets involved with local community issues. The Churchill Square branch can make even a trip there seem bearable.

Waikika Moo Kau
11a Kensington Gardens, North Laine, Brighton BN1 4AL
T: 01273 671117
Mon-Sun: 9am-6pm, open until 7pm on Sat

42 Meeting House Lane, The Lanes, Brighton BN1 1HB
T: 01273 323824/01273 604483
waikika@bt.conect.com
Sun-Wed: 11am-6pm, Thurs-sat: 11am-11pm

A Juicy favourite in The North Laine with a welcome to complement the size of the meals. Order a mezze for the entire family and you'll be pushing it to finish the plate.

Despite its popularity, the laid back staff don't try to move you on once you've finished your coffee, and the smiles are genuine. Could be the influence of all those Buddhas and gods on the walls. Look out for the lucky dice night; throw a dice and you get a meal for free.

Woodies
Kingsway, Hove BN3 4QT
T: 01273 430300
www.woodiesdiner.com
Tues-Thurs: 12pm-9pm, Fri-Sat: 10am-9.30pm, Sun: 10am-8pm

Not little Woody Cook's own diner, although Norm, Zoë and little Woody can often be seen sharing a burger here, so near is it to their own mansion on the beach. This is more Happy Days comes to Hove with Harley Davidson nights and rock'n'roll evenings keeping the 50's spirit alive along with specially rocker named 8 pounders.

PUBS

Unless otherwise stated, pub opening times are Mon-Sat: 10:30am-11pm, Sun: 12pm-10.30pm.

The Alibi

22 Victoria Terrace, Hove BN3 2WB. T: 01273 733983
Mon-Fri: 3pm-11pm, Sat: 3pm-11pm, Sun: 12pm-10.30pm

Set up by food writer Katie Stewart (The Guild Of Food Writers Cookery Journalist Of The Year in 2000),

great food's served Wednesday to Sunday in a non-smoking, child-friendly area. Serving times will be extended as summer approaches and there are plans for an outside bar and garden. It's also popular with local kite surfers.

The Barley Mow

92 St George's Rd, Kemp Town, Brighton BN2 1EE
T: 01273 682259

A traditional pub with velvet covered pews and a lovely friendly

atmosphere. The food is home-made and served well into the night (about 10pm). The fish is fresh from Shoreham. The Mexican-style chilli con carne with rice and fired potato skins (£6.25) is one to try if you're hungry. The menu changes weekly and is different at the weekend.

The Basketmakers

12 Gloucester Rd, North Laine, Brighton BN1 4AD
T: 01273 689006

Not a virgin wall in sight. Cigarette

cases, Victorian toffee boxes, photographs and old posters compete for space in one of Brighton's best-loved pubs. Popular with art students, lecturers and sort of clientele who appreciate its intimate atmosphere and cask-conditioned ales.

The Bath Arms
3-4 Meeting House Lane, The Lanes, Brighton BN1 1HB
T: 01273 329437

With guest ales which change every week, if you like to sample beer this is the place for you. Full of old Brighton memorabilia, The Bath Arms is a good refuge after a shopping trip around the Lanes. It attracts a young crowd who somehow manage to chat above the deafening background music.

The Black Lion
14 Black Lion St, The Lanes, Brighton BN1 1ND
T: 01273 711884

One of the chain of Zel pubs – which signifies a bit of class, friendly staff and a good selection of beer, or one of the faceless makeovers that have become the scourge of Brighton since the London explosion, depending on which side of the fence you sit on. Juicy sits on the former – there's little wrong with friendly staff and good beer. Dark and stylish, this is where you'll find local media types.

The Bristol Bar
Paston Place, Kemp Town, Brighton BN2 1HA
T: 01273 605687

The Bristol's punters range from the cool and collected, to Kemp Town dignitaries and singleton women. Set just across the road from the sea, the Bristol has wonderful views and they serve proper coffee all day long and the usual standard pub grub between 12 and 2:30pm (but not curiously at weekends), so why doesn't the landlord turn the largely unused car park into a garden?

The Caxton Arms
36 North Gdns, North Laine, Brighton BN1 3LB
T: 01273 207762

Tucked away in a side street near the station, this is a two level affair. Upstairs is a decent bar, all proper beer and pumps. Downstairs is a bit clubbier and very comfortable.

The Charles Napier
57 Southover St, Hanover, Brighton BN2 2UE
T: 01273 601413
Mon-Thurs: 4pm-11pm, Fri and Sat: 12pm-11pm, Sun: 12pm-10.30pm

Longstanding local community pub with great beer that makes it very popular with the forty-something social worker and teacher crowd. Check out the upstairs sofas once you're there.

The Colonnade
10 New Rd, Brighton BN1 1UF
T: 01273 328728

Gloriously luvvie and packed to the gills with actors in residence at The Theatre Royal next door. Expect to see famous faces and wannabes merging with the portraits adorning the walls. A tip: If you're going to the theatre; order your interval drinks here rather than the theatre bar if you want time to enjoy your V&T.

The Constant Service
96 Islingword Rd, Hanover, Brighton BN2 2SJ
T: 01273 607058
Mon-Fri: 3pm-11pm, Sat and Sun: 12pm-10.30pm

A favourite among Brightonians, but more an evening than daytime haunt.

The Cricketers
15 Black Lion St, The Lanes, Brighton BN1 1ND
T: 01273 329472

Graham Greene's favourite is the oldest pub in Brighton, and the olde interiors are gorgeous. Popular with tourists and office parties.

Doctor Brighton's
16 Kings Rd, The Lanes, Brighton BN1 1NE
T: 01273 328765

If this looks like a run-of-the-mill traditional seaside pub, but it's quickly obvious that looks can be deceiving. Dr. Brighton's is a legendary welcoming local without the cliqueyness of other gay pubs. Official host of the pre Wild Fruit shenanigans, there's no room for mundane traditions here. They've even got 21 different flavoured schnapps on offer.

The Dragon

58 St Georges Rd, Kemp Town, Brighton BN2 1EF
T: 01273 690144

Cosy local bar with a Caribbean and Spanish tapas menu. Our reviewer wasn't too impressed with the Caribbean offering; though apparently, they don't make jerk chicken like his old mum does.

The Druid's Head

9 Brighton Place, Brighton BN1 1HJ
T: 01273 325490

Close to the Open Market, the Druid's Head used to cater solely for market workers but that's all changed now. The clientele spreads right across the spectrum from 18-year-old student to the old locals nursing their half a Guinness. Music mags are scattered over the tables, and it likes to play its music loud. Popular with students, the staff will not only wait on your table, but also give you a free lollypop.

The Eagle

125 Gloucester Rd, North Laine, Brighton BN1 4AF
T: 01273 607765

With the Jubilee St development still waiting to reinvent the North Laine, this chic, arty, vegan bakery is a smart move by the boys behind the Hop Poles. The menu is mouth-wateringly fusion while the interiors are earthy metals and solid wood.

The Earth and Stars

46 Windsor St, North Laine, Brighton BN1 1RJ
T: 01273 772282

Eco, fully-environmentally balanced pub with a full organic menu. Everything here is organic: from the food to the cigarettes to the beer to the hemp T-shirts the bar-staff wear. Waste is recycled, they've applied for permission to put up solar panels, and just ask them about the carbon footprints.

The Eddie

Upper Gloucester Rd, Brighton BN1 3LQ
T: 01273 329540
Mon-Fri: 3pm-11pm, Sat: 12pm-11pm, Sun: 12pm-10.30pm

What used to be "The Game of Life", is slightly out of the way but close to Brighton Station. A nice, chilled-out place to have a quiet pint or two.

The Fiddler's Elbow

11-12 Boyce's St, The Lanes, Brighton BN1 1AN
T: 01273 325850

The Fiddler's Elbow is a traditional Irish pub – authentically Irish as opposed to some of those themed pubs – complete with low ceilings, slightly mad looking old men and, best of all, cheap Guinness. Always quiet enough to find a seat but still with a good atmosphere, The Fiddler's is a perfect drinking hole for winter evenings and Sunday afternoons. If you're looking for somewhere a bit busier, try the Full Moon next door. If you're lucky, there might be live Gaelic music.

The Fishbowl

74 East St, Brighton BN1 1HQ
T: 01273 777505
www.zelnet.com

A great place to kick the night off to a good start. It's packed every night with a young and stylish crowd enjoying the laid back atmosphere, cheap cocktails and regular DJ's.

The Fortune of War

157 Kings Rd Arches, Brighton BN1 1NB. T: 01273 205065

Maybe it's because this pub is so reliant on passing tourist trade that it lacks atmosphere, but seafront places often do. Never mind, you can't have everything. The Fortune is

always popular as a meeting place in the summer to sit outside and bask in the Brighton seaside atmosphere.

The Freemasons
39 Western Rd, Hove BN3 1AF
T: 01273 732043

One of the best central pubs – and a haven from shopping hell. The Freemason's has recently been bought from the people behind The Snowdrop in Lewes and as we went to press were preparing a new menu. Check out www. juicymapmider.co.uk for our review.

The Full Moon
8 Boyce's St, The Lanes,
Brighton BN1 1AN
T: 01273 328 797

An institution and a hangout for Brighton's young and beautiful who go for its relaxed vibe and organic Sunday roasts. The bar is mostly a chemical-free zone with organic beer, wine and cider on offer.

The George
5 Trafalgar St, North Laine,
Brighton BN1 4EQ
T: 01273 681055

Juicy award-winning pub in 2002, this is one of the best places in the North Laine for lunch, the food is largely (and famously) vegetarian and vegan (separate cooking pans are used for each). Burgers, nachos, sausage and mash, ploughmans, Thai fishless cakes and Japanese salad – something for everyone. Food is served all day and kids are allowed in until 8.30pm, and they can eat anything on the menu for £2.25. The roaring fires make it the cosiest pub in The North Laine.

The Geese Have Gone Over the Water
16 Southover St, Hanover,
Brighton BN2 9UA
T: 01273 607755

Open mic nights and live Irish folk music nights.

The Great Eastern
103 Trafalgar St,
North Laine,
Brighton BN1 4ER
T: 01273 685681

One of the most popular pubs in Brighton frequented by trendy young things and old regulars alike. The bar staff are friendly and efficient, food is served between 12pm and 4pm and they make the best Bloody Marys in town.

The Greys
105 Southover St, Hanover,
Brighton BN2 2UA
T: 01273 680734
www.greyspub.com
Mon: 5.30pm-11pm, Tues-Wed: 11am-3pm, 5.30pm-11pm, Thurs-Sat: 11am-11pm, Sun: 12pm-10.30pm

Despite the fine old selection of Belgian beers, The Greys – another of the many Hanover pubs – is the best place in town to hear proper acoustic folk and country. Check their website to find out what's on.

The Hampton
57 Upper North St,
Montpelier, Brighton BN1 3FH
T: 01273 325425

Zel's The Hamptons is now a trendier, friendlier place to be than before the takeover, with good food and cocktails.

The Hanbury Arms

83 St Georges Rd, Kemp
Town, Brighton BN2 1EF
T: 01273 605789

A cracking comedy night has
rejuvenated The Hanbury Arms.
Shaped like an Indian temple, the
drinking space is minimal but does
great party nights, including
Stick It On every second Saturday
where you can choose your top
five tunes. It can be a wild party.
The Ballroom next door to the
pub specialises in the weird and
wonderful, and holds nights like
jazz, DIY DJing, manga screenings.

The Hand In Hand

33 Upper St James St, Kemp
Town, Brighton BN2 1JN
T: 01273 602521
The teeniest pub in Brighton known
for brewing their own beer and
having a diverse range of drinkers
in such a small place. Oozing with
character, the Victorian ceilings
are splendid, as is its incredible
collection of ties hanging from
every available space. Popular with
ageing thespians and sea captains,
it is worth a visit if you can find a
place to squeeze in at the bar.

The Hanover

Queens Park Rd, Hanover,
Brighton BN2 9ZB
T: 01273 679902

Opened last year by the people
behind the original Pub with No

Name, No Name café and The
Reservoir, this is where comedy and
drinking get equal space, and fills
the gap in the market for a nice mid
market pub in the Queen's Park/Elm
Grove/Hanover borders.

The Heart In Hand

North Rd, North Laine,
Brighton BN1 1YD
T: 01273 683320

A stone's throw from all the action
in the busy North Laine this is a
quiet pub to hide away from the
crowds. It's popular with market-
traders of Upper Gardner Street,
so there's always the chance of

securing a bargain over a pint.
The Heart In Hand is a small but
comfortable pub with a superior
selection of beers and nibbles, and
a jukebox stacked with classics from
Marvin Gaye to Tim Buckley.

Hectors House

51 Grand Parade, Brighton BN2
9QA. T: 01273 688869

Hectors House is popular with
students. They lounge about here
on tired looking sofas any night of
the week drinking cheap plonk and
discussing their good intentions to
get up tomorrow morning and go to
their lectures. There are a couple of

shabby pool tables and a DJ booth, which belts out Jungle and hip-hop. The vibe in here is urban but still relaxed and friendly. Not the place to go for a glass of Sauvignon Blanc; the only choice of wine here is red or white.

The Hop Poles

13 Middle St, The Lanes, Brighton BN1 1AL. T: 01273 710444

Small, lively and trendy pub, popular with students and media types from the nearby Brighton Media Centre. The friendly bar staff serve excellent food all day. In the evening, things get a bit more intimate, with tables lit by dripping candles, and the food even better. It can get a bit cramped, so make sure you get there early if you want a table. Very fine music, and there's a small garden at the back.

The King and Queen

13 Marlborough Place, Brighton BN1 1UB
T: 01273 607207
Mon-Thurs: 11am-11pm, Fri-Sat: 11am-12pm, Sun: 12pm-10.30pm

A great place to have a big Sunday roast and watch The Match on one of the four TV screens. It's packed with the thousands of foreign students and freshers who make Brighton their spiritual home.

The Lion and Lobster

24 Sillwood St, Brighton BN1 2PS. T: 01273 327299
Mon-Wed: 11am-11pm, Thurs-Sat: 11am-12pm, Sun: 11am-11pm

Cosy, traditional pub popular with a 30-something crowd, so get there early if you want a seat. The lager's organic (Bittburger and Warsteiner), and the live Irish music on Sundays helps the one-course roast lunch (£6.50) go down a treat.

The London Unity

131 Islingword Rd, Hanover, Brighton BN2 9SH
T: 01273 681285

Part of the Hanover pub Mafia, and loved by locals who come for the warm atmosphere, roaring fire, stripped floors and sounds of hippy hits from times gone by. During Happy Hour (4.30-6pm) pints are £1.70. Surprisingly not studenty – yet.

The Mash Tun

Church St, Brighton BN1 1UE
T: 01273 684951

Funky pub with two floors depending on your mood: slouching sofas upstairs and more prim pew-like chairs below. Deliberately employing the best-looking bar staff helps to give the place a bit of a buzz. During the day there are newspapers on tap and coffee served. Just the way it should be.

Mrs Fitzherberts

25 New Rd, North Laine, Brighton BN1 1UG
T: 01273 682401

A cosy and intimate atmosphere where you can eat tapas, canoodle in the cubby holes or just enjoy drinking in central Brighton.

The Nelson

36 Trafalgar St, North Laine, Brighton BN1 4ED
T: 01273 695872

A proper, old-fashioned local. The beer is excellent and the staff well trained.

The New Vic

31 Richmond Rd, Fiveways, Brighton BN2 3RL
T: 01273 675906
Mon-Fri: 4pm-11pm, Sat: 1pm-11pm, Sun: 1pm-10.30pm

A cosy little local pub with bar and lounge areas plus a secluded outdoor area. Tuesday's 'Rowdy Pub Quiz' draws in a fun crowd.

The Office

8 Sydney St, North Laine, Brighton BN1 4EN
T: 01273 609134

A young and trendy crowd flock to this pub in the heart of the North Laine. The décor is light and airy, the music chilled and unobtrusive and the food authentic Thai. They're renowned for their extensive selection of exotic spirits such as cachaca, a Brazilian sugar cane drink, and if there's a new product out they'll probably have it. Each table comes with a spirit bible to help you choose your poison. For novelty value try the flavoured schnapps or shooter of the month. But if it all gets a bit too calm and sophisticated, they also do jelly vodkas.

The Open House
146 Springfield Rd, Fiveways, Brighton BN1 6BZ
T: 01273 880102

There's a roomy bar area complete with table football plus a more intimate lounge area with low-slung tables and sofas. While you're waiting for your date, check out the artwork, the walls display work by local Fiveways artists. When the sun comes out, all the families invade the large decked garden area. Once a real neighbourhood pub, the clientele has become a bit younger and more interested in the vodka nights these days. The food's not as good either – probably because students don't eat.

The Pond
49 Gloucester Rd, North Laine, Brighton BN1 4AQ
T: 01273 621400

In a novel gesture, pots hang from the ceiling like stalactites. Bit of a locals' pub, the food is good value and generous.

The Prince Albert
48 Trafalgar St, North Laine, Brighton BN1 4ED
T: 01273 730499

Unassuming little pub just down the road from the station, The Albert is the preferred watering-hole of Brighton's clubbing giants. When they're not spinning discs, they join in with the pool, darts, and table football. There's comedy and even a monthly Manga film night in the function room, which is also used for gigs. The Prince Albert shares its owner with Concorde 2, so anyone wanting tickets for whatever the Next Big Thing is can ask for Chris.

Princess Victoria
22 Upper North St, Brighton BN1 3FG. T: 01273 325491

This is the pub your mates mean when they tell you to meet them at the purple pub. It serves the 25-35 crowds looking for a nice cosy place just off the main drag to have a drink, although it does get packed at for the big sporting events on TV.

The Prodigal
80 East St, The Lanes, Brighton BN1 1JU
T: 01273 748103

A big, cavernous place with plenty of room, The Prodigal was originally three bars that were then knocked through in 1997. It's one of largest pre-club bars – well, it's perfect seafront location sees to that – and usually your quiet pint of foamy ale comes complete with a banging soundtrack, especially at weekends. But that's a regular drinkers problem. Sunday roasts from £4.95 with the sea view thrown in for free. It's child-friendly until 7pm, and a 30% NUS discount with a large sofa area makes it a student favourite.

Pub With No Name

58 Southover St, Hanover, Brighton BN2 9UF
T: 01273 601419
Mon-Thurs: 3pm-11pm, Fri-Sun: 12pm-10.30pm

Juicy Award-winning pub in the heart of Hanover. There's no sign outside but you'll know it when you find it. The wooden tables, guest DJs and cool ambience attract the young and hip crowd, as well as large sections of Hanover community. Upstairs there is an exhibition space for local artists, which is also used as a function room for private parties. At weekends families move in, attracted by the covered deck for kids at back. The menu is pub grub, Brighton style. A fine choice of meals, half vegetarian, most for around a fiver.

The Pull and Pump

1 Clarence Gdns, Brighton BN1 2EG. T: 01273 328263

Just out of the way from Churchill Square and the main shopping

area, this place is great for escaping crowds and grabbing a pint. Although the pub itself is small, the benches out front are designed for an afternoon drink in the sun. The good range of drinks and promotions, as well as friendly staff, make this well worth checking out.

The Queen's Head

3 Steine St, Kemp Town, Brighton BN2 1TE
T: 01273 602939

If the Freddie Mercury picture hanging outside isn't enough to tempt you inside this gay local, the home-cooked food will. There are DJs two or three times a week. Student night on Tuesday with drink offers. The £5 for any baguette or jacket and a pint/glass of wine/soft drink is a popular offer. Sunday Roast (£5.95) is 'ab fab' and 'well endowed' says the chef, Mrs Mark. Not intimidating as some gay bars can be. The upstairs lounge is available for private hire – free. At the weekends it's a lively place to drink before cruising round to Envy or Revenge.

Regency Tavern

32 Russell Square, Brighton BN1 2EF. T: 01273 325652
Wonderfully camp pub tucked behind Regency Square where landlord Chris Ryan is more Bet Lynch than Alex Gilroy and serves his pints under the watchful eye of a bunch of gold cherubs. At last orders, a glitter ball replaces the standard lighting as the PA croons

a midnight tune to its largely gay clientele. Sunday lunch is exquisite, although Chris compares it to the first day at the Harrods sale. No booking so get there early. The vegetarian menu is one of the big pulls and the loos are possibly Brighton's most glamorous.

The Roundhill

100 Ditchling Rd, Fiveways, Brighton BN1 4SG
T: 01273 697497

Recently refurbished with a new lounging area and deep red decor, The Roundhill has all the requisite features for a local pub – pool table, decent grub, newspapers and regular music nights. Sunday night's pub quiz has a dedicated following with the student crowd.

Royal Pavilion Tavern

3 Castle Square, Brighton BN1 1FX. T: 01273 827641

A Regular Joe kind of pub, big with students. which harbours a well kept secret upstairs in the form of The Tavern club or Pav Tav (see Clubs chapter).

St James's

20 Madeira Place, Kemp Town, Brighton BN2 1TN
T: 01273 626696

So Kemp Town that it dresses up as a bar, there's a huge choice of spirits including rare stuff you won't find elsewhere in Brighton. DJs play seven nights a week for a mixed bag of drinkers. St James's has same chef as The Office and will unveil a new Thai menu soon. The menu is organic with a wide range of veggie options.

Shakespeare's Head
Spring St, Brighton BN1 3EF
T: 01273 204680

The crowd consists of mainly regulars and shoppers. There is a pool table and a function room you can rent for about £30.

Shakespeare's Head
1 Chatham Place, Seven Dials, Brighton BN1 3TP
T: 01273 329444

Only in Brighton would you find a pub with a tiled bar, giant Elizabethan-clad dummies, purple walls and backgammon tables lit by night-lights in glass jars. The perfect place to hangout with friends, while cool jazz plays in the background.

The Sidewinder
65 Upper St James St Mews, Kemp Town, Brighton BN2 1RF
T: 01273 679927

Hip yet unpretentious, The Sidewinder is popular with students, media types and all those who love a laid back urban atmosphere. The large garden is perfect to spend hot summer evenings in or afternoons with the family. One of the best places for a quiet lunch in Kemp Town, the mezze of olives, roasted peppers and houmous goes down particularly well. Sausage and mash with a difference (£4.95) or choose from a selection including leek, cheddar, mushroom and sun dried tomato sausages.

The Slug and Lettuce
4 George St, Hove BN3 3YA
T: 01273 733359

Perfect for watching the world go by in this pedestrianised area of Hove.

The Smugglers
10 Ship St, The Lanes, Brighton BN1 1AD. T: 01273 328439
Mon-Sat: 12pm-11pm Sun: 7:30pm-10.30pm

One of Brighton's oldest pubs is now a student haven with pool and table football. Dripping with bric-a-brac downstairs, it's an ironworker's dream of a pub with the most bizarre relics of other worlds lending no particular theme. If you're waiting for the pool table, you could always have a nose to find out if the rumours of the underground tunnels have any truth.

Star of Brunswick
32 Brunswick Street West, Hove BN3 1EL
T: 01273 771355

The Star of Brunswick is something of a Brighton-drinker's institution.

For those who want a late night, there's the option to pay £2 and you can booze till 1am.

The Station
100 Goldstone Villas, Hove BN3 3RU. T: 01273 733660
Mon-Thurs: 12pm-11pm, Fri-Sat: 12pm-1am, Sun: 12pm-10.30pm

Cool drinking den next to Hove Station for youngsters who don't care about the chilly atmosphere. It's open late Thursday to Saturday and if you're going for food, try the oven-baked pizzas. There's a 2 for 1 cocktail deal on Sundays.

The Sussex
33 East St, The Lanes, Brighton BN2 3DD. T: 01273 327591

It's real tourist time here, but when the sun shines and you're sitting outside listening to the jazz band playing in the Square... Who cares?

Three Jolly Butchers
59 North Rd, North Laine, Brighton BN1 1YD
T: 01273 608571

Newly refurbished, The Three Jolly Butchers is smart and relaxing, and has started to get itself as a bit of a reputation for somewhere to hang out. You can get a selection of sandwiches, paninis, homemade lasagne, frittatas and bakes all for between £3 and £5.

The Western Front
11 Cranbourne St, Brighton BN1 2RD. T: 01273 725656

The Western Front is kind of sparse inside with a tatty Mediterranean feel, a mixed bag of daytime punters, rusty tables and laid-back jazz. The staff, the food and the building itself seem relaxed and cool without really trying. At lunchtime it's still quite relaxed, at night it gets heaving. .

The White Horse
30 Camelford St, Kemp Town, Brighton BN2 1TQ
T: 01273 603726
A gay pub for all ages that still has the warm atmosphere of the local it once was. One of the few gay pubs to still have a pool table.

Victory Inn
6 Duke St, The Lanes, Brighton BN1 1AH
T: 01273 326555

Right in the middle of The Lanes, The Victory is a nice place for a spot of outdoor summer sunshine, and on Sunday if the fancy takes you, they do roasts upstairs.

The Waggon and Horses
10 Church St, North Laine, Brighton BN1 1UD
T: 01273 602752

With all the alternative trendy places in The North Laine, this is one of the few places left where you can get a decent Ploughman's. The traditional name means they do traditional pub grub as well. The crowd is young, but not studenty.

The Walkabout Inn
67a West St, Brighton BN1 2RA
T: 01273 719364

The Australian-themed Walkabout is very large, has very friendly staff and attracts a young, lively crowd. There is a live band on a Friday night playing Rock classics.

The Walmer Castle
95 Queen's Park Rd, Hanover, Queens Park, Brighton BN2 2GH. T: 01273 682466
Mon-Sat: 12pm-1am, Sun:12pm-12pm-30am

An increasingly popular place for the young and gorgeous. Expect it to be lively whatever night you go. They do a lovely jerk chicken Sunday lunch and complete the mood with a reggae soundtrack.

William IV
4 Church St, North Laine BN1 1UJ. T: 01273 683365

On the junction of two main streets in the North Laine, you'd be forgiven for expecting this pub to cater for the student and tourist crowd. With respect to both students and tourists, it's better than that. .

The Windmill
69 Upper North St, Brighton BN1 3FL. T: 01273 202475
A cheery, welcoming pub for locals, which extends its welcome to lots of pre-clubbers on the weekends.

BARS

Alfresco

26 Kings Rd Arches, Brighton
BN1 2LN. T: 01273 206523
www.alfrescobrighton.co.uk
Sun-Thur: 12pm-9pm, Fri-Sat:
12pm-10pm

More restaurant than bar, but given
that it's got Brighton's best sunset
viewpoint overlooking what's left
of the West Pier, it's the perfect
place to hang out and sip a vodka
or three. The staff have got a bit of
an attitude, but let's not concern
ourselves about that: that's their
problem.

Ali Cats

80 East St, Brighton BN1 1NF
T: 01273 220902
www.alicatsbar.com
Mon-Sat: 3pm-11pm, Sun: 3pm-
10.30pm. Happy Hour: Tue-Sat:
3pm-8pm, Mon: 3pm-11pm, Sun:
3pm-10.30pm

If louche lounging is what's in
your heart, this is the place for
you. Ali Cats is, in every sense, an
underground dive. Where are the
windows? There are no windows.
Where's the air? No air. But it's
louche and chilled and there's
regular DJ spots, cult movies every
night and reasonably priced booze.

Bar Valentino

New Rd, Brighton BN1 1UF
T: 01273 727766
www.elmexicano.co.uk
elmexicano@youtopia.co.uk

Tues-Sat: 7pm-11pm
Happy Hour: Tue-Sat: 5pm-7pm

Managed by the guy who ran the
once glorious Blue Parrot two doors
down, this is an intimate, plush and
sexy 20 seater with great cocktails
from £5.50. Non-smokers report
that it's too smoky by 10pm but it's
a good option to The Colonnade or
Quod if you're going to the theatre.

Black and White Bar@Hotel Seattle

Waterfront, Marina, Brighton
BN2 5WA. T: 01273 665444
Mon-Fri: 5pm-11pm, Sat: 12pm-11pm,
Sun: 12pm-10.30pm

Great cocktails and atmosphere in
this black and white themed bar
with Beatles photos adorning the
walls. On a Saturday night though,

the vibe is more" I Wanna Hold Your
Hand" than "Let It Be".

Brighton Rocks

Rock Place, Kemp Town,
Brighton BN2 1TF
T: 01273 601139
Mon-Sat: 11am-11pm,
Sun: 12pm-10:30pm

Run by the people who have just
sold Hotel Nineteen, this cocktail
bar is where Kemp Town's style gurus
spend their money. It's also open for
lunches with a late kitchen cooking
up huge organic Sunday lunches and
homemade desserts like strawberry
and vodka cheesecake. Three all
organic courses will set you back
around £15. By Easter they hope to
whizz up large bowls of char grilled
chicken salads for around £8 and
serve them on the decked patio.
They've got DJs in most Friday nights.

Browns

34 Ship St, The Lanes,
Brighton BN1 1AH
T: 01273 323501
www.browns-restaurants.co.uk
Mon-Fri: 9am-11pm, Sat: 10am-
11pm, Sun: 12pm-11pm

Bang in the centre of town,
this tends to be the meeting
place for anyone who works
around here and who fancies a nice
glass of wine rather than a pint
down one of the locals. A useful
place to meet people, but make
sure you get it right because next
door is Brown's restaurant.

Candy Bar

129 St James's St,
Brighton BN2 1TH
T: 01273 622424
www.thecandybar.co.uk
Mon-Sat: 5pm-2am, Sun: 5pm-
10.30pm. Happy Hour:
Mon-Fri: 5pm-7pm

Sister of the legendary lesbian
London bar, The Candy Bar has
grown up and moved to a new
venue in Kemp Town. Decorated
in dark pink with images of naked
ladies gracing the walls, this bar
provides diversity with a pool
table in one corner, dance floor
in the other and tucked away
seating in which to enjoy a long
drink. The staff are friendly and the
atmosphere is relaxed. They operate
an open door policy so that all
friends of gay girls are welcome.

Charles Street

8 Marine Parade, Kemp Town,
Brighton BN2 1TA
T: 01273 624091
www.charlesstreetbar.com
info@charlesstreetbar.com
Bar: Mon-Sun: 12pm-11pm, Club:
Mon, Thur-Sat: 10.30pm-2am
Happy Hour: Mon-Sun: 5pm-9pm

A slice of metro-chic in this two-
level bar (Charles Street) and club
(Envy) on the seafront. The swish
downstairs bar, Charles Street,
offers daytime table service and
food, sofas, strategically lit standing
room and a glam walkway for that
all-important entrance.

Easy

9 Cranbourne St, Brighton BN1
2RD. T: 01273 710928
Mon-Sat: 11am-11pm, Sun: 12pm-
10:30pm

Bang in the centre of town next
to Churchill Square, this is a bit of
a refuge from the madness of the
shops and the beer monsters in
West Street. Stylistically similar to
the Polar Bars; in fact, didn't we spot
the same stools?

The Fish Bowl

74 East St, The Lanes, Brighton
BN1 1HQ. T: 01273 777505
Mon-Sat: 12pm-11pm, Sun: 12pm-
10.30pm. Happy Hour: Mon-Thur:
5pm-7pm

One of the first pre-club bars, this is
a great place to kick the night off to
a good start. Everything here is just
that little bit fishy: fish shaped beer
fonts, pillar fish bowls on the bar,
metal sharks and original artwork.
It's packed every night with a young
and stylish crowd enjoying the laid
back atmosphere, cheap cocktails

and regular DJ's. There are two floors with full table service – and the food's not bad either.

The Fringe Bar

10 Kensington Gdns,
North Laine, Brighton BN1 4AL
T: 01273 623683
Mon-Sat: 11am-11pm,

Sun: 12pm-10.30pm

Comedy and DJ nights at this cool North Laine bar café. Passing the Hookah round at the end of the evening is one of those activities that brings people together. And wash your mind out if

you weren't thinking hubble bubble.

Gemini Beach Bar

127 Kings Rd Arches, Brighton
BN1 2FN. T: 01273 327888
Mon-Sun: 12pm-12am

The largest and liveliest of the

bars on the seaside strip, Gemini epitomises summer in Brighton. Chrome seats spill out onto the promenade where carefree drinkers get an unrivalled view of the sea. Impromptu skate boarding stunts and live jazz bands help give the continental atmosphere a Brighton twist. By dusk the party's moved inside the cosy bar where securing a seat is as important as being noticed. The small capacity makes Gemini fairly exclusive at weekends when the rich and famous come to mingle in the mellow ambience.

The Grand

Kings Rd, Brighton BN1 2FW
T: 01273 224321
www.grandbrighton.co.uk
Mon-Sat: 11am-11pm, Sun: 12pm-10.30pm

Popping into The Grand for your pre-prandial is something that everyone does at least once. You might be disappointed by the lack of genuine grandeur, but you'll probably have plenty to giggle at. If you can forgive the gin and tonics served in wine glasses, go for the pianist in an ill-fitting syrup who makes Les Dawson look like a member of the Philharmonic – a real treat.

Grand Central

29-30 Surrey St, Brighton BN1 3PA. T: 01273 329086
Mon-Sat: 11am-11pm, Sun: 12pm-10.30pm

Chic pub/café/bar with dark leather Chesterfields, good food and a little patio for when the sun shines. For art lovers, the Nightingale Theatre upstairs is particularly avant garde. Opposite Brighton Station, it's a perfect place to wait for your train.

Ha! Ha!

2-3 Pavilion Buildings, The Lanes, Brighton BN1 1EE
T: 01273 737080
www.hahaonline.co.uk
brighton@hahaonline.co.uk
Mon-Sat: 11am-11pm, Sun: 12pm-10.30pm

Opposite the Pavilion and Al Duomo pizzeria, Ha! Ha! is smart and chic: all shiny dark wood and leather. It can feel a bit metallic; the sort of place where there are mirrors everywhere and the bar staff look better than you, but it is very well situated and serves every purpose.

Hotel du Vin

Ship St, The Lanes, Brighton BN1 1AD. T: 01273 718581
www.hotelduvin.com
info@brightonhotelduvin.com
Mon-Sat: 11am-11pm, Sun: 12pm-10.30pm

Sexy, dark and leathery, this is the place to take a secret lover before sneaking up to the hedonistic heaven upstairs. Hotel du Vin is for grown ups though; forget the cocktails and settle back into the deep Chesterfields with a glass

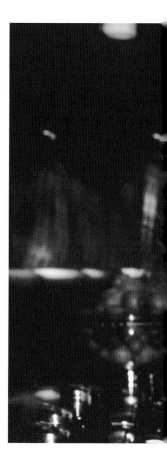

of champagne or any one of the fabulous wines on the vast list, nibble the olives and pistachios and indulge in a bit of celeb spotting.

Kai Bar

32 Brunswick St West, Hove BN3 1EL. T: 01273 771355
Lurking beneath the unsuspecting Star of Brunswick club there's the Kai Bar, dark and small and all things that an after hours bar should be. A couple of quid and you're in. You can get food past midnight and there are DJs, if you care.

Karma

The Waterfront, Marina,
Brighton BN2 5WA
T: 01273 818000
**Mon-Sat: 5pm-2.30am,
Sun: 5pm-1.30pm.**

New swanky bar down in the Marina
and, yes, the Marina can be a bit of
a souless place, but check out those
opening times. It wasn't open as we
went to press, but they describe it
as having a Moroccan theme and
being aimed at the 35 plus market.

"Chilled atmosphere, joss sticks and
champagne". A curious combination,
but if they're open till 2.30am...

Koba

135 Western Rd, Montpelier,
Brighton BN1 2LA
T: 01273 720059
www.kobauk.com
info@kobauk.com
**Mon-Sat: 5pm-11pm,
Sun: 5pm-10.30pm.**

Winner of the 2002 Juicy Award

for Best Bar – and you can't get a
better recommendation that that.
As you might expect from the
man who set up the original
Oriental Hotel, Koba is chic
and stylish, small but cool.
Go through the door and up
the stairs and you're in an
environment out of Wallpaper
magazine; from the purple
velvet panels lining the walls to
the deep, dark wood tables and
matching stools. It sounds a bit
melodramatic, but it works. It also
gets very crowded on weekends.

Koba Private Members Bar

135 Western Rd, Montpelier,
Brighton BN1 2LA.
T: 01273 720059
www.kobauk.com
info@kobauk.com
Mon-Sat: 7pm-2am, Sun: 7pm-12.30am

A discrete spot in one of the busiest parts of town, Koba's private members' bar is set at the back of Koba, the kind of place where you'd only go if you knew it was there, or if a friend had recommended it. Opened late last year, it's already giving The Sussex Arts Club a run for its money, with corporate events taking place in its lush surrounds.

Kruze Cafe

7 Marine Parade, Kemp Town,
Brighton BN2 1TA
T: 01273 608133
Mon-Sat: 12pm-11pm, Sun: 12pm-10.30pm

Kruze is one of those places on the seafront by the pier that tourists flock to, and it's a good a meeting point as any. The food is traditional, and replaces the a la carte menu this year. They have just opened their upstairs area to welcome families.

Legends

31 Marine Parade, Kemp Town,
Brighton BN2 1TR
T: 01273 624462
www.legendsbar.co.uk
Mon-Sat: 11am-11pm, Sun: 12pm-

10.30pm. Happy Hour: Sun: 12pm-2pm, 5pm-9.30pm, Mon-Thur: 5pm-9.30pm, Fri-Sat: 5pm-7pm

The bar for the seafront New Europe Hotel, but don't let that put you off. It's vibrant and funky, serves shooters and some food, and the music isn't too loud to stop you having a comfortable social experience. Thursday and Sunday nights are cabaret, Monday is karaoke, Tuesday is music hall (karaoke with a keyboard and a drag queen) and on Wednesdays it's a full house for bingo and quiz night. Legends is the official warm-up bar for Revenge and there's usually some free tickets up for grabs if you ask behind the bar.

The Market Diner

19 Circus St, Old Steine,
Brighton. T: 01273 608273
One of the few properly legendary places in town. Open all night, The Market Diner is one of those statutory post-club places where everything looks better than it probably is, largely on account of the fact that everyone's pupils are just that little bit skewed.

Oriel Bar@Rendezvous Casino

Marina, Brighton BN2 5UT
T: 01273 605602
www.lciclubs.com
7 days 6pm-2am

Free (but compulsory) membership allows you to drink late and then

pop downstairs to indulge in a little American and Electronic Roulette, Blackjack, Casino Stud Poker as well as dice and slots. There's a private high stakes room and separate card room with poker classes for beginners. The Oriel Bar often gets high-jacked by private parties making it off-limits to other members, but there's always the bar in the main gaming room.

Penthouse

1 Phoenix Place, Old Steine,
Brighton BN2 9ND
T: 01273 603974
Mon-Sat: 5pm-11pm,
Sun: 5pm-10.30pm.
Happy Hour: Mon-Sun: 5pm-7pm

A little bit of a hidey-hole and like all hidey-holes, a bit of a treat. It's upstairs from The Freebutt, so unless you've got a mate who knows about it or you like indie music you're unlikely to chance upon it. But it's a sweet sofa filled bar with drinks and pizzas and music.

The Pussycat Club

176 Church Rd, Hove BN3 2DJ
T: 01273 735574
www.pussycat-club.co.uk
Mon-Sat: 5pm-1.30am

Fifty quid to watch women cavorting with poles in tiny thongs and strategically placed sequins? Cheap at half the price.

Riki-Tik

18a Bond St, North Laine,
Brighton BN1 1RD
T: 01273 683844
Mon-Sat: 12pm-11pm, Sun: 12pm-
10.30pm. Happy Hour: Mon-Sun:
4pm-8pm

Primarily a pre-club bar where
glamour and lager are dished
out in equal measure. Playstation
junkies, Internetters and dressed
up clubbers are who you'll find in
this stylish den. DJs get the young
and hip clientele going around six
nights a week. On Fridays, fight
through the crowded ground floor
and relax with a cocktail in the
more salubrious upstairs lounge bar.
Those who find it all too much can
ask at the bar for a Playstation and
pretend that they are alone in their
front room.

The Reservoir

1 Howard Rd, Hanover,
Brighton BN2 9TP
T: 01273 269728
Mon-Fri: 4pm-11pm, Sat: 12pm-
11pm, Sun: 12pm-10.30pm

Comfy sofas downstairs and a
stylish garden in this cool bar on the
edge of Hanover. Run by the people
who won the first Juicy Award for
best pub back in 2000 for The Pub
With No Name (now sold on), you
know what to expect.

Saqqara

155 North St, Brighton BN1 1EA
T: 01273 778600 F: 01273
220734
www.saqqara-bar.co.uk
Mon-Sat: 12pm-11pm; Sun: 12-
10.30pm

Huge space with décor and statues
straight out of Egypt. Popular with
the cocktail, pre-club brigade, they
do a two-course menu by night,
and astonishingly cheap nibbles at
lunchtime; the risotto and lamb hot
pot were both £2.95, probably one

of the reasons why it's packed at lunch times with lunching shoppers, grannies and just about anyone you can think of. In the evening, it's more discerning; even Jordan wasn't allowed in on a Friday night.

The Squid and Starfish
78 Middle St, The Lanes, Brighton BN1 1AL
T: 01273 727114
Mon-Fri: 4pm-11pm, Sat-Sun: 3pm-11pm. Happy Hour: Mon-Sun: 4pm-9pm

Squid claims to be Brighton's original pre-club bar. It's stylishly designed, all retro-kitsch and funky lights, vibrant orange walls and

Mexican style mosaic bar. Popular with a funky, laid back crowd who happily hang around while enjoying bargain priced shooters and chilled tunes on the stereo, its central location makes it a natural choice for clubbers heading down to the beach. It's the official pre-club bar to Superstars and Chopper Choons at The Zap and you can get your free entry on Mondays and Wednesdays here and queue-jump.

Sumo
9-12 Middle St, Brighton BN1 1AL. T: 01273 749465
Sun-Wed: 3pm-11pm, Thurs-Sat: 1pm-11pm. Entrance: £2-£4

This is where the fashion conscious converge to look cool and collect new friends. The friends may not last much more than the night, but hey, that's why the boys come back, and why the girls are divided in their opinion.

The Tin Drum
95 Dyke Rd, Seven Dials, Brighton BN1 3JE
T: 01273 777575
43 St James's St, Kemp Town, Brighton BN2 1RS
T: 01273 624777
10 Victoria Grove, Hove, Hove BN3 2LG
T: 01273 747755
www.tindrum.co.uk
Mon-Fri: 11am-11pm, Sat: 10.30am-

11pm, Sun: 10.30am-10.30pm

Where The Tin Drum opens its doors, so the nearby house prices set off for space. A social barometer in Seven Dials, Hove and Kemp Town, this is the bar where drinks and food may be Polish, but the clientele is largely not. Try the Zakushki, traditional Polish bar snacks served on blinis (£2.75-£3.50), or the more substantial Salmon Gravadlax at £5.50. There's an on-line food ordering service. (See Restaurant section).

The Station

Goldstone Villas, Hove BN3 3RU. T: 01273 733660
Late night drinking Friday and Saturday – by which time even the purple pool tables look good.

Sussex Arts Club

7 Ship St, The Lanes, Brighton

BN1 2AD. T: 01273 727371
www.sussexarts.com
Mon-Wed: 11am-11pm, Thur-Sat: 11pm-2pm, Sun: 7.30pm-10.30pm

The Sussex Arts Club was the first attempt to fulfil the need for a Soho House in Brighton, and dingy as it is, it still draws the media types in. History plays a part in this: it's been a members' bar since the mid-19th century. Members pay £160 a year, with a renewal rate of £85 to get a drink after the pubs close. As well as the members bar, there are 250 plus events in the domed Ballroom, eight hotel rooms (open to the public), and club nights such as Da Do Ron Ron, the UK's only 1960's female vocal only club, the Brighton Jazz Club, the longest established jazz club in the south-east and corporate and private events. Temporary membership can be arranged with 48 hours notice.

AIN'T YOU LOT GOT HOMES TO GO TO? LATE NIGHT DRINKING AND PRIVATE CLUBS

You don't want to go to bed but you don't know someone who knows something that's going on that night and you don't want to get your ears hammered in a club full of kids who should be doing

their O Level revision and...
and... where do you go?
Getting a drink after hours in
this country is still a test of
ingenuity in this country. The
legal ones are lusted here, ok,
so you'll need membership
for some of them. So test
that ingenuity.

Charles Street and Envy
8-9 Marine Parade, Kemp

Town, Brighton BN2 1TA
T: 01273 624091
Koba Bar
135 Western Rd, Brighton BN1
2LA. T: 01273 720059
Kai Bar
32 Brunswick St West, Hove
BN3 1EL. T: 01273 771355
The Market Diner
19 Circus St, Old Steine,
Brighton T: 01273 608273.
The Pussycat Club

176 Church Rd, Hove BN3 2DJ
T: 01273 735574
Sumo
9-12 Middle St, The Lanes,
Brighton BN1 1AL
T: 01273 749465
Sussex Arts Club
7 Ship St, The Lanes, Brighton
BN1 2AD. T: 01273 727371
The Station
Goldstone Villas, Hove BN3
3RU. T: 01273 733660

CLUBBING

CLUBBING IN BRIGHTON

Brighton clubbers just don't take themselves seriously. They'd would rather go out in a pair of faded jeans and a Desil t-shirt, mess around, then crash back to whoever happens to be throwing a party. Some of the best times are when the DJs and decks go alfresco for Pride, when the Kemp Town clubs deck themselves out in rainbows and everyone dances all day in Preston Park or on the beach at Norman Cook's Big Beach Boutique.

Monday to Sunday there's plenty to keep everyone entertained. In winter most clubbers go into hibernation, but summer in the city is unlike anywhere else. Laze on the beach all day before tripping over to the pub on the beach, The Fortune of War, for your favourite tipple and watch the sun go down. Then... Make a dash to the loos, change your top, apply a slick of mascara and dance all night.

West Street
West Street is not what Brighton is about. Teenie boppers totter along with Alco-pops floating round their blood. Out-of-towners, drawn like moths by the bright lights and girls in mega micro-minis – well, belts – and terrifying parties of Hens and Stags. Clubbing is cheap Monday to Thursday and that's when the students hit town. Should you want to – and God knows why you would – you'll find this crowd in Creation, The Event or Weatherspoons.

Alternative
In England's hedonistic home there are some great alternative nights, so grab a cab to Va Va Va Voom at The Concorde 2 through the summer or Supercharged at The Funky Buddha on a Thursday. For a fancy dress night to remember everyone is invited to Margot's Party at The Hanbury Ballroom or maybe you'd like to have a go at salsa in Club New York. Just beware the short, greasy men.

Gay

There is a great gay vibe in Brighton clubs, which are all gay friendly, but for a real giggle, try Harlequin for karaoke and wonderful cabaret. Creation hosts Wild Fruits once a month and with Monday night being the official end of the weekend here The Honey Club on a Sunday night or Sunday Sundae at Audio (formerly The Escape) sees gay, straight, young and old all seeing in the coming week.

Late Bars

Late Bar Culture is becoming a big thing in Brighton. Young things with daddy's cash, local celebs, entrepreneurs and property tycoons all strut their stuff to smooth R'n'B just enough to get noticed but not enough to mess up their carefully straightened hair (and that's just the boys). Find them in Sumo on a Friday or Saturday night or Snafu 24. With the new late licensing laws, bars where you can drink, dance, chat, and sit down all under one roof look set to become more and more popular.

All That Jazz

For a softer sound Casablanca offers jazz and funk, or for modern jazz try The Jazz Place. The Concorde 2, which used to be the home of jazz still has the occasional night.

Ravers

Finally, the hardcore merchants, the tireless stalwarts of the rave era determined to keep going till they pass out. Legends of the Dark Black has recently moved to the unlikely venue of The Event and has been well received, Mr Scruff is an old timer at The Concorde and Meltdown at The Beach still pulls the crowds and some top MCs. For those more into house music, Hed Kandi at The Honey is a really great night, but beware of the queues.

CLUBS

Arc
160 Kings Rd Arches, Brighton
BN1 1NB. T: 01273 770505
www.arcbrighton.co.uk
Mon-Sat: 10pm-2am
Entrance: £3-£6

This trendy seafront spot is a bar by day and a club by night. There is a sun patio (summer only) at the front with Thai food on offer during the day. Entry is usually free, with drinks at fairly reasonable prices. Gorgeous (Funky house) is on Friday, Holdup! (new indie night) is on Saturday.

Audio
10 Marine Parade, Kemp Town, Brighton BN2 1TL
T: 01273 606906
www.audiobrighton.com
info@audiobrighton.co.uk
Tue-Thurs: 10pm-2am, Fri and Sat: 10pm-3am. Entrance: Tue-Thurs: £2-£6, Fri-Sat: £5-£10

Set in a perfect Art Deco building just the Kemp Town side of the Brighton Pier, and with the huge success story of its forerunner The Escape, Audio is bound to be a winner. Even Stompaphunk have left The Funky Buddha for it.

Babylon Lounge
Western Esplanade, Kingsway, Hove BN3 4FA
T: 01273 207100
Mon, Wed and Sun: 11am-5pm, Tues, Thu, Fri and Sat: 11am-5pm, 9pm-2am. Entrance: Tue: £5, Thu: £5, Fri: £6-£10, Sat: £5

Hove's only seafront club, with sex gods Adonis Cabaret giving the hens a thrill every Friday, The Candystore serving up indie tunes on a Saturday, families celebrating naming ceremonies on its lawns, Hove promenaders sipping hot chocolate by day and salsa kings and queens shaking their booty on Tuesdays.

The Beach
171 Kings Rd Arches, Brighton
BN1 1NB. T: 01273 722272
www.thebeachbrighton.co.uk
Wed-Thurs: 10pm-2am, Fri-Sat: 10pm-3am. Entrance: £2-£10

Beach bar/cafe by day, throbbing heart of the seafront by night, everyone goes to The Beach at least

once. This diverse seafront club/day bar has an open music policy that caters for all, with each night having its own sound: Drum'n'bass showcase Meltdown Monthly and new Seb Fontaine residency Type (last Friday of every month). Voodoo (party tunes and dance anthems) Thursday, Fever (commercial dance) Saturday. With its wee sibling, Minimelt going strong every Tuesday at the Ocean Rooms, Meltdown monthly is still one of Brighton's premier drum'n'bass nights. Hot, heavy and hectic, queues are likely and so are hen parties.

Brighton Gloucester

27 Gloucester Place, Brighton BN1 4AA. T: 01273 688011
Mon-Sat: 10pm-2am
Entrance: £2-£6

In an attempt to cater for all and

capture the diversity of Brighton, The Gloucester has found a large alternative following. If you're more interested in moshing the night away then the Gloucester is your place. Super good (Funk, Soul and Hip-hop) on Thursday, Sindrome (Alternative) on Tuesday. Most Saturdays are Back to School where the entrance decreases considerably if you're wearing school uniform (and no, they don't mean starched white shirts and itchy jumpers).

Casablanca

2 Middle St, The Lanes, Brighton BN1 1AL. T: 01273 321817
Mon-Sat: 9.30pm-2am
Entrance: £3-£7

Not the most cutting edge club, but one of the most popular. Two

floors of jazz and funk with the odd bit of salsa and 70's disco thrown in. Upstairs the front half of a purple Beetle fits two turntables and one DJ quite nicely, while downstairs live bands play every weekend. Nights such as Sambanation and Love Bug are a great alternative to the sometimes-bland offerings down at the seafront and with a friendly atmosphere and good service. We once saw a whole crowd of clubbers entertained by a troupe of drummers during a power cut here. Now how many clubs can offer that?

Club Mango

1 Preston St, Brighton BN1 2HN. T: 01273 323161
Mon-Sat: 10pm-2am
Entrance: £5

Formally BN1, Club Mango has a

different theme every night of the
week. Go on Mondays for the Tequila
party, Wednesday for African night
if you are looking to try something
new, Thursday is total cheese with
70's and 80's, Friday is the club most
popular night with R'n'B and rap
and Saturday is time for salsa. It's
small enough to have a party vibe,
and there's no stress to get your
latex hotpants out for the occasion.
Unless, of course, you want to.

Club New York
11 Dyke Rd, Brighton BN1 3FE
T: 01273 208678
Mon-Sat: 8pm-2am
Entrance: £0-£5
Brighton's main salsa club starts off
with salsa dancing lessons before the
full club experience starts. Later in
the night, house and funk are played
upstairs and Latin and salsa is played
downstairs. Spanish Party is on
Thursdays with '70s to present day
party tunes on Friday and Saturday.

Concorde 2
Madeira Shelter Hall Madeira
Drive, Kemp Town, Brighton
BN2 1EN. T: 01273 772770
www.concorde2.co.uk
info@concorde2.co.uk
Fri-Sat: 10pm-4am, Mon-Thurs:
8pm-12am. Entrance: £6-£20

Arguably the best music venue in
town, a legendary club, and a multi
Juicy Award winner, the Concorde is
one of the things that Brighton does
best. The Big Beat Boutique on every
other Friday with the likes of Fatboy

Slim often playing. Don't miss Etch
(the Mr Scruff extravaganza) on
the first Friday of the month. Solid
Ground (drum'n'bass) is on the
last Saturday of the month and Va
Va Voom comes to town once in
a while with its feather boas and
thigh length boots, so keep your ear
to the ground for a wild night out.

Core Club
12-15 Kings Rd, Brighton BN1
1NE. T: 01273 326848

www.brightoncharterhotel.
co.uk
brightoncharter@fsbdial.co.uk
Fri and Sat: 9pm-2am
Entrance: Fri: £5, Sat: £8
Its recent refurbishment has
allowed the Core Club to come out
of the shadows and gain a better
reputation. Its new look plays host
to lots of live DJ's with funky house,
the most common sound. Open
every weekend and occasionally
during the week.

music rather than trendy toilets, this is the place to be on a Saturday night. Ninja Tune's Phonic Hoop is a beautiful mish-mash of old-skool, hip-hop, jazzy breaks, drum'n'bass – anything goes as long as the emphasis is firmly on funk and every tune's a floor filler. Nights: Imprint (hip-hop) is on Thursday and Soul City (hip-hop, old skool) on Friday.

Envy
Marine Parade, Kemp Town, Brighton BN2 1TA
T: 01273 624091
Mon-Sun: 10.30-2am. Entrance: £1.50 on Mon to £8 at the weekend
Formerly Pool, this is Brighton's late night dance, drink and cabaret bar on the seafront – particularly for those who staggered into Charles Street, the bar downstairs a few hours earlier. Home to nights like Perfumed Gardens and Coco Latte, and through the week classics Funktion, Pump, XXL and Bootylicious.

The Event II
Kingswest, West St, Brighton BN1 2RE. T: 01273 732627
www.event2nightclub.co.uk
event2-brighton@luminar.co.uk
**Tue, Fri and Sat: 9.30pm-2am
Entrance: Tue: £2-£3, Fri: £4-£5, Sat: £5.50-£7.50**
This club claims the title of busiest in Brighton, and offers commercial dance and party music for the masses in a large, pretty faceless setting. Drinks are cheap but be prepared to queue for the bar. Home to Beat Down, one of the best live hip-hop nights around

Creation
78 West St, Brighton BN1 1AL
T: 01273 321628 F: 01273 203916
www.creationbrighton.com
**Tues, Thurs, Fri and Sat: 9pm-2am
Entrance: Tue and Thurs: £3, Fri: £6, Sat: £8**

On the site of what was once Paradox/Barcelona, but after a £5m refit later, it's pretty much the same. Three different rooms,

three different types of music with everything changing through the week. It's big and populist and Event-like, and once a month gay night Wild Fruit comes down to play.

Enigma
10 Ship St, The Lanes, Brighton BN1 2RA. T: 01273 328439
**Thurs-Sat: 10pm-2am
Entrance: £4**
Not the chicest club in town, but for those whose priority is great

(www.stickiton.co.uk), the legendary DIY night on Saturday where you, the public, can line up to play DJ for 15 minutes. Opening times vary depending on what's going on, so you might have to check their website or phone ahead for those big nights.

Harlequin

Providence Place, Brighton BN1 4GE. T: 01273 620630 www.harlequin-brighton.co.uk One of Brighton's most popular gay clubs with outrageous drag and karaoke keeping the punters queuing around the corner.

(we've heard of people travelling from Manchester and Liverpool to go to these events), long standing south coast drum'n'bass extravaganza, Legends of the Dark Black, come to play once a month.

Funky Buddha Lounge

169 Kings Rd Arches, Brighton BN1 1NB. T: 01273 725541 www.funkybuddha.co.uk info@funkybuddha.co.uk Mon-Sat: 10pm-2am. Entrance: £3-4

A Juicy Award winning club, it's been created with an eye on design and is one of the few clubs to take its shape into consideration. It boasts state of the art light and sound equipment. Supercharged (breaks and beats) on Thursday still pulls in the punters. They have also welcomed Thank Funk On Fridays for those who love funk and party tunes.

Funky Fish Club

19 Marine Parade, Kemp Town, Brighton BN2 1TL. T: 01273 696961 www.funkyfishclub.co.uk Fri-Sat: 10pm-2am Entrance: £4-£5 The hot and heaving Funky Fish is the option for those who can't be bothered to get dressed for clubbing, but are still looking for a good party. It's known for its friendly atmosphere with clubbers and staff sharing the experience.

Hanbury Ballroom

83 St George's Rd, Kemp Town, Brighton BN2 1EF T: 01273 605789 www.zelnet.co.uk Mon-Sat: 5pm-3am Entrance: £3-£7

All sorts of things go on at the Hanbury, but check out Stick It On

Honey Club

214 King's Rd Arches, Brighton BN1 1NB. T: 01273 202807 www.thehoneyclub.co.uk info@thehoneyclub.co.ukin Mon and Tue: 10pm-2am, Wed: 9.30pm-2am, Thurs: 10pm-2.30am, Fri: 10pm-3am, Sat: 10pm-4am, Sun: 9pm-2am. Entrance: £3-£10

The Honey Club is a sophisticated and stylish haven for dance types who like their hotpants sparkling and their bra tops fluffy. It's the closest Brighton has to a 'super club' with three gleaming bars, Tardis-like toilets, a spacious chill out room in the back arch and a balcony bar. The music changes through out the week from disco, to drum'n'bass, through to hip-hop and finishes with dance anthems and house. Cream touches down here on the first Friday of each month, and Hed Kandi on the last.

The Jazz Place

10 Ship St, The Lanes, Brighton
BN1 2RA. T: 01273 328439
Fri-Sat: 10pm-2am
Entrance: £4

If modern jazz is your thing – jazz
funk, Afro-jazz, Latin jazz, whatever
– this will be your Nirvana. Down
in this small, dark basement DJ Russ
Dewbury – the man behind the
Festival Jazz Bop – spins a sweat-
soaked array of discs that, thanks to
a conversation-killing sound system,
sound fab. It's the sort of place where
people go to dance rather than pose.

The Joint

37 West St, Brighton BN1 2RE
T: 01273 770095
Thurs-Sat: 10pm-2am
Entrance: £5
Smoky basement club with kitsch,
cosy seating and an intimate (it's the
red lighting that does it) that aims to
emulate a Boho beatnik vibe. If you're
into lounge and all that easy listening
thang, then this is the place for you.
Dynamite Boogaloo (disco trash) is
the top night on Thursday.

Midnight Blues

Grand Hotel, Kings Rd,
Brighton BN1 2SW
T: 01273 321188
www.midnightblues.co.uk
midnight.blues@virginnet.co.uk
Fri-Sat: 9pm-2am. Entrance: £5-£10

This clubs caters for 30 to 40-year-
olds who are looking for a good

time with music anywhere between
the 60's and modern. Also look out
for DJ Floppy Johnsen who has quite
a local following.

The Ocean Rooms

1 Morley St, Brighton BN2 9RA
T: 01273 699069
www.oceanrooms.co.uk
info@oceanrooms.co.uk
Mon-Sat: 10pm-2am
Entrance: £3-£8

Said to have the best sound
system in town, the Ocean Rooms
is about quality acts and DJs in
a plush, sophisticated setting.
Spread over three floors, this BEDA
(Bar, Entertainment and Dance
Association) Club of the Year has a
cushioned – walled restaurant on
the middle floor and glowing UV
tabletops in the basement bar. It's
dark, atmospheric, and perfect for
that big night out when it's all about
the music. Nights: Minimelt (Drum
n Bass) on Tuesdays, Substance
(various, tops) on Fridays, BoyGirl
(House) on Saturday.

Penthouse

1 Phoenix Place, Brighton BN2
9ND. T: 01273 603974
www.zelnet.com
freebutt@zelnet.com
Mon-Sat: 5pm-11pm, Sun: 5pm-
10.30pm. Entrance: free

Imagine a pre-famous Jarvis Cocker
and Debbie Harry drinking cheap
lager and discussing the merits

of electroclash vs indie in your
sitting room in 1969 and you've got
the feel of this place. Favourite
hang out for bands playing in the
Freebutt downstairs, top nights
include Chicks With Decks (Thurs)
Stop Making Friends (Fri) Electronic
Goodness (Mon).

Po-Na-Na

75-79 East St, The Lanes,
Brighton BN1 1NF
T: 01273 777904
www.ponana.co.uk
Mon-Sat: 9am-2am.
Entrance: £5-£10

A late night bar with the feel of a
club. It's well decorated with relaxing
booths and chilled out areas and a
small dance floor. Expect a mix of
music that includes popular dance,
hip-hop and R'n'B and attracts a
diverse set of people at weekends
ranging across all age groups.

Pressure Point

33 Richmond Place, Brighton
BN2 9NA. T: 01273 702333
www.pressurepoint.me.uk
Sun-Wed: 8pm-12am, Thurs-Sat:
10pm-2am. Entrance: £1-£10

Smartened up under new
management and finally making use
of its capabilities as a live music
venue with the excellent Cable Club
(Sun, Mon, Tues), The Pressure Point
has always showcased the decent
up and coming Brighton bands.
It's full of duffel coats and sharp

haircuts shyly eyeing each other up, the sweat pours off the walls, and occasionally you'll witness a truly great new band moment.

Revenge

32 Old Steine, Brighton BN1 1TR. T: 01273 606064 F: 01273 621063

www.revenge.co.uk

admin@revenge.co.uk

Mon-Thur and Sun: 10pm-2am, Fri and Sat: 10pm-3am. Entrance: Mon: free, Tue-Thur: £3, Fri: £6.50, Sat: £8.50, Sun: £4.50

Voted Weekend Club of the Year for two years running by gay magazine "Boyz", Revenge is Brighton's premier gay club. Although its main appeal

lies in the gay market, Revenge has a strong straight following as well, mainly because the lack of attitude and booty-shaking music. Cabaret Queen, Maisie Trollope struts her stuff on Wednesdays, Lollipop is a fun and frivolous night hosted by a gaggle of top drag hags, and look out for the stripper nights if you're into that kind of thing.

Royal Pavilion Tavern

3 Castle Square, Brighton BN1 1FX. T: 01273 827641
Mon-Sat: 12pm-11pm,
Sun:12pm-10.30pm

A Regular Joe kind of pub which harbours a well kept secret upstairs in the form of The Tavern club or Pav Tav. Once the bar shuts, it's time to shimmy upstairs for a Sixties showdown on Saturday nights, or the rock/indie nights on Wednesdays and Thursdays. MFI (Mad For It) celebrates everything Mancunian mid-week.

Sumo

9-12 Middle St, Brighton BN1 1AL. T: 01273 749465
Sun-Wed: 3pm-11pm, Thurs-Sat: 1pm-11pm . Entrance: £2-£4

This is where the fashion conscious converge to look cool and collect new friends. The friends may not last much more than the night, but hey, that's why the boys come back, and why the girls are divided in their opinion.

Volks Tavern

Madeira Drive, Kemp Town, Brighton BN2 1PS
T: 01273 682828
www.volksclub.co.uk
info@volksclub.co.uk
Mon-Sun: 9pm-2am
Entrance: £1-£7

Volks always was the perfect antidote to both the big, showy nightclubs and the bigger name beachfront places, and it still is. Despite opening the basement and expanding, it's still groovy and slightly down-at-heel. Bargain beer prices and cheap entry have long attracted a loyal following of friendly up-for-it clubbers. Strictly Reggae on Monday, Lunacy Soundsystem (techno, breakbeat and drum'n'bass)on Friday, The Funktion (funk, soul and hip-hop) monthly Saturdays.

Zap

189 Kings Rd Arches, Brighton BN1 1NB
T: 01273 202407
www.thezapbrighton.co.uk
Mon-Sat: 10am-3am
Entrance: £5-£8

The oldest and the first. With two main rooms and a maze of arch shaped corridors to explore, The Zap is the original raver's playground. Nights include: Wasted Youth (indie) on Monday; Sin (Wild Fruit night) on Thursday; Ice (R'n'B and hip-hop) on Fridays.

GAY

Brighton offers gay boys and girls a safe, diverse and vibrant city all within reach of the ultimate chill out venue... the beach. Whether you're looking to party, kickback or both there is something on the gay scene to tickle every fancy (even the naughty ones)

There are bars and clubs in abundance and no visit would be complete without a trip to Revenge for hands in the air fun. Charles St is the place to be seen and of course a must for the girls is The Candy Bar.

Feeling hungry? Veggie cafe Gardenia and Bona Foodie deli on St James Street are well worth a visit or for something a little special head to The Strand, just around the

corner from the ever friendly Dr Brighton's.

If you want to try something a little 'alternative' then Brighton has it all from acupuncture to Zen. Evolution offers a range of classes including yoga, life drawing and Bollywood dancing. The Pink Pamper will do just that with hair, facial and body treatments.

Whatever your scene, Brighton will have something to give to you. This city by the sea is out and proud – give it a go – you won't regret it.

Indra

LESBIAN BRIGHTON

One of the best things about Brighton for gay girls is not just that there are so many lesbians, but that

so many are visible. In summer there often seem to be such a lot of dykes out and about that the buzz you get never really goes away.

Yes, it might seem at first glance that bars and clubs for lesbians are thin on the ground, but much of Brighton has such a polysexual mentality that you can guarantee meeting other women in many of the gay/mixed/whatever venues in town. However, for purely lesbian pubs and clubs there's the Marlborough (open until 11pm) and the Candy Bar (open until 2am), and on the first Friday of the month glammed-up girls go dancing at Wet Pussy at Envy. Club nights come and go with such frequency in Brighton that it's worth while keeping an ear to the ground to find out if there's anything new on at the moment. The Queen's Head is a gay pub that has a trendy lesbian clientele (and the bisexual group meet there on Thursday evenings). For bi-curious types Dynamite Boogaloo at the Joint on a Thursday is awash with beautiful drunken students looking for someone to snog on the seats round the back. The Bedford Tavern has a lesbian and gay real ale drinkers group that meet on the last Friday of every month – there really is something for everyone.

BLAGSS (Brighton Lesbian and Gay Sports Society) is a getaway from the boozy atmosphere found at the places above – although there are often social events organised, as well as meetings for various sports including tennis, cycling and swimming. If you prefer footy, Brighton Bandits is a football club for gay men and lesbians.

GLAM (Gay and Lesbian Arts and Media) run courses in all kinds of things. Tickled on Gardner Street sells sex toys for girls. And for all sorts of advice and help, from finding a flat to getting counselling, the lovely people at Switchboard are available every day from 5-11pm on 01273 204050.

Stephanie Lam

websites & addresses

Revenge
32 Old Steine, Brighton BN1
1TR. T: 01273 606064

F: 01273 621063
www.revenge.co.uk

Charles St
8 Marine Parade, Kemp Town,
Brighton BN2 1TA
T: 01273 624091
www.charlesstreetbar.com

Gardenia
2 St James Street, Kemp Town,
Brighton BN2 1RE
T: 01273 686273

Bona Foodie
21 St James's St, Kemp Town,
Brighton BN2 1RF
T: 01273 698007

The Strand
6 Little East Street, The Lanes,
Brighton BN1 1HT
T: 01273 747096

Dr Brighton's
16 Kings Rd, The Lanes,
Brighton BN1 1NE
T: 01273 328765

Evolution
2 Sillwood Terrace, Brighton
BN1 2LR. T: 01273 204204
www.evolutionarts.co.uk

The Pink Pamper
1 St James St, Kemp town,
Brighton BN2 1RE
T: 01273 608060
www.thepinkpamper.co.uk

The Marlborough Tavern
4 Princess St, Old Steine,
Brighton BN2 9RD

Tel: 01273 570028
the_marlborough@hotmail.com

The Candy Bar
129 St James's St, Brighton BN2
1TH. T: 01273 622424
www.thecandybar.co.uk

Pool
Marine Parade, Kemp Town,
Brighton BN2 1TA
T: 01273 624091

The Queen's Head
3 Steine St, Kemp Town,
Brighton BN2 1TE
T: 01273 602939

The Joint
37 West St, Brighton BN1 2RE
T: 01273 770095

Tickled
15 Gardner St, North Laine,
Brighton BN1 1UP
T: 01273 628725 F: 01273 606720
www.tickledonline.co.uk

www.bedfordtavern.com
(Western St, 01273 739495)

www.brightonbothways.org
(Brighton Bisexual Group)

www.blagss.com

www.banditsfc.org

www.glam-brighton.co.uk

www.switchboard.org.uk/
brighton

SHOPS

PEE WEES

SANDPIPER
BOOKS

Check www.juicymapminder.co.uk for hundreds more shops, including chain stores, department stores, DIY and supermarkets

ARTS AND ANTIQUES

Art Asylum
80c St James St, Kemp Town, Brighton BN2 1PA
T: 01273 626426
M: 07890 744217
www.artasylumgallery.co.uk

Contemporary pop art/graphic canvases from the chilled out classics to modern day icons. Limited edition prints available and commissions welcome.

Art Republic
13 Bond St, North Laine, Brighton BN1 1RD
T: 01273 724829
F: 01273 746016
www.artrepublic.com
Mon-Fri: 9.30am-6pm, Sat: 9am-6pm, Sun: 11am-5pm

Fine art poster, print and framing gallery. Check out the latest exhibitions online and what's on worldwide. A nice touch – they let you check out a picture at home to see if it suits you first. Expert advice and friendly staff.

Brick a Brack
25 Gloucester Rd, North Laine, Brighton BN1 4AQ
T: 01273 697300

sue@bric-abrick.demon.co.uk
Mon-Fri: 9am-5.30pm,
Sun: 12pm-4pm

Beautiful selection of second hand furniture that looks good as new, and lovely leather sofas at great prices.

Brighton Architectural Salvage
33-34 Gloucester Rd, North Laine, Brighton BN1 4AQ
T: 01273 681656
Tue-Sat: 10am-5pm

If you're looking for a beautiful restored fireplace this is the place to come. Sometimes you might find the odd cast iron bath or railings, but it's all a bit of a lucky dip. Don't expect the word 'cheap' to pass your lips.

Brighton Artists Gallery
108a Dyke Rd, Seven Dials, Brighton BN1 3TE
T: 01273 711016
www.baggallery.co.uk
alicia.murphy@baggallery.co.uk
Tues-Sat: 11am-6pm

Brighton Artists Gallery provides an outlet for local artists to exhibit, sell and develop their work with new exhibitions every month. It's a great place to tap into all the talent Brighton has to offer, and often puts on prestigious shows such as last year's Man Ray.

Brighton Designers And Makers
39 Sydney St, North Laine, Brighton BN1 4EP
T: 01273 671212
Mon-Sat: 10am-6pm,
Sun: 11am-5pm

Fantastic local talents show their work in this shop and gallery. They have monthly exhibitions with the artist of the month working downstairs. Over 140 local artists sell their wares here at very reasonable prices.

Brighton Pottery Workshop
94 Trafalgar St, Brighton BN1 1NB. T: 01273 601641
www.workshoplinepttery.co.uk
workshop.stocker@talk21.com
Tues-Sat: 10am-5.30pm

Traditional ceramics fashioned on the work found in Brighton in the 18th century. Resident potter Peter Stocker is more than happy for you to sit and watch as he creates that perfect masterpiece.

Chameleon Gallery
13a Prince Albert St, The Lanes, Brighton BN1 1HE
T: 01273 324432
www.chameleongallery.org
info@chameleongallery.org
Mon-Sat: 10am-6pm,
Sun: 11am-4pm

Bright, vibrant contemporary gallery.

there are often some real bargains here. There are special designs to order, and classes – adult and children's – are available.

Kensington Yard
77-78 North Rd, North Laine, Brighton, E Sussex BN1 1YD
T: 01273 689405
Mon-Sat: 10am-6pm, Sun: 11am-5pm

Specialists in 1930's stripped oak and Art Deco furniture plus decorative objects and textiles from the 1920's and 1930's. A great place to go if you need a new dining table and chairs.

Dermot and Jill Palmer Antiques
7-8 Union St, North Laine, Brighton BN1 1HA
T: 01273 328669
www.jillpalmerantiques.co.uk
Mon-Sat: 9am-6pm

Somewhere on the three floors you'll find something to suit your budget, with the emphasis on European – largely French – antiques for the home and garden. They also have a warehouse of furniture to tempt you and your purse strings further.

Economy
82 St George's Rd, Kemp Town, Brighton BN2 1EF
T: 01273 682831
www.economyofbrighton.co.uk
Mon-Sat: 9am-5pm, Sun: 11am-5pm

If you need some stationary – from the obvious to the oddest – this is the place. Pens, papers, glue, stickers; name it, they've got it. It's great for all your handicraft needs and it's got everything to entertain your kids.

Ivy White
45 Church Road, Hove, BN3 2BE
Tel 01273 203202
Tues and Wed: 11am-5.30pm,
Thurs-Sat: 10am-6pm
Beautifully restored Antique Pine and fine furnishings. Plus a selection of charming gifts for that country cottage feel.

J S Carter Antiques
14 Prince Albert Square, Brighton BN1 1HE
T: 01273 206091
Mon-Sat: 10am-6pm

With eight rooms of furniture, among the restoration there are some beautiful Edwardian mahogany pieces. Although it can be expensive, expect to find designs you wouldn't see in any usual antique shop.

Kemp Town Terracotta
5 Arundel Rd, Kemp Town, Brighton BN2 5TE
T: 01273 676603
Mon: 2pm-6pm, Tues-Sat: 9am-6pm
Terracotta glazed pots and tableware from £2 to £100. It's always worth checking the seconds;

Lanes Armoury
26 Meeting House Lane, The Lanes, Brighton BN1 1HB
T: 01273 3211357
www.thelanesarmoury.co.uk
enquiries@armsandarmour.
co.uk
Mon-Sat: 10am-5.15pm

Voted the best antique and collectibles shop in Great Britain by the Miller's Antique Guide. Mark, the owner, has all types of military armour and weapons from every period. A real haven for boys – and it doesn't matter what age they are.

Moth
104 Trafalgar St, Brighton BN1 4ER. T: 01273 696914
Tues-Sat: 10am-6pm, open some Sun: 12pm-3pm

A marvellous shop of timeless elegance tucked in at the end of Trafalgar Street. Here you can browse through antique painted armoires, decorative chaise lounges, marble wash stands and sink units. All items come from France and are very reasonably priced – hence the large turn around of stock. The lovely owners go to France every three weeks, so it's worth popping in often.

North Laine Photography
Unit 24, New England House
New England Rd, Brighton BN1
4GH. T: 01273 686506
www.northlainephotography.
co.uk
Mon-Sat: 10am-5.30pm, Sat: 11am-4pm

Brighton's most famous images in calendars and prints.

RP Inman
98 Colleridge St, Montpelier,
Brighton BN3 5AA
T: 01273 774777
r.p.inman@talk21.com
Mon-Fri: 9am-5pm

You take your chance with any auction, but this is one of the most consistent in terms of good finds.

Snooper's Paradise
7-8 Kensington Gdns, North
Laine, Brighton BN1 1HB
T: 01273 602558
snoopersparadisebrighton@bt
internet.com

Mon-Sat: 9.30am- 5.30pm, Bank
Holidays and Sunday: 11am-4pm

Never was a place better named. Snooper's is a real Aladdin's Cave. Two floors of flea market heaven, browse through the endless stalls of bric-a-brac and collectibles and you're sure to find exactly what you're looking for and more besides. Furniture upstairs and Tuff Tarts clubbing gear on the ground floor.

BOOKS

Borders
Churchill Square Shopping
Centre, Brighton BN1 2RG
T: 01273 731122
www.bordersstores.co.uk
www.churchillsquare.com
Mon-Sat: 8am-10pm, Sun: 11am-5pm

If you could find a shop with comfy chairs, a cafe and books to browse, where staff know their books, records and films and where there's even story time for children on Saturdays at 11am, well, how nice would that be?

Brighton Books
18 Kensington Gdns, North
Laine, Brighton BN1 4AL
T: 01273 693845
Mon-Sat: 10am-6pm

One of the best second hand bookshops in town. Paul and Catherine buy and sell top quality

titles covering topics such as biographies art, design and 20th century literature.

City Books
23 Western Rd, Hove BN3 1AF
T: 01273 725306
www.citybookshove.co.uk
citybooks@connectfree.co.uk
Mon-Sat: 9.30am-6pm, Sun: 11am-4.30pm

Short listed this year for The Daily Mail Independent Book Shop of the year, this is what book shops should be like. Already voted by locals as the best shop around, their excellent fiction department has lured authors like P.D.James, Nick Hornby, Will Self, Jamie Oliver, Dave Eggers, John Mortimer, Louis de Bernieres, Michael Moore, Louise Rennison, Iain Banks, Penelope Lively, Michael Frayn and Sandi Toksvig. They also have excellent sections devoted to children's books, travel, music, poetry, local history and alternative health.

Colin Page
Duke St, The Lanes, Brighton
BN1 1AG. T: 01273 325954
Mon-Sat: 9.30am-5.30pm

A great selection of antiquarian books on architecture, antiques, art and rare books.

David's Book Shop
3 Sydney St, North Laine,
Brighton BN1 4EN
T: 01273 691012

davidcomics@yahoo.co.uk
Mon-Sat: 9.30am-5.30pm, Sun:
11am-5pm

Toys, comics, collectibles, and the best pocket money buys in town. A great place to find cult releases.

Kemp Town Bookshop
91 St George's Rd, Kemp Town, Brighton BN1 4EN
T: 01273 682110
Mon-Sat: 9am-5.30pm

Small good quality bookshop with a wide range of topics, gift wrap and cards. Their ordering service is excellent with books often delivered the next day and the helpful staff know what they are talking about. When they open after a refurbishment programme in May, they'll have a little cafe there too.

Sussex Stationers
55 East St, The Lanes, Brighton BN1 1HN
T: 01273 328032
37-37a London Rd, Brighton BN1 4JB
T: 01273 691626
50 Western Rd, Hove BN1 2EB
T: 01273 204700
James St, Kemp Town, Brighton BN2 1TH
T: 01273 608229
Mon-Fri: 9am-5.30pm, Sat: 9am-6pm, Sun: 11am-5pm

A Sussex institution and excellent

local stationery chain that also sells popular fiction and non-fiction.

13 Travel
14 Pavilion Buildings, Castle Square, Brighton BN1 1EE
T: 01273 739313 F: 01273 774710
Mon-Sat: 10am-6pm, Sun: 11am-5pm

Large shop selling all the things you would need to prepare to go travelling – whether it be a month long hike along The Himalayas or camping in Wales. There are plans to dig deep into the Prince Regent's tunnels under the shop and set up a Trailfinders' style travel agency.

Waterstone's
71-74 North St, Brighton, E Sussex BN1 1ZA
T: 01273 206017
www.waterstones.co.uk
Mon/Wed-Fri 9am-7pm; Tues: 9.30-7pm; Sat: 9am-6pm; Sun: 11am-5pm
Large bookstore with its own in-store charts so you can check off all the must reads of the season.

BOUTIQUES

Acacia
94a Gloucester Rd, North Laine, Brighton BN1 4AP
T: 01273 688401
Mon-Wed: 10.30am-5.30pm, Thurs-Sat: 10.30am-6pm, Sun: 12pm-5pm

French style boutique with cutting edge designs. Ranges include Chloe,

Roland Mouret, Yanuk, House of Jazz, shoes by British designer Audley and accessories by Button Brothel. Not cheap, but what you'd expect from high-end fashion.

Badger for Men
25 Bond St, North Laine, Brighton BN1 1RD
T: 01273 722245 F: 01273 719131
Mon-Fri: 9.30am-5.30pm, Sat: 9.30am-6pm, Sun: 11am-5pm

Upmarket trendy shop filled with men's clothes and shoes. Stockists of Schott, Hush Puppies, Timberland, Rockport and Birkenstock.

Badger for Women
26 Bond St, North Laine, Brighton BN1 1RD
T: 01273 325421 F: 01273 719131
Mon-Fri: 9.30am-5.30pm, Sat: 9.30am-6pm, Sun: 11am-5pm

Designer lines include Great Plains, Duffer, Evisu and Diesel.

Brief Encounter
13 Brighton Square, The Lanes, Brighton BN1 1HD
T: 01273 208404
www.brasbras.com
Mon-Fri: 10am-5pm, Sat: 10am-5.30pm, Sun: 10am-4pm

Beautiful lacy designer underwear and a choice of great swimwear. Stock includes La Perla, Lejaby, Chantelle, Cotton Club and Aubade.

She also has an unusual range of bags by local designer Iam Mai.F.

Cutie
33 Kensington Gdns, North Laine, Brighton BN1 4AL
T: 01273 697957
Mon-Sat: 10am-5.30pm, Sun: 12am-5pm

Barbie girl collection of t-shirts, dresses etc and great selection of funky pants. In the back you'll find the beanbag boudoir stocking every kind of beanbag and throw.

East
51 East St, The Lanes, Brighton BN1 1HN. T: 01273 776711
www.east.co.uk
Mon-Fri: 9.30am-5.30pm, Sat: 9.30am-6pm, Sun: 11am-5pm

Gorgeous Asian inspired clothes and accessories that look particularly fine on the larger woman. They also look good on thin women, but anything looks good on thin women.

Coast
59 East St, The Lanes, Brighton BN1 1HN. T: 01273 821305
Mon-Sat: 9.30am-5.30pm, Sun: 11am-5pm

New in Brighton, Coast offers a beautiful collection of elegant day and evening-wear at a middle-of-the-road price.

Covet
16 Gloucester Rd, North Laine, Brighton BN1 4AD
T: 01273 609515 F: 01273 609513

Lynne Aveyard has been in fashion for over 20 years and has brought her expertise to women who want a bit of flair. Designers like Issey Miyake, Xile and Margret Howell.

Garden
39b Sydney St, North Laine, Brighton BN1 4EP
T: 01273 692691
Mon-Fri: 9.30am-5.30pm, Sun: 11am-5pm

Designer outlet where the fashion is local and exclusive to Brighton and Hove.

Glass House

16 East St, The Lanes, Brighton BN1 1HB. T: 01273 326141
www.the-glasshouse.com
Mon-Sat: 9.30am-6pm, Sun: 11am-5pm

Stylish and creative clothing range for women of all sizes looking for arty and elegant designs. Imagine a cross between Ghost and Armani and you're almost there. At last designs for women without model figures who have (physically and spiritually) outgrown Top Shop. Particularly good for taller women too.

Gog

24 Dukes Lane, The Lanes, Brighton BN1 1HL
T: 01273 727232
Mon-Sat: 10am-5.30pm

Small boutique selling contemporary designer menswear for label-freaks including Burberry and Juicy Couture.

Gog

24 East St, The Lanes, Brighton BN1 1HR. T: 01273 749505
Mon-Sat: 10am-5.30pm

Just like the menswear shop – but for women.

Gresham Blake

8 Bond St, North Laine, Brighton BN1 1RD
T: 01273 609587
www.greshamblake.co.uk

info@greshamblake.co.uk
Mon-Sat: 10am-6pm, Sun: 11am-4pm

Tailor to the likes of Zoë and Norman. Prices start from £600 for hand-made designs.

Hemp Shop

22 Gardner St, North Laine, Brighton BN1 1YB
T: 01273 818047
www.thehempshop.net
shop@thehempshop.net
Mon-Sat: 10am-6pm, Sun: 11am-4pm

It's amazing what you can make out of hemp. Beautiful stylish clothes in earthy hues, accessories and bags.

Igigi

37 Western Rd, Hove, Brighton BN1 1UP. T: 01273 734160
Mon-Sat: 10am-6pm

Zoë the owner has an eye for classical yet fashionable clothing. All her pieces are collectibles to build a wardrobe that is unlikely to date. Designs are limited and change often.

Ju-Ju

24 Gloucester Rd, North Laine, Brighton BN1 4AQ
T: 01273 673161 F: 01273 684411
www.jujubrighton.co.uk
Mon-Sat: 11am-6pm, Sun: 11am-5pm

Good quality fashion seconds and some new stock.

Jump The Gun

36 Gardner St, North Laine, Brighton BN1 1UN
T: 01273 626777 F: 01273 626555
www.jumpthegun.co.uk
Mon-Sat: 10am-6pm

A shrine to the Mod age. The Vespa in the window gives you a good idea of what you can find and the Paul Weller look-alike will guide you around his fantastic good quality clothes designs.

Long Tall Sally

10 East St, North Laine, Brighton BN1 1EB
T: 01273 731791
Mon-Sat: 9.30am-5.30pm, Sun: 11am-5pm

A range of casual and classic clothes for the taller woman. Now a range for the taller teenage too.

Magick

1-2 Shop 2, Sydney St, North Laine, Brighton BN1 4EN
T: 01273 686568
www.magickgaile.com
gaile_magick@hotmail.com
Mon-Fri: 10am-5.30pm, Sat: 9am-6pm

The place to go for underwear with a difference. Choose between sexy corsets (which you can have made to measure), baby dolls and teddies.

Mango

4 North St, The Lanes,
Brighton BN1 1EB
T: 01273 203355
www.mango.es
**Mon-Fri: 9.30am-5.30pm, Sat:
10am-6pm, Sun: 11am-5pm**
One of Spain's finest exports has
finally arrived in Brighton offering
good quality, affordable high
fashion European women's wear and
accessories.

Masquerade

40 Preston Rd, Brighton BN1
4QF T: 01273 673381
Mon-Sat: 10am-5pm, Sun: 11am-5pm

Tonight, Matthew, I'm going to be...
Fancy dress, costumes and the best
selection of masks in town. Don't
even think of browsing yourself; this
is a Mr Benn experience where you
give yourself over to the team and
emerge the spit of James Bond/Rita
Hayworth/Alice in Wonderland.

Minky

26 Sydney St, North Laine,
Brighton BN1 4ET
T: 01273 604456
32 Sydney St, North Laine,
Brighton BN1 4ET
T: 01273 604490
www.iloveminky.com
Mon-Sat: 10am-6pm, Sun: 12pm-5pm

Both sell men and women's street
wear from London (Marvel and
Burro), each shop has different stock.
No.26 has Glitzy Tarts stock upstairs.

Moist

20 Dukes Lane, The Lanes,
Brighton BN1 1HL
T: 01273 2205544
Mon-Sat: 10am-6pm, Sun: 12pm-5pm

Cool streetwear for the young
who've got a bit of cash.

Mottoo

12 Duke St, The Lanes,
Brighton BN1 1AH
T: 01273 326633
15 Duke St, The Lanes,
Brighton BN11BG
T: 01273 771093
**Mon-Sat: 9.30am-6pm,
Sun: 11am-5pm**

Upmarket designer wear. Stockists

include Nicole Farhi, Fake London,
Ted Baker and John Smedley.

Nilaya

38 Kensington Gdns, North
Laine, Brighton BN1 4AL
T: 01273 697096
www.nilaya-online.com
Mon-Sat: 10am-6pm, Sun: 11am-5pm

Truly beautiful collections from
Marlane Burge, Marilyn Moore, BZR
and Alice Astrid. Clothes that you'd
think would more likely to be found
in Notting Hill than in Brighton. They
also have Ginka and Orka bags and
pretty knitwear and jewellery.

Profile

35 Dukes Lanes, The Lanes,
Brighton BN1 1BG

Designer, nearly new styles at reasonable prices. Stuart and Angela will kit you out in the perfect Armani, Chanel, Gucci or Prada (to name a few) for a fraction of the price. They even have a good selection of beautiful Voyage cardigans at rock bottom prices.

Route One
3 Bond St, North Laine,
Brighton BN1 1RD
T: 01273 323633
www.routeone.co.uk
Mon-Sat: 9.30am-5pm, 11am-5pm

Street wear and alternative sports equipment. DC trainers, skateboard hardware, maps and videos.

Simultane
37 Trafalgar St, North Laine,
Brighton BN1 4ED
T: 01273 818061/01273 608426
www.simultane.co.uk
info@simultane.co.uk
Mon-Sat: 10am-6pm, Sun: 11am-5pm

Boutique and fashion label which is one of Brighton's best success stories: They sell their own label into the uber-style boutiques like The Cross in Notting Hill, designers/ owners Sarah Arnett and Amanda Sullivan come from the stables of Paul Smith, Agnes B, Tracey Boyd and Nicole Farhi. Simulatane also stocks designs from stars such as Antoni & Alison, Cutler and Gross, and emerging labels like Cazza. Exclusive stockists of Miller Harris fragrances.

T: 01273 733651
Mon-Sat: 9.30am-5.30pm, Sun: 11am-5pm
5 Dukes Lanes, The Lanes,
Brighton BN1 1BG
T: 01273 323275
Mon-Sat: 9.30am-5.30pm, Sun: 11am-5pm

Designer clothing for women. Stocks Armani, Hugo Boss, Joseph and now Prada and Helmut Lang.

RE-AL
7 Dukes Lane, North Laine,
Brighton BN1 1BG

T: 01273 325658
Mon-Sat: 10am-5.30pm, Sun: 11am-5pm

Everything for the skateboard and roller kid, plus accessories.

Revisions
3 Pool Valley, The Lanes,
Brighton BN1 1NJ
T: 01273 207728
www.revisionsclothing.com
Mon-Fri: 10.30am-5.30pm, Sat: 10am-6pm

Specs of Brighton
22 Kensington Gdns, North
Laine, Brighton BN1 4AL
T: 01273 676796
www.specsofbrighton.com
Mon-Fri: 9am-5.30pm, Sat: 9am-6pm

Cool eyewear in the heart of the
North Laine.

Starfish
25 Gardner St, North Laine,
Brighton BN1 1UP
T: 01273 680868
www.starfishretroclothing.com
Mon-Fri: 10.30am-6pm, Sat: 10am-
6pm, Sun: 11.30am-5.30pm

Second hand retro clothing and
accessories.

To Be Worn Again
24a Sydney St, North Laine,
Brighton BN1 4EN
T: 01273 680296
51 Providence Place, London
Road, Brighton BN1 4GE
T: 01273 624500
tobewornagain98@yahoo.co.uk
Mon-Sat: 10am-6pm, Sun: 12pm-5pm

Largest second-hand clothing
warehouse in Brighton. In the Sydney
Street shop you'll find a top selection
of second-hand clothes, including
leather, fake fur, shoes, coats and
knitwear. Upstairs houses the
Brighton Retro Furniture that stocks
everything you'll need to recreate the
perfect 1960's/1970's home.

Urb
40 Middle St, The Lanes,
Brighton BN1 1AL
T: 01273 325336
www.urbclothing.co.uk
urb@nistral.co.uk
Mon-Sat: 10am-6pm, Sun: 12pm-5pm

Urban wear for boys. Complete the
look with backpacks, sunglasses and
baseball caps.

Walk In Wardrobe
89 Western Rd, Hove,
Brighton BN3 1JB
T: 01273 775583
Mon, Tues, Thurs and Fri: 10.30am-
5.30pm

Large rental section of evening
gowns and good quality second
hand clothes plus new French
designer clothes for sale.

Yellow Submarine
12 Kensington Gdns, North
Laine, Brighton BN1 4AL
T: 01273 626435
www.yellowsubmarineretro.
co.uk
Mon-Sat: 10am-6.30pm, Sun: 11am-
5.30pm

Sister shop to the one in Covent
Garden. The two girls who run this
one are young and fun. They stock
great retro men and women's gear
and furniture with new accessories.
They promote local bands and have
big plans for the future.

CHILDREN

Abstract
35 North Rd, North Laine,
Brighton BN1 1YB
T: 01273 693737
www.abstractuk.com
info@abstractuk.com
Mon-Sat: 10am-5.30pm

Bernadette started off with a
sewing machine and a market
stall and now has a successful and
beautiful line in fleece outfits and
pram blankets. Custom designed
Moses basket blankets and linings
and linen cotton range for the
summer have made her brand
noticeable in the streets. They're
also stockists of the Baby Hut
cotton sling and baby hammock

Cat and Mouse
17 Sydney St, Brighton BN 4EN
T: 01273 600145
www.catandmousekids.co.uk
info@catandmousekids.co.uk
Mon-Fri: 9.30am-5.30pm, Sat:
10am-6pm

Designer wear for children aged up
to 16. They have their own designs as
well as Oiliy, Kenzo, Quik Silver and
French Connection.

Daisy Daisy
33 North Rd, North Laine,
Brighton BN1 1YB
T: 01273 689108
www.daisydaisy.me.uk
Mon-Sat: 10.30am-5pm

Great Expectations
42-44 Lewes Rd,
Brighton BN2 3HQ
T: 01273 622993
www.gtexpectations.co.uk
Mon-Sat: 10am-5.30pm

Wooden toys and cutie romper suits, eco-nappies and hand painted birthday cards, this is the place for parents and kids with style and conscience. Stockists of the Baby Hut cotton sling and baby hammock.

Mooch
19 Kensington Gdns, North Laine, Brighton BN1 4AL
T: 01273 693510
Mon-Sat: 9.30am-5.30pm

More café than toyshop, but it's all hand-made so if you're stopping for a coffee anyway, you could always snap up that little something for your spare presents drawer. You do have a spare presents drawer, don't you?

Dials
86 Dyke Rd, Brighton BN1 3JD
T: 01273 823003
Mon-Fri: 9.30am-5.30pm

Ever so cute collection of children's clothes and accessories for kids up to seven. They produce their own cool funky t-shirts and now supply stuff for the mums like shoes, bags, cushions and home ware.

Gamleys
64/68 Church Rd,
Hove BN3 2FP
T: 01273 733002
www.gamleys.co.uk
Mon-Sat: 9am-5.30pm
Sussex's own toy store where you can buy just about anything, but still get the olde toyshop touch. There's a smaller one in Churchill Square but it doesn't have the same feel.

Traditional wooden toys, little fairy outfits, miniature toy soldiers, cowboys and Indians, which makes this a huge hit with kids. Their new clothing range was so successful that the second hand clothes had to go. Kit out your little darlings in the chicest of outfits like beautiful suede dresses, and wrap your baby in the Baby Hut cotton sling and baby hammock.

Dancia
8 Western St, Brighton BN1 2PG
T: 01273 719001
www.dancia.co.uk
dancia@line1.net
Mon-Fri: 10am-5.30pm, Sat: 9.30am-5pm

Professional dancewear with uniforms for the various local dance schools.

National Schoolwear Centre
44 Blatchington Rd,
Hove BN3 3YH
T: 01273 739676
www.ncshop.co.uk
Mon-Sat: 9am-5pm

The only shop that sells the generic uniforms for all the schools in the area, although the odd thing you may need to go to John Lewis for. Accessories too, plimsolls, bags, ballet and swimming kit.

Toby Tiger
11 Gardner St, North Laine,
Brighton BN1 1YUP
T: 01273 710610 F: 01273 710610
www.tobytiger.com
Mon-Sat: 10am-6pm,
Sun: 12pm-4pm

Zoë Mellor sells her own brand
fleece children's clothing here for a
fraction of what you would pay in
the London stores. The shop also
stocks little hand-made leather
shoes, traditional toys and t-shirts
and baby-grows.

Wigwam Baby
93 Preston Drove, Brighton
BN1 6LD T: 01273 554056
F: 01273 554056
www.wigwamstore.com
Mon-Sat: 10am-5pm

Everything for the designer parent
with pre-pregnancy stages to
kids clothes, accessories and toys
(including wooden) for up to age
eight. Stockist of the Baby Hut
cotton sling and baby hammock.

FABRIC

C&H Fabrics
179-180 Western Rd, BN1 2BA
T: 01273 321959
Mon/Wed-Sat: 9am-5.30pm;
Tues:9.30-5.3pm
Three floors of everything you could
imagine for your dressmaking needs.
The staff could be more helpful but
you can't have it all.

Fabric Land
76 Western Rd, Brighton BN1
2HA T: 01273 822257
www.fabricland.co.uk
Mon-Sat: 9.15am-5.30pm
Two floors of gorgeous fabrics and
haberdashery, with a great remnant
box for the kids to use their pocket
money on. More groovy than good
old C&H, this is where budding
young designers can play with ideas.

Fabric Warehouse
42 George St, Kemp Town,
Brighton BN2 1RJ
T: 01273 620744
Mon, Tue, Thurs, Fri and Sat:
9.30am-5.30pm, Wed: 9.30am-3pm

An excellent selection of unusual
and discount fabrics sold at very
reasonable prices including curtain
material selection. Top service too.

Fabric Wear
51 Gardner St, North Laine,
Brighton BN1 1UN
T: 01273 605512
Mon-Sat: 9.30am-5.30pm
All the usual zips, silks, needles
and fabulously cheap and exotic
sari materials for your individual
creation.

Southern Handicrafts
20 Kensington Gdns, North
Laine, Brighton BN1 4AL
T: 01273 550044
Mon-Sat: 10am-5.30pm, Sun:
11am-5pm

If you can't find your fabric here,
chances are you won't find it
anywhere. The one stop shop for
serious dressmakers.

Velvet
37 Gardner St,
North Laine, Brighton
BN2 1RJ
T: 01273 326007
www.velvetstore.co.uk
Mon-Fri: 10am-5.30pm, Sat: 10am-
6.30pm, Sun: 11am-5pm

Homing fearlessly into the
mass of Brighton's hippy chic who
can run up a skirt out of a net
curtain (and do), Velvet is a
pleasure dome of fabrics and
haberdashery happiness. They've
even got the pattern books that
your mum used to wade through
in John Lewis, but with enough
sequins and sew-on rose buds
to make sew-your-own a
thoroughly trendy experience.

FLOWERS

Amaryllis
10 Upper Market St,
Hove BN3 1AS
T: 01273 321999/07974 403381
www.amaryllis/hove.com
flowers@amaryllis-hove.com
Mon-Sat: 10am-7pm,
Sun: 10am-6pm

Dutch flowers, plants and
terracotta pots at this beautiful and
individual new flower shop.

Botanica

18 Gardner St, Brighton BN1
1UP T: 01273 686377
Mon-Fri: 10am-5.30pm,
Sat: 10am-6pm

Once a huge florist in the North
Laine with plans for becoming
part of the Winter Gardens in
Jubilee St, this is now a gorgeous
flowers and chocolate shop on the
other side of the road.

Flower Stand

St Johns Church Palmeira
Square, Hove BN2 3JP
T: 01273 711711
www.theflowerstand.co.uk
Mon-Sun: 9.30am-8pm

This buzzy flower stand is a real find,
and people really do travel from all
over the city to get their Kangaroo
Paw, Proteas and Gingers, Irises and
Tulips. It's all served with the kind of
passion you don't find in the average
florist.

Flowers by Best

42a Ship St, The Lanes,
Brighton BN1 1AF
T: 01273 205040
www.flowersbybest.brighton.
co.uk
Mon: 10am-4pm, Tues and Wed:
9am-5pm, Thurs-Sat: 10am-6pm

Top quality flowers and designer
hand tied bouquets with an unusual
selection.

Gunns

6 Castle St, Brighton BN2 3HQ
T: 01273 07490
13-14 Sydney St, North Laine,
Brighton BN3 8BG
T: 01273 683038
Mon-Thurs: 9am-5.30pm, Fri:
9am-6pm

Large family owned, friendly florist
selling a wide selection of plants
and flowers at really good prices.
Brighton is famous for its florists,
and Gunns is one of the reasons.

Rhubarb

181 Edward St, Kemp Town,
Brighton BN2 2JB
T: 01273 626993
Mon-Fri: 9am-5.30pm, Sat:
10.30am-4.30pm

One of the most creative and
unusual florists in town.

FOOD SHOPS

Audrey's Chocolates

16 Regent Arcade, East St, The
Lanes, Brighton BN1 1HR
28 Holland Rd, Hove BN3 1JJ
T/F: 01273 735561
www.audreyschocolates.co.uk
Mon-Sat: 9am-5pm

Hand made chocs made on the
premises and wonderful Easter eggs
made to order. They're expensive,
but how often do you buy hand-
made chocolate?

B.Right.On

56 Greenways, Ovingdean
BN2 7BL. T: 01273 705606
www.chillypepperpete.com
brightfoods@hotmail.com
Mon-Sat: 10am-6pm

Miranda and Pete deliver home
cooked organic meals to your
door with a fantastic selection of
cuisines and cultures: wild salmon
teriyaki, fragrant rice and wasabi/soy
dressing, Thai fishcakes, or a host
of vegan and vegetarian delights.
Exceptionally good value, and you
should try out their range of chillies.

Bona Foodie

55-56 Western Rd, Hove BN3
2JQ T: 01273 727909
21 St James's St, Kemp Town,
Brighton BN2 1RF
T: 01273 698007
Mon-Sat: 9.30am-6pm,
Sun: 11am-**4pm**

A deli with a difference. Selling
the usual range of meat, cheeses
and fancy foods they also have a
good range of organic products
and items for people with allergies.
You can choose to take away the
prepared meals or indulge yourself
in the small but pleasant café at
the back. The range of marmalades,
curds, chutneys, pickles, and
relishes is reason enough to take
a peak. Champagne mustard is
recommended for those with
expensive taste.

Butlers Wine Cellar

247 Queen's Park Rd, Queen's
Park, Brighton BN2 9XJ
T: 01273 698724

F: 01273 622276
www.butlers-wineceller.co.uk
Tues and Wed: 10am-6pm, Thurs-
Sat: 10am-7pm

Henry Butler sells speciality wines
for connoisseurs. He is also one of
the Brighton Wine School tutors
and holds wine tastings at gourmet
dining clubs such as The Seattle.

The Canteen Deli
18 Rock St, Kemp Town
Brighton BN2 1NF
T: 01273 682689
Mon-Sun: 9am-6pm, opening
times may vary
Faisal comes from the most
prestigious of foodie backgrounds
(Roux, Marco Pierre White, who he
worked with at The Canteen – hence
the name), and has stocked this
quiet little part of Kemp Town with
the most must-have deli items this
side of Notting Hill. The only place
you'll get Ventrusca, a Spanish tuna
delicacy, in the UK, this will have the
likes of Cate Blanchett and the other
residents of nearby Sussex Square
and Lewes Crescent queuing up.

C.H. Mears
33 Marshalls Row, Brighton
BN1 4JS. T: 01273 670711
Mon: 7am-1pm, Tues-Sat: 7am-5pm
Freshest fruit and veg at the Open
Market

Cherry Tree
107 St James's St, Kemp Town,
Brighton BN2 1NF
T: 01273 698684

Mon-Fri: 8.30am-5pm, Sat: 9am-6pm

Sun dried vegetables and bowls full
of home-made couscous, houmous
and all things Mediterranean.

Choccywoccydoodah
27 Middle St, The Lanes,
Brighton BN1 1AL
T: 01273 381999
www.choccywoccydoodah.
com
Mon-Fri: 10am-6pm, Sat-Sun:
10am-5pm

Chocolate art at this nationally
recognised cake shop. Ask for
anything you can imagine, and
they'll spin it into chocolate for you.

Coriander Deli
4 Hove Manor, Hove St,
Hove BN3 2DF
T: 01273 730850
www.corianderbrighton.com
Mon-Sat: 10am-8pm, Sun: 10am-4pm

Newly opened deli selling the
locally sourced and organic products

used in the owners' gorgeous
restaurant next door.

Fish at the Square
2 St George Rd, Brighton BN2
1EB. T: 01273 680808
Mon-Fri: 9.30am-5.30pm
Famed first for their homemade
fishcakes and their fishing friendly
opening times, Nigel and Freia Sayers
are now winning new customers
for their fish friendly approach to
fishmongery. Endangered species like
cod, monkfish, skate and swordfish
are off the menu, as are the
fishcakes now. Apparently the good
middle class of Kemp Town were
fighting in the streets over them...

Gourmet Gift Shop
11 Church St, The Lanes,
Brighton BN1 1UD
T: 01273 818163
www.hampersbypost.com
Mon-Sat: 10am-5pm, Sun: 12pm-4pm

A world of different types of
panettone, pandoro and pastas,
home made sauces and specialities
from around the world. They also do
hampers to order on the website.

Infinity Foods

25 North Rd, North Laine,
Brighton BN1 6DA
T: 01273 603563
www.infinityfoods.co.uk
Mon-Sat: 9.30am-6pm,
Sun: 11am-4pm

Workers co-op and part of
Brighton's fabric, this is the place to
buy anything organic and healthy,
stock up on flyers about meditation
and yoga, and make friends of a like
mind.

Kemp Town Deli

108 St George's Rd, Kemp
Town, Brighton BN2 1EA
T: 01273 603411
Mon-Sat: 8am-6pm,
Sun: 10am-3pm

The queues at lunchtime spell out
the popularity of this store. They
sell fresh juice, croissants and
pastries, homemade soups and the
usual deli stuff, but the exception
is in the quality. They also have a
cappuccino bar.

Kudos Foods

The Food Shop, Church Lane,
Brighton BN8 6AS
T: 01273 811118
www.kudosfoods.co.uk
orders@kudosfoods.co.uk
Mon-Thurs: 9.30am-3pm, Fri:
9.30am-6pm, Sat: 9.30am-3pm,
deliveries after 5.30pm

Delicious gourmet home
delivery service using the freshest
local produce. Book yourselves a
dinner for eight and then pretend
that you are that domestic god/
dess. Kudos are very discreet. Prices
start from £2.95 for a chicken liver
parfait to rich chocolate torte for 12
to 16 people at £15.95.

Le Grand Fromage

10 East St, Shoreham-by-Sea
BN43 5ZE. T: 01273 440337
www.legrandfromage.co.uk
Mon-Sat: 7.30am -6pm

L'Esprit du Vin has a fabulous
selection of fine wines (including
organic) while Le Grand Fromage
stocks unusual and quality cheeses
for that perfect accompaniment.
You can order your goods from the
website.

L'Esprit du Vin

10 East St, Shoreham-by-Sea
BN43 5ZE. T: 01273 440337
www.legranfromage.co.uk
Mon-Sat: 7.30am -6pm

L'Esprit du Vin has a fabulous
selection of fine wines (including
organic) while Le Grand Fromage
stocks unusual and quality cheeses.

Little Farmhouse Deli

20 Richardson Rd, Hove BN3
5RB. T: 01273 722481
Mon-Sat: 8am-2.30pm
Locally sourced products such as
Sussex High Weald organic sheep

cheeses, and local meats make this
deli different from other local food
shops. The owner, Rob Silverstone,
is a chef so take your time if you like
to talk food.

Montezuma Chocolates

15 Duke St, The Lanes,
Brighton BN1 1AH
T: 01273 324979
www.montezuma.co.uk
Mon-Sat: 9.30am-6pm,
Sun: 11am-5pm

Organic orgasmic chocolate, with
a great children's range and famous
truffles. Mail order available.

Oki Nami

12 York Place, Brighton BN3 2DJ
T: 01273 677702
Mon-Sat: 10.30am-6.30pm,
Sun: 1pm-5pm

Japanese shop and deli bar which
suffers only for its location off
London Road. Takeaway sushi
sets and delicious Japanese tit bits
make a delightful option to a sarnie
at lunchtime (for anyone with
wheat intolerances, Japanese is the
way to go). For those who can
linger longer, there's a seating area
on the first floor where you can get
stuck into your wasabi and
lust after the collection of
Hello Kitty crockery at the same
time. Happily, for the trillions of
Japanese students from St Giles
who make it their spiritual
home, it's a hop and a skip.

Sun: 10am-5pm

Two floors of gorgeous deli foods, with the atmosphere of a New York food emporium. Upstairs is the deli proper, with local cheese and meats, wines and olives. Downstairs is the restaurant and takeaway area (see Restaurants chapter), with more delights to prise your purse. Check out the lavender and honey ice cream.

Realfooddirect
Unit 4 level 3 New England House, New England St, Brighton BN1 4GH
T: 01273 621222
www.realfood-direct.com
Sat: 9am-6pm
An established small independent company that has been trading for almost four years in mainly organic products.

Sensational Food
57a George St, Hove BN3 3YD
T: 01273 723200
Mon-Sat: 9am-5.30pm

International and English sausages of any flavour imaginable, plus an extensive range of mustards, chutneys and continental provisions. Vegetarian sausages available.

Oliviers and Co
23a East St, The Lanes,
Brighton BN1 1HL
T: 01273 739840
www.oliviers.co.uk
Mon-Wed: 9.30am-6pm; Thurs-Sat 9.30am-6.30pm; Sun: 11am-5pm

If you love olives this is the place for you – there's an amazing array of olives and olive oils, both flavoured and natural, from France and Italy. They've got sauces, condiments, sweet and savoury biscuits, too.

Pickle Pie Organics
44 St Leonards Rd,
Hove BN3 4QR
T: 01273 275597
A family run baby food and toddler home delivery food business that has established a good reputation. Delivery is free.

Real Eating Company
86-87 Western Rd,
Hove BN3 1JB
T: 01273 774870
www.real-eating.co.uk
Mon-Fri: 9am-6pm, Sat: 9am-6pm,

Southover Wines
80 Southover St, Hanover,
Brighton BN2 9JE
T: 01273 600402
Mon-Sat: 10am-5.30pm

Obscure and eclectic collection of wine, ales and beer from around the world.

Thai Siam Food Market

41-42 Marshalls Row,
Brighton BN1 4JS
T: 01273 624233
Mon 7am-1pm; Tue-Thurs 7am-5pm; Fri 7am-6pm
In the Open Market on the London Road, this has some of the best Thai vegetables and spices in the city and supplies many of the local restaurants which claim that their ingredients are flown directly from Thailand. Silly really; if they pass a good tip on, they're much more likely to encourage loyalty among their fans.

The Cheese Shop

17 Kensington Gdns, North Laine, Brighton BN1 4AL
T: 01273 601129
Mon-Fri: 9.30am-5.30pm,
Sat: 9am-6pm
The name says it all really, although they do have a nice line in veggie pizza, focaccia and ciabatta bread to compliment your cheese.

The Lanes Deli and Pasta Shop

12b Meeting House Lane,
The Lanes, Brighton BN1 1HB
T: 01273 723522
www.lanesdeli.co.uk
slownorris1@hotmail.com
Mon: Sat 10am-6pm

Sun 11.30am-5pm
Once owned by the people who have now set up the Gourmet Gift Shop, it's still packed with fresh pasta and gorgeous goodies.

HI FI

Bang and Olufsen

44 Church Rd, Hove,
Brighton BN3 2FN
T: 01273 771888
F: 01273 321289
www.bang-olufsen.com
brighton@bang-olufsen.uk.com
Mon-Sat: 10.30am-5.30pm

A large selection of top of the range audio products designed by Bang and Olufsen. The quality of sound outshines many other products on the market, but they're pricey.

Powerplant

40 Church Rd, Hove BN3 2FN
T: 01273 775978
www.powerplant.co.uk
sales@powerplant.co.uk
Tues-Sat: 10.30am-5.30pm

A professional company selling high quality home cinema and hi fi systems. A must have for those with sensitive ears, refined taste and an accommodating wallet.

HOMES AND INTERIORS

Adam Flude Rugs

93 North Rd, North Laine,

Brighton BN1 1YB
T: 01273 689922
www.cityrugs.co.uk
rugs@fluderugs.co.uk
Mon-Sat: 10am-5pm, Sun: 10am-4pm

A distinctive and friendly shop that is said to have the largest selection of rugs in the UK.

Ananda

24 Bond St, North Laine,
Brighton BN1 4AQ
T: 01273 725307
F: 01273 207474
www.ananda.co.uk
info@ananda.co.uk
Mon-Sat: 10am-5.30pm, Sun: 11am-5pm

Stunning furniture, rugs and hangings from south east Asia. The shop's been established for 30 years, and the good folk who run the place know their stuff.

Arts and Crafts Home

28 Gloucester Rd, North Laine, Brighton BN1 4AQ
T: 01273 600073
Mon-Sat: 10am-5pm

If you need inspiration for your home, this is the place to come. Retro furniture, wallpapers, fabrics, designer paints and arts and crafts.

Blend

53 Upper North St, North Laine, Brighton BN1 3FH

T: 01273 739111

www.blend-design.co.uk

Mon-Sat: 10am-5pm, Sun: 12pm-5pm

Lighting, furniture, and home accessories like cushions and glasses from European designers such as Mooi, Marcel Wonders, Edward Van Vleet and Sharon Marsdon (who's just had an exhibition at The V&A).

Bluebell

5 & 6 Church St, North Laine, Brighton BN1 1US

T: 01273 699546

Mon-Sat: 9.30am-6pm, Sun: 11.30-6pm

Relocated from Kensington Garden, Bluebell is now on the corner of Church Street and Bond Street, but still tempts you with gorgeous things you really don't need for the garden you really don't have. Still, you can always find a space for a little watering can, can't you?

Bo Concept

Churchill Square Shopping Centre, Brighton BN1 2TF

T: 01273 730008

www.boconcept.co.uk

contracts.uk@boconcept.com

Mon-Sat: 9am-7pm, Thurs: 9am-8pm, Sun: 11am-5pm

Sleek contemporary furniture in a variety of styles and veneer including the popular Wenge look. It's all delivered flat packed but can

be assembled for an extra charge. Give plenty of time when you order though, as delivery can take an age.

Bonsai KO

45 Sydney St, North Laine, Brighton BN1 4EP

T: 01273 621743

www.bonsai-ko.co.uk

Mon-Sat: 9.30am-6pm

Such a tranquil little shop. The owner is friendly and knows all there is to know about caring for Bonsai trees. He has worldwide orders and stocks books and tools to help you along.

Brewers

49 New England St, North Laine, Brighton BN1 4GQ

T: 01273 570243

F: 01273 693592

www.brewers.co.uk

Mon-Fri: 7.30am-5pm, Sat: 8am-1pm

Brewers exceptionally knowledgeable staff and fantastic stock make it the decorators' paint shop. Not only do they sell Fired Earth, John Oliver and Farrow and Ball, but if you find a paint range you like they will order it for you.

Brunswick Interiors

130 Cowper St, Brighton BN3 5BL. T: 01273 206982

Mon-Sat: 9am-5pm

Interior haven for the perfectionist.

Caz Systems

17-19 Church St, Brighton BN1 1RB

T: 01273 204794

www.cazsystems.com

Mon-Sat: 10am-6pm, Sun: 11am-4pm

Contemporary lighting and furniture. Beautiful Philippe Stark perspex stools, and colourful plastic chairs and designer styles.

Chair Maker

54 Western Rd, Hove BN3 1JD

T: 01273 777810

www.chairmaker.co.uk

Tues-Sat: 10am-6pm

Family-owned furniture designer and maker combining new designs with old methods. Frames are made from solid kiln dried beech with all the joints glued, screwed and doweled, Chesterfields nailed, deep-buttoned and Thunderbirds sleek blind-seamed.

Cologne and Cotton

13 Pavilion Buildings, Castle Sq, Brighton BN1 1EE

T: 01273 729666

Mon-10am-6pm; Sun 11am-5pm

Everything for the boudoir from proper linen to French antique beds, expensive toiletries and gorgeous perfumes.

Decorative Arts

27 Gloucester Rd, Hove, Brighton BN3 1JB

T: 01273 676486

www.decart.net
info@decart.net
Mon-Sat: 10am-5.30pm

Stripped chunky oak handcrafted furniture, leather sofas and contemporary soft furnishings.

Domus
2 Union St, The Lanes,
Brighton BN1 1HA
T: 01273 737356
Mon-Sat: 9am-5.30pm,
Sun: 11am-5pm

Stylish contemporary home ware and kitchenware, 1950's tin toys and children's accessories. Large selection of Alessi products.

Egg and Spoon
15 St George's Rd, Kemp Town,
Brighton BN2 1EB
T: 01273 608884
Mon-Sat: 9.30am-5.30pm

Stylish contemporary kitchen and tableware. Stockists include Rosle, Francis Francis espresso cups and saucers in fabulous designs, and Eva if you're looking for something outside the norm.

EFDC
147 North St, Brighton. BN1 1RE
T: 01273 326039
F: 01273 749059
Mon-Sat:10am-6pm
Sun 11am-5.30pm
The Elephant Furniture Design

Company sells a more contemporary line of the furniture and lighting that you'll find at the bigger Elephant department store in The Lanes. The shop is divided into two halves, the Italian designers such as Molteni sofas and Dada kitchens – all with a price tag to match. The EFDC own brand which, while still not cheap, means you have the choice of paying for the posher names. A corner sofa on the Italian side of the shop will be £4500 while the EFDC will be £3225.

Elephant
1 Duke St, Kemp Town,
Brighton BN1 1AH
T: 01273 731318
Mon-Sat: 10am-6pm,
Sun: 10am-4pm

This Duke Street department store stocks elegant and tasteful colonial style furniture. On three floors with fine lighting, textiles and accessories.

Em Space
20 Sydney St, North Laine,
Brighton BN1 4EN
T: 01273 683400
Mon-Sat: 10am-6pm, Sun: 12pm-4pm

Cool cards and gift-wrap. Check the local artists work while you're there.

England at Home
32 Ship St, The Lanes,
Brighton BN1 1AD
22b Ship St, The Lanes,
Brighton BN1 1AD
T: 01273 205544/01273 738270

F: 01273 723109
www.england@home.co.uk
Mon-Fri: 10am-6pm, Sun: 12pm-5pm

Contemporary funky furniture and cool accessories such as heart shaped leopard print cushions. A great place for a gift or to update your home.

Evolution
42 Bond St, North Laine,
Brighton BN1 1AD
T: 01273 205379
Mon, Tues and Wed: 10am-5.30pm,
Thurs, Fri and Sat: 10am-6pm, Sun: 11am-5pm

An interiors store that helps Buddhists work together, with their profits going to charitable projects. There's a beautiful selection of Indonesian goodies including brightly coloured wooden mobiles and toys, ceramics, glass, textiles and everything for the tasteful eclectic home. Gifts include books and cards.

Fired Earth
15c Prince Albert St, The Lanes, Brighton BN1 1HF
T: 01273 719977
www.firedearth.com
brighton@firedearth.com
Mon-Sat: 9.30am-5.30pm, Sat: 10am-5.30pm

The ultimate in natural stone tiles, natural flooring and bathroom

House
82 North Rd, North Laine,
Brighton BN1 4EB
T: 01273 571674
Mon-Sat: 10am-6pm,
Sun: 12pm-5pm

Best described as a mini Heals and, as the name suggests, stocks everything you would need for your home: cushions, leather bound stationery, mirrors, lights, shades etc and beautiful Mongolian skin cushions.

In My Room
35 Gloucester Rd, North
Laine, Brighton BN1 4AQ
T: 01273 675506
www.inmyroom.co.uk
Tues-Fri: 10am-5.30pm, Sat: 9am-6pm, Sun: 11am-4.30pm

Classic retro furniture and decorative objects especially designed by owners Michelle and Oliver Learmonth, with contemporary pieces made by Oliver. Both have been collectors for 15 years and have collected original pieces from classic designers such as Charles James, Eero Saarinen and Verner Panton. An ever-changing collection well worth a browse.

accessories (look out for the stunning stone basin). Be prepared to spend some money – quality and individuality doesn't come cheap. Installation and full interior design service available.

Gaff
66 Trafalgar St, North Laine,
Brighton BN1 1RD
T: 01273 819202
www.gaffrugs.co.uk
Mon-Sat: 10am-5.30pm,
Sun: 11am-3.30pm

If you're tired of run of the mill flooring this is the place to come to. Design your own, any shape and

style is not a problem. They also have their own designs if you're stuck for inspiration and a colour matching service.

Habitat
Churchill Square, Brighton BN1 2TB
T: 01273 324831
Mon-Wed: 9am-7pm, Thurs:
9am-8pm, Sat: 10am-7pm, Sun:
11am-5pm

Habitat has managed to get itself back to the standard that it was once famous for. New designers have increased its reputation, with cutting edge design now fairly affordable.

Java
103 Blatchington Rd, Hove,
BN3 3YG. T: 01273 711132
java331@hotmail.com
Mon-Sat: 10am-5pm

Hove has gone Indonesian in the last year, with traders following

the removal vans down Portland Road and quickly shipping their furniture into Blatchington Road before the relocators have had time to think of a colour scheme. With Jugs and Bazaar just down the road, Habitat hasn't got a chance.

Jugs

44 Blatchington Rd, Hove BN3 3YN. T: 01273 719899
www.jugsfurniture.co.uk
Mon-Sat: 9.30am-5pm,
Sun: 12pm-2pm

Two floors of Indonesian, Mexican and African furniture, objects and hangings at the kind of prices that make you realise that carting that cabinet back from Bali wouldn't have been such a great idea. If you

can't find what you want, try Java just down the road.

MacDougall Rose

12 Richmond Parade, Brighton BN2 9QD
T: 01273 606241 F: 01273 685854
www.duluxdecoratorcentres.co.uk
Mon-Fri: 7.30am-5pm, Sat: 8am-1pm

Apparently only for professionals, with Dulux specialists and trade accounts, they're also very helpful and welcoming to Joe Public.

Martha's Barn

47 Norway St, Portslade BN4 1AE
T: 01273 699360 F: 01273 676300
www.marthasbarn.co.uk

Mon-Sat: 9.30am-6pm,
Sun: 12pm-5pm
Martha's Barn has moved to Portslade but the vast space in their new warehouse is well worth your trip. They house an excellent stock of Chinese furniture and accessories, and specialise in bespoke leather and suede sofas. If the one they have in the showroom fits your room you can have that delivered rather than made to order.

Metal Guru

2 East St, The Lanes, Brighton BN1 1NF. T: 01273 207755
www.metalguru.co.uk
Mon-Sat: 10am-5.30pm (Tuesdays Closed), Sun: 12pm-4pm

Bespoke iron and metal furniture.

Parker Bathrooms

80 Dyke Rd, Seven Dials, Brighton BN1 3JD
T: 01273 329829
Mon-Fri: 9am-5.30pm, 10.30pm-3pm
Contemporary and traditional bathroom furniture. They have the largest range of taps, showers and bathroom equipment in Sussex and much is made especially for them.

Pure

20-21 Chatham Place, Seven Dials, Brighton BN1 3TN
T: 01273 735331 F: 01273 734229
www.pure2k.com
info@pure2k.com
Tues-Sat: 10am-5pm

Rachel scours the country for classic original furniture from the 1950's to the 1980's and now has the Knoll range. She offers a design service and will source for you. Stockists of Vitra and her selection of vintage wallpapers are a real find. Designs include works from Arne Jacobson, Robin Day and Vernerpanton. Glass and ceramics available too.

Red House Furniture

34 Upper St James's St, Kemp Town, Brighton BN2 1JN
T: 01273 696737
www.redhousefurniture.co.uk
info@redhousefurniture.co.uk
Mon, Wed, Thurs, Fri and Sat: 10am-5.30pm, Sun: 10am-4.30pm

Beautifully designed contemporary furniture with all the mod cons.

Roost

26 Kensington Gdns, North Laine, Brighton BN1 4AL
T: 01273 625223
Mon-Fri: 10am-5.30pm, Sat: 10am-6pm, Sun: 12pm-4.30pm

Contemporary collection of design items for the home, lights, kitchen accessories and paper items.

Shop

28a Gloucester Rd, North Laine, Brighton BN1 4AQ
T: 01273 600477
Mon-Sat: 10am-5.30pm
It's a great name for a place that sells a stunning collection of furniture, textiles and accessories from the Swat Valley in Pakistan and north and east Africa. Affordable and beautiful.

Sneek

34 St James's St, Kemp Town, Brighton BN2 1RG
T: 01273 679648
www.sneekltd.com
Mon-Fri: 11am-7pm, Thurs: 11am-8.30pm Sat: 10am-7pm, Sun: 12-5pm

Hand made furniture, interiors and amazing wall panels.

Souk

4 Little East St, The Lanes, Brighton BN1 1HT
T: 01273 776477
Mon-Fri: 9.30am-6pm, Sat: 10am-5pm

Everything imaginable from Morocco, with a beautiful line in ornate lamps, furniture, ceramics, tiled tables, kilims and accessories.

Steamer Trading

35 Ship St, The Lanes, Brighton BN1 1AB
T: 01273 227705
www.steamer.co.uk
Mon-Sat: 10am-6pm, Sun: 11am-5pm
Three floors of designer kitchen gear including Global, Wusthos, Kitchen Aid, Dualit, Hackman, Daggia, Alessi, and a coffee shop on the fourth.

Suttons Home Furnishings

56 Church Rd, Hove BN3 2FP
T: 01273 723728
F: 01273 730837
Mon-Sat: 9am-5.30pm

Interior design service as well as latest ranges of designer fabrics and wallpapers such as Designers Guild, Zoffany's and Osbourne and Little.

The Floor

32 Gloucester Rd, North Laine, Brighton BN1 4AQ
T: 01273 602894
Tues-Fri: 10am-5pm,
Sat: 10.30am-4.30pm
Expensive but interesting selection of carpets, runners, rugs and tiles.

Tucan

29 Bond St, The Lanes, Brighton BN1 1AD
T: 01273 326351 F: 01273 325149
www.tucan.co.uk
tucanretail@btinternet.com

Mon-Sat: 10am-5pm,
Sun: 11.30am-4.30pm

Brightly coloured home accessories
and gifts from Latin America.
Children's wooden toys, funky
furniture, jewellery and much more.

Valentina
212 Church Rd, Hove BN3 2DJ
T: 01273 735035
Mon-Sat: 10am-5pm

Beautiful French wooden and iron
antique beds, and a small selection
of antique Louis XV and VI armoires.

Vanilla
23 Ship St, The Lanes,
Brighton BN1 1AD
T: 01273 725538
vanillahome@msn.com
Mon-Fri: 10.30am-5.30pm, Sat: 10am-
6pm, Sun: 12pm-5pm

Contemporary ultra sleek furniture,
leather, lighting, ceramics and mirrors.

Villa and Hut
40 Sydney St, North Laine,
Brighton BN1 4EP
T: 01273 696787/01273 696787
www.villaandhut.com
Mon-Sun: 10am-6pm

Furniture from Java, Indonesia and
Malaysia and trinkets from Morocco.
They've also got a huge warehouse in
Portslade stacked with more goodies.

Yashar Bish
96 Gloucester Rd, North
Laine, Brighton BN1 4AP
T: 01273 671900
www.yashar-bish.com
Mon-Sat: 10am-6pm, Sun: 12pm-4pm

Wide selection of rugs, kilims and
textiles from Turkey. There are also
fabulous lamps, beads, ornate inlaid
backgammon sets and village soaps.
Upstairs you'll find antique Turkish
pots and Anatolian village artefacts.

JEWELLERY

All That Glitters
9 Meeting House Lane, The
Lanes, Brighton BN1 1HB
T: 01273 733217
www.all-that-glitters.co.uk
Mon-Sat: 9am-5.30pm,
Sun: 12pm-5pm

Fashion accessories meets up market
jewellery with prices more Churchill
Square's than Bond Street.

Appendage
36 Kensington Gdns, North
Laine, Brighton BN1 4AL
T: 01273 605901
Mon-Sat: 10am-5.30pm

Lovely collection of contemporary
jewellery and gifts made by local
artists at affordable prices. Hand-
made bags, copper heart key rings
and John Castle's reclaimed wood
lamp bases and painted shades.

Big Ears
143a North St, Brighton BN1 1RE
T: 01273 326292 F: 01273
326292
Mon-Sat: 10am-6pm,
Sun: 11am-5pm

Funky, modern jewellery at good
prices, a favourite with teens.

Conberts
16 Sydney St, North Laine,
Brighton BN1 1UP
T: 01273 625222
www.conberts.co.uk
conberts@btopenworld.com
Mon-Sat: 10am-6pm,
Sun: 12pm-6pm

An unusual combination of
olde worlde teashop and
contemporary jewellers. Christian
designs the jewellery – although
he sells other designers' work
too, and Ray runs the tearoom
with a mouth-watering selection
of teas from all over the world.
All the jewellery is mounted in
ornate gilt frames, and you can
browse as you sip.

Flux
48 Market St, The Lanes,
Brighton BN1 1HH
T: 01273 738784
www.flux.co.uk
Contemporary jewellery by 26
different designers including Flux's
own Alex and Goodwin, and Nicky
Morris, winner of The Best Jeweller
Award 2003

Grains of Gold

52 Meeting House Lane, The
Lanes, Brighton BN1 1HP
T: 01273 777197
Mon-Sat: 9.30am-6pm

Specialists in platinum and
contemporary jewellery
with quality certified diamonds.
Design service available.

Jeremy Hoye

22a Ship Street, The Lanes,
Brighton BN1 1AD
T: 01273 777207
www.jeremy-hoye.co.uk
Mon-Fri: 10.30am-5.30pm, Sat:
10.30am-6pm, Sun: 12pm-5pm

Contemporary designer
jewellery, mainly in silver.
Wedding bands, engagement
rings with diamond and semi
precious stones available too.

Julian Stephens

37 Gloucester Rd, North
Laine, Brighton BN1 4AQ
T: 01273 692110
www.julianstevens.com
Tues-Sat: 10am-6pm

One of the best contemporary
silverware and jewellery designers
in Brighton, Julian offers both a
bespoke service, his own and select
others collections which include
elegant tableware and unusual gifts.
All work is done on the premises
and now offering workshops.

Rina Tairo Jewellery

26 Clifton Terrace, Brighton,
BN1 3HB
T: 01273 733822
www.rinatairo.com
rina.rinatairo.com
Born in Helsinki, she studied fine
art before discovering her talent
for jewellery design. The individual
pieces are fresh and exciting, in gold
and silver and a wide selection of
precious gems. Look out for a shawl
made entirely out of fine silver
strands and gems. Rina's jewellery
has been used in films such as Emma
and Love Actually. There are plans
for a new shop at 13 Prince Albert
Street in the near future.

Silverado

30 Meeting House Lane, The
Lanes, Brighton BN1 1HB
T: 01273 326756
www.silverado.co.uk
mail@silverado.co.uk
Mon-Fri: 10am-5.30pm, Sat:
9.45am-5.45pm, Sun: 11am-5pm

Large selection of silver rings at rock
bottom prices, plus contemporary
silver jewellery.

Soma

24 Meeting House Lane, The
Lanes, Brighton BN1 1HB
T: 01273 321332
Mon-Fri: 10am-6pm,
Sun: 11am-5pm

Contemporary silver and semi
precious jewellery, supporting

local designers. They've recently
introduced engagement and
wedding rings with precious stones
set in platinum or white gold.

MUSIC

Across the Tracks

110 Gloucester Rd, North
Laine, Brighton BN1 4AP
T: 01273 677906
Mon-Sat: 10am-6pm,
Sun: 12pm-5pm

Packed with boxes of second-hand
vinyl, from 60's rock to 90's old
skool hip-hop to what is perhaps
the best collection of country music
in town. Take time to browse and
you'll unearth a gaggle of forgotten
classics, usually at good prices.

Banging Tunes

91 Trafalgar St, North Laine,
Brighton BN1 4ER
T: 01273 571605
www.bangingtunes.com
info@bangingtunes.com
Mon-Sat: 12pm-6pm

Formerly known as Klik Klik Whirly
Beep Beep (can't imagine why they
changed the name), Banging Tunes
is one of those 'does what it says on
the tin' shops. It stocks all kinds of
music – as long as it's banging.

Borderline

41 Gardner St, North Laine,
Brighton BN1 1UP
T: 01273 818611

Mon-Sat: 10am-5.30pm,
Sun: 11am-5pm

A lovely browers shop, the sort of place where you go in looking for Tim Buckley and come out with King Tubby. A great cross-genre selection – from hip-hop to soul and funk classics, break beats, and drum'n'bass – and it's not only the modern nonsense you get at most record shops. The staff are sweet and warm and helpful and if you look carefully and you'll dig up a few bargains.

Covert Records
39a Sydney St, The Lanes,
Brighton BN1 3AG
T: 01273 624774
Mon-Sat: 11am-6pm, Sun: 12pm-5pm

Vinyl only, underground music shop. Specialists in techno, house, break beat, electro and electronica.

Rounder Records
19 Brighton Square, The Lanes,
Brighton BN1 1HD
T: 01273 325440
philshop@btconnect.com
Mon-Sat: 9.30am-6pm, Sun:
10.30am-6pm

A bit of an institution, Rounders has been here since the 60's, it has the biggest section of vinyl in Brighton. The staff are keen (bet they've all seen High Fidelty a thousand times) and hugely helpful. It's the place to come for tickets for local gigs.

Wax Factor
24 Trafalgar St, The Lanes,
Brighton BN1 4EQ
T: 01273 673744
F: 01273 694229
Mon-Sat: 10.15am-5.30

This shop is great for collectors and those wanting to just browse in the hope of finding a surprise. Tucked away at the end of the North Laine, it's easy to miss but well worth a visit for those who have some time to kill. There are hundreds of original 7" and 12" classics on two floors, from Led Zeppelin and The Beatles to Sinatra and Benny Goodman for big-band swingers. If you want to buy a book on feminism or philosophy or get a tape of Dire Straits, before sitting down for a quick coffee, it's all here. A gem.

RETAIL THERAPY

Brighton Bead Shop
39 Sydney St, North Laine,
Brighton BN1 4AQ
T: 01273 671212 Mail order service: 01273 740777
Mon-Sat: 10am-6pm, Sun: 11am-5pm

Bead kits for all ages and skills plus rows and rows of individual beads to suit all budgets for your own individual design.

Belle Boutique
32 Kensington Gdns, North
Laine, Brighton BN1 4AL

T: 01273 621135
www.belleboutique.biz
Mon-Sat: 11am-5.30pm

The best of France available in Brighton. Natural beauty products, hand-made soaps and organic honeys. It's even got an oxygen bar – a perfect hangover cure, energy boost and detox.

Blue
20 Church St, North Laine,
Brighton BN1 1RB
T: 01273 700370
www.bluecrafts.co.uk
Mon-Sat: 10am-5.30pm

Arts and crafts made by local artists. Ceramics, cards, jewellery, natural earth coloured clothes. Beautiful hand-made kiddies shoes.

Castor and Pollux
164-165 King's Rd Arches,
The Beachfront,
Brighton BN1 1NB
T: 01273 773776
www.castorandpollux.co.uk
Tues-Fri: 12pm-4pm, Sat and Sun: 11am-5pm

Lovely new gift shop on the beach-front with a bizarre and eclectic mix of lifestyle gifts and furnishings. Books, throws, jewellery – it's all here. They specialise in illustrator art and hand-made gifts and there's a pottery studio on site. They also have the widest selection of hand made cards in the city.

Cissymo
88 Western Rd, Brighton BN3
1JB. T: 01273 202008
38 Sydney St, The Lanes,
Brighton BN1 1EP
T: 01273 607777
25 Church St, The Lanes,
Brighton BN1 1RB
T: 01273 205060
www.cissymo.co.uk
Mon-Sat: 10am-5.30pm

Designer stuff for your bathroom,
cool loo seats and shower curtains,
plus an array of cards, kitsch
accessories and fabulous gifts.

Cup Cake
98 St George's Rd, Brighton
BN2 1EE. T: 01273 624134
Mon-Sat: 9.30am-5.30pm

Kids designer clothes by Petit Bateau,
Powell-Craft and wellies by Aigle,
soft toys and hand made mobiles.
The stock is European, pricey but the
perfect place for a special treat.

Departure Shop
19 Gardner St, Preston Circus,
Brighton BN1 1UP

T: 01273 572100 F: 01273 572111
www.departureshop.com
info@departureshop.com
Mon-Fri: 9am-5.30pm, Sat: 9am-6pm

Everything for the traveller.
Beautiful contemporary luggage and
accessories. Books, maps, beauty kits,
sunglasses and seasonal accessories.

Foley and Fitch

13 New Rd, North Laine,
Brighton BN1 1UF
T: 01273 775218
Mon-Fri: 9am-5.30pm, Sat: 9am-6pm
Sister company to The Dials, this
store houses all for anyone who
obsesses about style. Exclusive
stockists of Cath Kidston products,
fabrics, furnishings and books with
temptations from Liberty, Heirs and
Graces, Little Shrimp and Neisha
Crossland stationery. They have their
own label of wrap around dresses
and elegant coats.

Fossil 2000

3 Kensington Place, North
Laine, Brighton BN1 4EN
T: 01273 622000
www.fossil2000.co.uk
Tues-Sat: 10am-5.30pm, Sun:
11am-4pm

Everything is on display and ready to
be touched and handled, including
a huge array of Grade A crystals and
ammonite, dinosaur teeth and eggs,
exclusive fossilised seabed stone
with orthoceras inlaid crafted into
bowls, plates and goblets. Kids can

use the magnifying glass to check
out the dinosaur poo and flies
petrified in amber.

Hocus Pocus

38 Gardner St, North Laine,
Brighton BN1 1UN
T: 01273 572207
www.hocuspocus.co.uk
info@hocuspocus.co.uk
Mon-Sat: 10am-6pm, Sun: 11am-5pm

Hocus Pocus encourages the work of
quality crafts people in this New Age
store which sells tarot cards, crystals,
incense and has tarot consultations
available. Everything for the
alternative with an open mind, with
a clinic upstairs for those wanting to
go further into their own minds.

Lavender Room

16 Bond St, The Lanes,
Brighton BN1 1RD
T: 01273 220380
Mon: 10am-5.30pm, Tues-Sat:
10am-6pm, Sun: 12pm-5pm

A gorgeous combination of shabby
chic and delicate lace and silks,
floaty dresses, pj's and slippers,
knickers and girly accessories. And,
of course, the essential lavender eye
pillow. What do you mean it's not
essential?

Mac

6 Dukes Lanes, The Lanes,
Brighton BN1 1HL
T: 01273 720026
Mon-Sat: 9am-6pm

This sleek shop is more of a make-
up studio than a store and has the
goods to make a supermodel out
of all of us. Inexpensive prices and
helpful staff.

Malarkey

34 Bond St, North Laine,
Brighton BN1 1RD
T: 01273 722339
Mon-Sat: 10am-6pm, Sun: 11am-5pm

Individual gifts, cards and one-offs
for those who want something
different.

Mojoe

24 Church St, Brighton BN1 1RB
T: 01273 208708
Tues-Sat: 10am-6pm,
Sun: 12am-4pm

If you're into minimalism, this is for
you. Mojoe sells anything from hand-
made greetings cards, from the latest
sun lounger to unique pieces of art
for the wall. Moses (Mr. Mojoe) is as
an interior designer and worked at
Muji (the Japanese home/office very
minimal chain of stores throughout
the world), and has an excellent eye
for design and fashion.

Nail Zone

Churchill Square, Brighton
BN1 2EP
01273 736303
Mon-Sat: 9am-7pm
New York comes to Brighton. Once

you've done your shopping, treat yourself to a manicure and watch the world go by. A basic manicure costs £15.

Nasty Nip
36 North Rd, North Laine, Brighton BN1 1YB
T: 01273 601184
www.nastynip.co.uk
Mon-Sun: 12pm-6pm

Everything's imported from Japan and there's anything you might want, from Dog Water bottles to Madonna condoms. Mad kitsch stuff that's a bit pricey, but then again it all comes direct from the Mother country.

Neal's Yard
2a Kensington Gdns, North Laine, Brighton BN1 4AL
T: 01273 601464
www.nealsyardremedies.com
Mon-Sat: 9.30am-5.30pm,
Sun: 11am-4pm

Heavenly apothecary. Medicinal herbs, lotions and potions in the famous blue and purple bottles. Alternative music books. too.

Pardon My French
104 St George's Rd, Kemp Town, Brighton BN2 1EA
T: 01273 694479
www.pardonmyfrench.co.uk
Mon-Fri: 9.45am-5pm,
Sat: 10am-5pm

Anything and everything that's French, eccentric and classy.

Pecsniff's
45 Meeting House Lane, The Lanes, Brighton BN1 1HB
T: 01273 723292 F: 01273 733713
www.pecksniffs.com
info@pecksniffs.com
Mon-Sat: 10.30am-5.30pm, Sun: 11am-5pm
Specialist perfumery and aromatherapy shop selling soothing and effective blends of essential oils.

Pen to Paper
4 Sydney St, North Laine, Brighton BN1 4EN
T: 01273 676670
www.pentopaperonline.co.uk
info@pentopaperonline.co.uk
Mon-Sat: 1pm-6pm,
Sun: 11.30am-4pm

Unusually high quality accessories and stationery. Specialists in hand-made paper.

Pussy
3a Kensington Gdns, North Laine, Brighton BN1 3BH
T: 01273 604861
www.pussyhomeboutique.co.uk
Mon-Sat: 10am-5pm, Sun: 11am-5pm

Everything for the girly girl. Satin sheets and pillows, Babycham pyjamas, books, bags and accessories.

Pyramid
9a Kensington Gdns, North

Laine, Brighton BN1 4AL
T: 01273 607791
Mon-Fri: 10am-5.30pm, Sat: 10am-6pm, Sun: 11am-5.30pm

Beautiful 1940's cards, inlaid loo seats, gifts, cards and watches, with a large supply of Mathmos goods and Dr. Who products.

Rapid Eye Movement
23 Gardner St, North Laine, Brighton BN1 1UP
T: 01273 694323
Mon-Sat: 10am-6pm, Sun: 12pm-5pm

Contemporary home accessories. Cool Japanese items, watches and sunglasses.

Revamp
11 Sydney St, North Laine, Brighton BN1 4EN
T: 01273 623288
www.revampfancydress.co.uk
Mon-Sat: 10am-5.30pm,
Sun: 11am-5.30pm

Vast collection of fancy dress for sale or hire, plus accessories such as wigs, masks and boots. They have a good children's section and all the usual party gear like balloons etc.

She Said
11 Ship Street Gdns, The Lanes, Brighton BN1 1AJ
T: 01273 777811
www.shesaidboutique.com
Mon-Sat: 11am-6pm,

Velvet
27 Bond St, North Laine,
Brighton BN1 1RD
T: 01273 326007
www.velvetstore.co.uk
Mon-Fri: 10pm-5.30pm, Sat: 10am-6.30pm, Sun: 11am-5pm
10 George St, Hove BN3 4AL
T: 01273 775758
Mon-Fri: 9am-5.30pm,
Sat: 11am-5pm

Sun: 12pm-5pm, Closed on
Monday during winter

High-quality lingerie at affordable
prices, select couture party wear,
leather and latex, with boudoir
changing rooms downstairs. Exclusive
bags, jewellery and adult toys.

Tickled
15 Gardner St, North Laine,
Brighton BN1 1UP
T: 01273 628725
F: 01273 606720
www.tickledonline.co.uk
Mon-Fri: 11am-5.30pm, Sat:
10.30am-6pm, Sun: 12pm-5pm

The first shop in Sussex to cater
exclusively for women looking for
erotic adult toys and accessories.
With two shops in one, Tickled has
everything from satin bedding to
inflatable husbands, along with a
vast range of products for those
more daring, Check out the website
to plan the perfect dirty weekend.
Men only accompanied by women.

Rin Tin Tin
34 North Rd, North Laine,
Brighton BN1 1RD
T: 01273 672424
Mon-Sat: 11am-5.30pm

The ultimate in ephemera. Rick has a
fabulous collection of tins, toys and
prints plus a framing service.

Tsena
6 Bond St, North Laine,
Brighton BN1 1YB
T: 01273 328402/01273 328402
www.tsena.co.uk
info@tsena.co.uk
Mon-Sat: 10am-6pm, Sun: 11am-5pm

Original limited edition gifts, with
personalised embroidered cards
made by local artists like Laura
Windebank. They also stock Bob
and Blossom t-shirts for kids.
Leather and suede books in pastel
hews and personalised ceramics
for weddings etc. Plus glassware,
pewter and cards all designed by
local designers.

More interiors oriented than
its fabric sister shop in Gardner
Street, this is where you can finish
your house off with lampshades
and objects once you've run up the
curtains.

Wallace McFarlane
14 St George's Rd, Kemp Town,
Brighton BN1 1RD
T: 01273 297088
Mon-Sat: 10am-6pm

Wonderfully friendly and helpful
owners who stock an array of
delicious gifts and goodies.
Choose from the wide selection
of soaps and smellies and work
your way through the artistic talents
of local artists. They also
sell Cocoadance chocolate –
one of the finest hand-made
chocolates money can buy.

Winfalcon
28 Ship St, The Lanes,
Brighton BN1 1AD
T: 01273 728997
F: 01273 720411

www.winfalcon.com
winfalcon@dial.pipex.com
**Mon-Sat: 10.30am-5.30pm,
Sun: 11am-4pm**

With Tarot readers on hand to
tell you your destiny, this shop
sells all things alternative;
crystals, incense, dream catchers,
books and a healing centre
to put you back on track after
a day at the sales.

SHOES

Feet Inc
Unit 25 Churchill Square,
01273 732195 Bn1 2TD
www.feetinc.com
**Mon-Wed/Fri: 9am-7pm,
Thurs: 9am-8pm; Sun: 11am-5pm**

Cool brands like Histanatas,
Pikalonos, Riva, Ecco and
Joseph Feadel.

Ghita Shuy
17 St George's Rd,
Kemp Town, Brighton
BN1 1AH
T: 01273 885275
**Mon-Sat: 10am-5.30pm,
Sun: 11am-5pm**

Ghita's shop is also her work room
so if you're lucky you'll catch her
working on new designs. Her shoes
are beautifully made particularly the
pointed toed appliquéd flats –
apparently the designs come to her

in her dreams. All shoes are made to
order for children and adults.

Pullingers
9 Bond St, North Laine,
Brighton BN1 1RD
Mon-Sat 9-15am-5.30pm
T: 01273 725476
5 George St, Kemp Town,
Brighton BN1
T: 01273 670187
Good old-fashioned shoe shop
(and cobbler in the Kemp Town
shop) selling Church's shoes and Dr
Marten's for young and old.

Vegetarian Shoes
12 Gardner St, North Laine,
Brighton BN1 1UP
T: 01273 691913
www.vegetarianshoes.com
info@vegetarianshoes.com
Mon-Sat: 10am-6pm

Guilt free, animal friendly footwear.
Fashionable hardwearing styles
and the closest look to leather
you'll find.

SPORTS

Air Born Kites
42 Gardner St, North Laine,
Brighton BN1 1UN
T: 01273 676740
F: 01273 676752
www.airbornekites.co.uk
info@airbornkites.co.uk
**Mon-Fri: 10am-5.30pm, Sat: 10am-
6pm, Sun: 12pm-5pm**

Kites, hot air balloons, stomp
rockets and all you need for the
massively popular kite surfing.
Repairs and orders available.

Boost
15 Victoria Terrace, Kings Way,
Hove BN3 2WB
T: 01273 721100 F: 01273 721100
www.boostsports.com
info@boostsports.com
**Mon-Sun: 10am-5pm, closed on
Monday in winter.**

The brains and energy behind
Brighton's kitesurfing championships,
this is the place to get your gear,
your lessons and to meet anyone
who has anything to do with the
sport. Seb and Paul will organise
your weekend if you're coming
down for the thrill, with weekends
in Blanch House and Pelirocco,
evenings at The Alibi and long days
on the beach waiting for the waves.

Run
46 Blatchington Rd, Hove BN3
3YN. T: 01273 770972
www.run-shop.co.uk
info@run-shop.co.uk
**Mon-Fri: 11am-7pm,
Sat: 9am-6pm, Sun: 12pm-4pm,
closed all day Wed**

Running shop run by runners. Get
specialist advice from pros who
assess your running style and find
the right pair of shoes for you.
Pricey, but worth it if you're serious
about sport.

ARTS

CINEMAS

Cinematheque

9-12 Middle St, The Lanes, Brighton BN1 1AL.
T: 01273 384300
www.cinematheque.org
cinematheque@yahoo.com
Thurs and Sun: 8pm
Entrance Fee: £3.50, £3 cons, 50p
membership per year, payment by
cash only.
Founded in 1996, the Cinematheque, which seats 60, is run by a group of enthusiasts dedicated to screening films you won't find in any other cinema, from Russian films to early silent movies and digital shorts. Basically, if it's got subtitles and lacks a coherent narrative, it's in. It's not only outside the mainstream, it's outside the familiar art house circuit. They cover a wide range of cinema from experimental, animation, obscurities and rare classics, through to premiers and specialised festivals. A bi-monthly, open reel night screens films and works in progress submitted.

Duke of York's Cinema

Preston Circus, Brighton BN1 4NA
T: 01273 626261
www.picturehouses.co.uk
dukeofyorks@picturehouses.co.uk
Entrance Fee: Adults: £4.80-£5.80,
children: £3.50, members: £3.50-
£4.80, concs with ID: £3.50-£4.50

Grade II listed building and – this is the good part – the oldest cinema

showing films continuously in Britain. 'One-night only' showings are its speciality, so make sure you paste its calendar of events on your front door to avoid missing such one-offs and retrospectives. It's also the home of the November Brighton Jewish Film Festival. If you fancy a treat, there's one of the original balcony boxes remaining, which they rent out if you ask nicely. The Duke Of York's is also that curio, a place that treats you like an adult. Not only is there a licensed bar, but the auditorium is licensed so you can have a drink while watching the film. On Friday and Saturday there are late night shows, and Junior Dukes, the Kids' Club, takes place Saturday morning at 11am.

Odeon

Kingswest, West St, Brighton BN1 2RE
T: 01273 323317/0870 5050 007
www.odeon.co.uk

A big, old-fashioned, multi-screen cinema that boasts a built-in Haagen Dazs café, so at least if the film's rubbish, you can enjoy the ice-cream. Just remember to add 15 minutes to your timing – the ice-cream queue can take its time.

UGC

Marina Village, Brighton Marina, Brighton BN2 5UF
T: 08701 555145
www.ugccinemas.co.uk

A mega-screen multiplex showing

all the latest blockbusters. The main joy here is that it shows films at a remarkably civilised time; most evenings the main show doesn't start until 9pm. A UGC card allows you to see an unlimited number of films for £9.99 a month.

COMEDY AND CABARET

Joogleberry Playhouse

14-17 Manchester St, Kemp Town, Brighton BN2 1TF
T: 01273 687171
www.joogleberry.com
info@joogleberry.com
Mon-Sun: 12pm-1am
Entrance Fee: Prices various: £2.00-
£10.00. Happy Hour: 5pm-7pm
Cabaret theatre-bar where the talent is purely Kemp Town. One of the most successful crossovers of camp cabaret and gay night out, this is entertainment for anyone who's up for singing their heart out with the likes of 70's sensation, Viola Wills. Star-spangled walls and a Parisian skyline mural add to the atmosphere.

Kemp Town Crack @ The Hanbury Ballroom

St George's St, Kemp Town, Brighton BN2 5UP
T: 01273 605789
www.zelnet.com
Entrance Fee: £5.00 (£3.00 conc)
Comedy is necessarily a hit-or-miss affair, but at least at The Crack the bar stays open late. The Thursday night Kemp Town Crack is as near you'll get to an old style Comedy Store atmosphere in Brighton.

Komedia

44-47 Gardner St, North Laine,
Brighton BN1 1UN
T: 01273 647100
www.komedia.co.uk
admin@komedia.co.uk
Mon-Fri: 10am-10pm, Sat: 10am-
10.30pm, Sun: 1pm-10pm

Not just the place for comedy,
Komedia was originally set up
to bring European-based visual
and physical theatre to Brighton.
Specialising in fringe productions,
the Komedia is the place to go for
performance theatre or kids' drama.
Komedia's International Theatre has
been honoured by The Institute Of
International Theatre For Excellence,
and there's even a Komedia at the
Edinburgh Festival now.

Prince Albert

Trafalgar St, North Laine,
Brighton BN1 4ED. T: T:
01273 730499
info@concorde2.
co.uk
Third Mon of every
month: 8pm-11pm
Entrance Fee: £2

Regular comedy nights at this well-
loved pub near the station.

GALLERIES

Art Asylum

80c St James St, Kemp Town,
Brighton BN2 1PA
T: 01273 626426
www.artasylumgallery.co.uk
simon@artasylumgallery.co.uk
Thurs-Sat: 11am-6pm

Simon Etheridge displays his own
work at Art Asylum. He specialises in
contemporary pop art and prices for
an original start at £250.

Art Republic

13 Bond St, North Laine,
Brighton BN1 1RD
T: 01273 724829 F: 01273 746016
www.artrepublic.com
info@artrepublic.com
Mon-Sat: 10am-5pm, Sun:
11am-5pm

Dealing mainly in prints and
posters of famous works, Arts
Republic also sells limited
editions of Simon Dixon's
work, a local artist
specialising in Pop Art.

Brighton Artists Gallery of Contemporary Art

108a Dyke Rd,
Seven Dials, Brighton
BN1 3TE

T: 01273 711016
www.baggallery.co.uk
alicia@murphy@baggallery.
co.uk
Mon-Sun: 10am-5pm

BAG provides an outlet specifically
for local artists to exhibit their
work at rents they can afford. It's
well worth a visit to pick up some
bargains.

Brighton Designers and Makers

39 Sydney St, North Laine,
Brighton BN1 4ET
T: 01273 671212
Mon-Sat: 10am-6pm, Sun: 11am-5pm

Two floors of local artists work
including ceramic, glass work,
painting and jewellery. There is a
monthly exhibition of a new work.

Brighton Media Centre Gallery

20-21 Old Steine, Brighton
BN1 1AL
T: 01273 648300 F: 01273
384201
www.mediacentre.org
info@mediacentre.org
Mon-Sun: 11am-5pm
A small gallery which concentrates
on new media art such as
photography and installations.

Brighton Museum and Art Gallery

4-5 Royal Pavilion Buildings,
Brighton BN1 1EE

T: 01273 290900/01273 292871
www.brighton.virtualmuseum.
info visitor.services@brighton-
hove.gov.uk
Tues: 10am-5pm, Wed-Sat: 10am-
5pm, Sun: 2pm-5pm

Re-made and re-modelled, this is art
for art's sake. Packed with Brighton
history from Mods and Rockers
to Gay Brighton, it also (bizarrely)
houses one of the biggest collections
of Ancient Egyptian artefacts outside
The British Museum.

Burstow Gallery
Eastern Rd, Kemp Town,
Brighton BN1 1AL
T: 01273 697131
Mon-Sat: 11.30am-5pm, Sun: 2pm-
5pm
Gallery within Brighton College
quadrangle with four visual arts
exhibitions a year.

Chameleon Gallery
13a Prince Albert St, The Lanes,
Brighton BN1 1HE
T: 01273 324432 F: 01273 324432
www.chameleongallery.org
info@chameleongallery.org
Mon-Sat: 10am-5.30pm, Sun: 11am-
4pm

Chameleon gallery is on two floors
and exhibits paintings, sculptures and
hand blown glass work by local and
national artists.

Fabrica
Duke St, The Lanes, Brighton

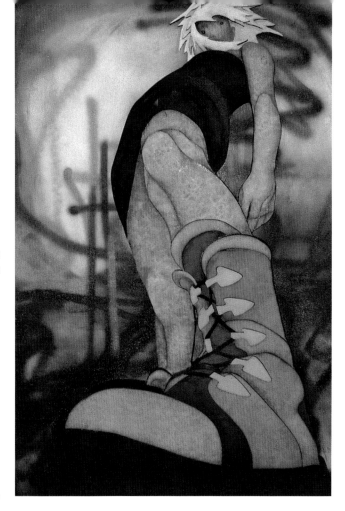

BN1 1AG. T: 01273 778646
www.fabrica.org.uk
info@fabrica.org.uk
Wed-Sat: 11.30am-5pm, Sun: 2pm-
5pm

Set in the beautiful, but redundant
Holy Trinity Church in the heart of
Brighton's shopping area, Fabrica is
a fantastic place to relax in if the
shopping gets too much. Sound
installations and bizarre puppetry are
the kind of thing to expect. Check

out the website to see what's on. You
can rent Fabrica for private functions
too; one juicy couple are even
getting married there this summer.

First Light Gallery
3 Nile St, The Lanes, Brighton
BN1 1HW. T: 01273 327344
www.firstlightclick.com
info@firstlightclick.com
Mon-Fri: 10am-5pm, Sat: 10.30am-
5pm, Sun: 1.30-4pm
A working photographic library with
a public gallery on the ground floor.

Gardner Arts Centre

University of Sussex, Falmer,
Brighton BN1 9RA
T: 01273 685861/01273 678551
www.gardnerarts.co.uk
info@gardnerarts.co.uk
Mon-Sun: 10am-7pm

Sussex University-based arty theatre
with a strong emphasis on the avant-
garde. Kids' pantos here tend to be
particularly worth a visit. Its venture
into kids' drama and interactive
theatre is a must for everyone under
the age of 10. Look out for the Earwig
kids' clubs in the summer.

George Street Gallery

4 George St, Kemp Town,
Brighton BN2 1RH
T: 01273 681852
gsg@onetel.net
Tues-Fri: 10am-5pm, Sat: 10am-3pm

Monthly exhibitions of local, national
and international artists.

Naked Eye

32 Western Rd, Hove BN3 1AF
T: 01273 204800/01273 775847
www.nakedeye.com
naked.eye@virgin.net
Mon-Sun:10am-6pm, closed on Tue.

A gallery that's been up and running
for four years. The owner, David
Donno, chooses the artwork
according to his own taste – quite
right, too – and deals in national and
international artists such as Charlotte
Atkinson.

The Old Picture Shop

2 Nile St, Brighton BN1 1HW
T: 01273 725609
Mon-Sat: 10.30am-5pm, Sun: 1pm-
4pm

An Aladdin's cave of new and antique paintings. This gallery is stuffed to bursting. Prices start at around £50.

Permanent Gallery

20 Bedford Place, Brighton BN1 2PT. T: 01273 710771
www.permanentgallery.com
info@permanentgallery.com
Thurs and Fri: 6pm-9pm, Sat and Sun: 1pm-6pm
A new artist-run gallery space in Brighton, which focuses on innovative, contemporary art – painting, photography and sculpture to audio visual to the public – while its poetry evenings have spawned Brighton's new Beatnik set. There's also limited edition books, fanzines, art magazines and independent publications. A good place.

Phoenix Gallery

10-14 Waterloo Place, Brighton BN1 2PT. T: 01273 603700 T: 01273 603704
www.phoenixarts.org
info@phoenixarts.org
Tues-Sat: 11am-5pm

Artists' co-op in an enormous '60's building with workshops for adults and children's open days all year.

QUODart

160 North St, Brighton BN1 1EA
T: 01273 772002
quodart@quod.co.uk
Mon-Fri: 10am-5pm

Linked to the restaurant next door,

QUODart is another of Brighton's new contemporary art galleries, aiming to showcase the work of emerging, pre-dominantly Brighton-based contemporary artists.

Space Gallery and Café

10 Western Rd, Brighton BN3 1AE
T: 01273 770083
www.synergygallery.co.uk
synergy.gallery@tiscali.co.uk
Tues-Sat: 10am-6pm

This smart chic gallery/café – all bright and modern and shiny – is an indication of how things are changing in Hove. A long way from the blue rinses of old.

Start Contemporary Gallery

8 Church St, The Lanes, Brighton BN1 1US
T: 01273 233984
www.startgallery.co.uk
mail@startgalleryco.uk
Mon-Fri 11am-5pm, Sat: 10am-6pm

Contemporary ceramics and glass at reasonable prices.

University of Brighton Gallery

Faculty of Arts and Architecture, Grand Parade, Brighton BN2 0JY
T: 01273 643012
www.brighton.ac.uk/gallery-theatre/ c.l.matthews@bton.ac.uk
Mon-Sat: 10am-5pm

The University of Brighton Gallery originates, shows and tours an eclectic range of international and national art, as well as local and student work from its own students. It features wide-ranging exhibitions, including multi-media and art installation pieces, but the highlight of the year has to be the graduate shows in June where you can pick up some real steals from the big names of the future.

Brighton Fishing Museum

201 Kings Rd Arches, Brighton
BN1 1NB. T: 01273 723064
www.museums.brighton-
hove.gov.uk visitor.
services@brighton-hove.gov.uk
Open all year: 9am-5pm

A window into a world gone by.
Right on the beachfront, most
people check this out during the
Brighton Festival, but this sweet
museum keeps the spirit of this
one-time fishing village alive. The
main museum arch is the focal
point of Brighton's fishing quarter.
It contains a 27ft beach boat, prints,
photographs and memorabilia of
Brighton seafront life from the
Regency days to the post-war
boom in pleasure boat operations.
The museum operates a 12-seater
passenger boat, Skylark, off the beach
in fair weather during the summer
months, but the more landlocked
might be more interested in the
two shellfish stalls, smokehouse and
smoked fish shop.

MUSEUMS

Booth Museum of Natural History

194 Dyke Rd, Hove BN1 5AA
T: 01273 292777 F: 01273 292778
www.booth.virtualmuseum.
info boothmus@pavillion.co.uk
Mon, Wed, Fri and Sat: 10am-5pm,
Sun: 2pm-5pm

Built in 1874 by Victorian ornithologist

Edward Booth to house his collection
of stuffed British birds, The Booth
is home to more stuffed birds than
there are in a stuffed bird shop, plus
insects, beasties and all manner of
things to do with natural history. It's
a spooky old place to hang around,
the sort of place where Peter Cushing
should play the curator. Activities are
organised during children's holidays,
and there are regular temporary
exhibitions and an educational service
for visiting schools. Entrance is free.

Engineerium

Off Nevill Road, Hove BN3
7QA
T: 01273 559583 F: 01273 566403
www.britishengineerium.com
info@britishengineerium.com
Mon-Sun: 10am-5pm
Entrance Fee: Admission: £4, Con
£3, family £12

This small boy's dream of a museum
is set in a beautifully restored

Victorian pumping station, housing an impressive collection of steam engines, from small toys up to a 10-metre-high beam engine. Exhibits include the Giant's Toolbox, an interactive exhibit explaining the principles of mechanical engineering, plus the giant has thoughtfully left belongings around the building for younger kids to spot. The staff are knowledgeable and very helpful.

Foredown Tower

Foredown Rd, Portslade BN41 2EW. T: 01273 292092
www.foredown.
virtualmuseum.info paula.
huntbach@brighton-hove.
gov.uk
Feb-Oct: Sat and Sun: 10am-5pm, Mid July to end Aug:Thurs-Sun: 10am-5pm
Entrance Fee: Adults – £2.50, Children – £1.60, Family Tickets – £6.40, Concessions-£1.85, B&H residents – £1.35, B&H schools – free, Group of 20 or more – £1.85

This fantastic converted Edwardian water tower is home to the only working camera obscura in the south east and hosts astronomy evenings for teenagers during holidays. It's the strangest thing, but offers outstanding views over the surrounding countryside.

Hove Museum and Art Gallery

19 New Church Rd, Hove BN3 4AB
T: 01273 290200/292827

www.hove.virtualmuseum.
info/ museums@brighton-hove.gov.uk
Tues-Sat: 10am-5pm, Sun: 2pm-5pm.

Based in a huge Victorian villa, the highlights include the South East Art collection of contemporary craft, a celebration of Hove's history as the home of early film-makers and the magical Wizard's Attic filled with 18th century toys.

Preston Manor

Preston Drove, Preston Park, Brighton BN1 6SD
T: 01273 290900/292771
www.prestonmanor.
virtualmuseum.info visitor.
services@brighton-hove.gov.uk
Tues to Sat: 10am-5pm, Sat: 11am-5pm, Sun: 2pm-5pm, Mon: 1pm-5pm
Entrance Fee: Admission: Adult £3.70, child (under-16) £2.15 family tickets available, concessions £3

Edwardian home of the Stanford family who once owned the whole area around Preston Park, Preston Manor dates from 1600 (rebuilt in 1738 and added to in 1905). Most of the furniture and fittings are more Upstairs Downstairs with mangles and smoothing irons, tin baths, as well as a butler's pantry. Check out the pets' cemetery in the walled gardens.

Royal Pavilion

Pavilion Gardens, Brighton BN1 1EE
T: 01273 290900
www.royalpavilion.org.uk
April-Sept: 9.30am-5.45pm, Oct-Mar: 10am-5.15pm
Entrance Fee: Adult £5.35, child £3.30, family ticket £14
Possibly the most sumptuous, ostentatious and hedonistic piece of architecture in the UK. When he was still Prince of Wales, the man who would later be known as King George IV had rented out the building when it was just a farmhouse. In 1787 the architect Henry Holland extended the farmhouse, but it was between 1815 and 1822 that things really

happened. George became Prince Regent in 1811 and instructed Nash to enlarge the building and create the Indian style Palace, as it is known as today. Decked out like a playboy's bordello it became the place for aristocratic hangers-on and the Prince's arty entourage to spend their spare time in. Make sure you get a guided tour through the fabulously over-the-top building for a feast of gossip and information. Kids love the stuffed swans in the kitchen's baking tins and Queen Victoria's princess-and-the-pea bed and expect to bump into The Beast or Aladdin around every corner. Storytelling and art sessions for kids during half term.

Sealife Centre

Marine Parade, Brighton BN2 1TB
T: 01273 604234/681843
www.sealife.co.uk www.slcbrighton@merlinentertainment.biz
Mon-Sun: 10am-5pm
Entrance Fee: Adults £7.95; Children £4.95

Not cheap, but the perfect place to take anyone from little Johnny to Granny on a rainy day. Creatively designed, it's a joy on the eye and is filled with more fish than there are stars in the sky. The rays can be fed and stroked, the seahorses are beautifully displayed in magnified glass and the shark tunnel is a treat for anyone scared of the misunderstood little loves. Check out www.sealife.co.uk for a virtual tour.

Toy and Model Museum

52-55 Trafalgar St, North Laine, Brighton BN1 4EB
T: 01273 749494/749494
www. brightontoymuseum.co.uk
info@brightontoymuseum.co.uk
Tues-Fri: 10am-5pm, Sat: 11am-5pm
Entrance Fee: Adults £3.50, Children £2.00, Family £9.00

It's easy to miss, but it would be a shame, for lurking under a bridge just below Brighton station is the very fine museum of toys and models. Highlights include Meccano and other construction toys, puppets and toy theatres. You can have a go at old-fashioned penny arcade games and early photographic animation through the working mutoscope. There are a number of beautiful dolls and rare dolls house furniture on display as well as a series of evocative military dramas.

ORGANISATIONS

Carnival Collective

113 Queens Rd, Brighton, BN1 3XG. T: 01273 625617
www.carnivalcollective.org.uk
lucy@carnivalcollective.org.uk

The Carnival Collective is one of Brighton's assets, a voluntary community samba organisation that gets the city by its goulies with a fabulously infectious stomp. They've been part of the festival scene for years and are a regular part of the calendar. Their grand design is to develop a yearly carnival to rival Rio. They do 10-week courses in samba drumming and dance leading to performance.

Same Sky

The Old Post Office, 1 College Rd, Kemp Town, Brighton BN2 1JA
T: 01273 571106 F: 01273 606668
www.samesky.co.uk
info@samesky.co.uk
Independent arts organisation responsible for a growing number of street arts in Brighton. The Children's Festival, with its staggering school made giant sculptures parading through the city on the first Saturday in May, is an example of how Same Sky inspire and teach local children.

THEATRE

Brighton Little Theatre Company

9 Clarence Gdns, Brighton BN2 1EG. T: 01273 205000
www.the-little.co.uk
tickets@the-little.co.uk
Plays start at: 7.45pm
Entrance Fee: Mon, Wed, Thurs, Fri, Sat, Sun: £7.00, Tues: £6.00

Tucked away at the end of a wee twitten off Western Road, the Little Theatre Co is the longest established amateur theatre company in Brighton. Formed in 1940, it stages about a dozen productions a year. Catch its annual outdoor performance at Lewes Castle.

Komedia

44-47 Gardner St, North Laine, Brighton BN1 1UN
T: 01273 647100/647101
www.komedia.co.uk
admin@komedia.co.uk
Mon-Fri: 10am-10pm, Sat: 10am-10.30pm, Sun: 1pm-10pm
Entrance Fee: Between £5 and £10

Not just the place for comedy, Komedia was originally set up to bring European-based visual and physical theatre to Brighton. Specialising in fringe productions, the Komedia is the place to go for performance theatre or kids' drama. Komedia's International Theatre has been honoured by The Institute Of International Theatre For Excellence,

and there's even a Komedia at the Edinburgh Festival now.

Malborough Theatre

4 Princess St, Old Steine, Brighton BN2 9RD. T: 01273 570028
the_malborough@hotmail.com
Entrance Fee: Tickets are usually around £5
The pub below is as camp as a row of tents, but the tiny upstairs theatre isn't always and there's often a good variety show to be had.

New Venture Theatre

Bedford Place, Brighton BN2 1RD
T: 01273 746118
www.newventure.org.uk
Entrance Fee: Usually £7.00-£8.50
Founded in 1947, this training ground of new writing and directing allows Brighton and Hove to witness some breathtaking new theatre and a few duds along the way. .

Nightingale Theatre

29-30 Surrey St, Brighton BN1 3PA
T: 01273 702563
Mon-Fri: 9am-11pm
Entrance Fee: Usually around £5.00
Once one of Brighton's best loved theatres, the Nightingale has long been known only to readers of history books. But life above Grand Central bar is looking up and new life is being breathed into the 90 capacity upstairs theatre. Stephan Berkoff is the new patron and plans to provide an exiting alternative to mainstream Brighton Theatre.

as the West End by the Sea, this is a drama house where you'll find enough Dolls Houses, Tell Me on A Sunday and Jesus Christ Superstar with a smattering of Ballet Rambert to keep everyone entertained. At Christmas it must be the best place in the country for panto.

VENUES

Brighton Centre

Kings Rd, Brighton BN1 2RG
T: 01273 290131/01273 779980
www.brightoncentre.co.uk
b-centre@pavillion.co.uk

Big and cavernous and squatting on the seafront in all its ugly Seventies concrete glory, spending a night in The Brighton Centre is about as appealing as a night out on platform 4 at the train station. The poor bar service only exacerbates the situation, but (and there's always a but) it is the only place in town for big bands to play. There's a plan to knock it down and create a new all-singing, all-dancing centre but when this might happen...

Sallis Benney Theatre

University of Brighton, Faculty of Arts and Architecture, Grand Parade, Brighton BN2 0JY
T: 01273 643010
www.brighton.ac.uk/gallery-theatre/theatrelistings.html
Entrance Fee: Concessions: NUS, over 60's, UB40's, university staff and students.
The University of Brighton's theatre, the Sallis Benney has a strong reputation for contemporary music, from classical and jazz to world, and past artists have included the Dave

Holland Quintet, Joe Lemvo, Trilok Gurtu, the Vienna Art Orchestra and Jan Garbarek. It's rarely open to the public except during the Festival.

Theatre Royal

New Rd, Brighton BN1 1SD
T: 01273 328488
www.theambassadors.com/theatreroyal

The oldest theatre in Brighton dating back to 1774 and scene to many a luvvie from Marlene Dietrich to Sir Larry himself. Positioning itself firmly

Concorde 2

Madeira Shelter Hall Madeira Drive, Kemp Town, Brighton BN2 1EN
T: 01273 772770/730468
www.concorde2.co.uk
info@concorde2.co.uk

An excellent booking policy and a bar almost as long as the walk home

along the seafront make this the best live venue in Brighton and one of the best venues of its size in the country. Known as the home of The Boutique, all kinds of acts also play here from Adam Freedland to Blu Cantrell, Roni Size to Raekwon. Prices lurk around the £10 mark.

The Dome

Church St, Brighton BN1 1UE
T: 01273 260821
www.brighton-dome.org.uk

The leading arts venue in the south of England with state-of-the-arts acoustics and the ability to turn itself to just about anything the event demands, this is the heartbeat of Brighton's art scene. The Dome is actually three venues: The Dome, The Corn Exchange and The Pavilion Theatre. Originally built as stables for the Prince of Wales in 1805, it was converted into a concert hall in 1867 and modernised in an art deco style in 1935. The recent restoration took the capacity to 1800 while retaining that Deco feel. It has a 1200 standing capacity or a theatre for 320. The Pavilion Theatre was built in 1935 as a 'supper room' but became a theatre soon afterwards. It has a 240 capacity seated or 350 standing.

Free Butt

1 Phoenix Place, Brighton BN2 9ND. T: 01273 603974
www.zelnet.com
freebutt@zelnet.co.uk
Along with the Pressure Point, this is indie heaven. Imagine a sticky floored

venue where it feels like the band is playing in your face and the sweat's running down the walls... Hang about; the band is playing in your face and the sweat's running down the wall. If that feels good, the Free Butt is for you. Tickets are usually around £5.

The Greys

105 Southover St, Hanover, Brighton BN2 9UA. T: 01273 680734
www.greyspub.com
chris@greyspub.com
Mon: 5.30pm-11pm, Tues and Wed: 11am-3pm, 5.30pm-11pm, Thurs-Sun: 11am-11pm
Entrance Fee: £5-£7
A fine old selection of Belgian beers aside – they're so in love with the stuff, they hold their own Belgian Beer Festival – this is the best place in town to hear proper acoustic music from folk to country.

Old Market

11a Upper Market St, Hove BN3 1AS. T: 01273 736222
www.theoldmarket.co.uk
Newly restored Romanesque forum in an old marketplace where the performance space is geared towards opera and acoustically correct theatre, though recently more respectable popsters have taken advantage of its civilised atmosphere.

Pressure Point

Richmond Place, Lewes Road, Brighton BN3 1AS
T: 01273 684501
Mon-Sun: 11.30am-11.30pm
Entrance Fee: £1.00-£6.00
Traditional indie venue above a pub. The walls are black and the floors are sticky after years of beer abuse. A good venue, and one of Brighton's stalwarts, if it's a guitar band you want, this is the place to look.

CHILDREN'S ACTIVITIES

ANIMALS

Mitchelswood Farm

Mitchelswood Farm, Newick,
Lewes BN8 4NH
T: 01825 722296 M: 07968
088974 F: 01825 724010
www.mitchelswoodfarm.com
seona@mitchelswoodfarm.
com
This riding school is for children only.
It is family run and prices start at £9
for half an hour for a novice, £12 for
one-hour group, and £12 for half an
hour private. They also run activity
days at £30 for a whole day or £15
for half a day or try a pony and pool
party at £15 per person for 3 hours.
All instructors are BSH qualified and
chosen for their childcare skills.

The Mohair Centre

Brickfield Farm, Laughton Rd,
Chiddingly, Lewes BN8 6JG
T: 01825 872457
Jacky and Martin run children's
courses in school holidays. Children
have the opportunity to learn
about all aspects of farming from
goat handling to spinning, shearing,
milking, tractor driving for the
older kids and making butter. Jacky
used to be a teacher so there is a
really nice mix of fun, learning and
discipline, which is essential on a
farm. Children return year after year.
Prices start from £20 and casual
visitors are welcome at the farm at
weekends. They also run an after
school activity club and will pick
your children up from schools in the
local area, give them tea at the farm
and keep them busy with things like
egg collecting until 6pm.

Rottingdean Riding School and Livery Yard

Chailey Avenue, Rottingdean,
Brighton BN2 7GH
T: 01273 302155
A great selection of lessons, all taken
by British Horse Society trained
instructors. Prices range between
£12-£15 per hour for a group lesson,
£15 for half an hour private lesson,
£15 for an hour hack and £6 for a
half hour lead. They also offer an
'Own a Pony' day for children. This
costs £35 and they get a hack, lesson
in stable management and lots of
competitions.

Sealife Centre

Marine Parade, Old Steine,
Brighton BN2 1TB
T: 01273 604233
www.sealifeeurope.com
Mon-Sat: 10am-6pm, Sun: 10am-
5pm
A fantastic old Victorian underwater
world, with little coves, ancient
shipwrecks and a glass tunnel
through a shark tank. Seahorses and
interactive information games, ray
feeding zones and even a bouncy

castle for afters. What more do kids
need to fire their imagination on a
rainy afternoon?

ARTS

Brighton Dome Youth Theatre Company

Church St, Brighton BN1 1UE
T: 01273 260821
www.brighton-dome.org.uk
Led by David Oyelowo of "Spooks"
fame, the Brighton Dome Youth
Theatre Company stages two
productions a year. Open to 16 to 21-
year-olds, it's an ideal launch pad for
really passionate talented youngsters
who may be hoping for a career in
the performing arts.

DANCE AND DRAMA

Alexandra Academy

11 Howard Rd, Elm Grove,
Brighton BN2 9TP
T: 01273 688991
Mon-Fri: 4pm-8.30pm, Sat: 9am-
12.30pm
Ballet, tap and modern classes which
keep Elm Grove and Hanover's little
girls looking like little girls for just
that bit longer.

Beacon Arts

Knoyle Hall, Knoyle Rd,
Preston Park, Brighton BN1
6RB. T: 01273 557124
www.beaconarts.co.uk
info@beaconarts.co.uk
Mon-Fri: 4pm-6.30pm
Centre for all types of dance for most
of Preston Park's little girls (and boys).

Dance Arts Studio

St Marys Hall, Surrenden Rd,
Brighton BN2 1HA
T: 01273 556313
Linda Forster is the younger
generation's dance angel from
Heaven. St Mary's Hall is a huge hall
with plenty of space for practicing
tap, ballet and modern, with exams
and shows for parents. She also holds
classes at Brighton College and other
venues in the city. After school.

Dance at The Dome

Church St, Brighton BN1 1UE
T: 01273 293524/01273 203032
www.brighton-dome.org.uk
pippa.smith@brighton-dome.
org.uk
Mon: 4.30pm, 5.45pm
Dance classes for 8-11 year olds and
11-18s at the glorious Dome.

Earwig Productions

7 Pembroke Avenue, Hove
BN3 5DA
www.earwig.mistral.co.uk/
summerga.htm
info@earwigproductions.co.uk
There are loads of ways of
entertaining the kids in the summer
holidays; you can plonk them in
front of the video, or cancel your life
for six weeks while you take them to
every pottery café, working farm or

picnic on the beach. Or you can sign
them up for Earwig's summer camps
at Brighton College and Gardner
Arts Centre where they'll learn
circus skills, singing, costume design,
drumming, drama and gain the kind
of confidence to make them shine.
The end of week shows will make
you cry.

Jo Cansell

Hanover Community
Centre, Southover St,
Hanover, Brighton
BN2 9UD
T: 01273 694873
Mon: 4pm-5:30pm, Tues: 4:30pm-
5:30pm, Wed: 4pm-4:30pm,Thurs:
5pm-6pm, term time only
No strict training, no exams, just
straight enjoyable ballet for little
bodies that are still growing.

Rox School of Dance and Drama

Unit 3, Hove Business Centre, Fonthill Rd, Brighton BN3 6HA
T: 01273 208513
Mon: 3.30pm-7.30pm, Tue: 3.30pm-7pm, Wed: 4pm-7pm, Thu: 4pm-9pm, Fri: 4pm-8pm, Sat: 10.30am-1pm
Modern, street and any other kind of dance you can shake your body to – for kids and grown ups.

Stonelands

170 Church Rd, Hove BN3 2DJ
T: 01273 770445
www.stonelandsschool.co.uk
dianacarteur@stonelandsschool.co.uk
Mon-Fri: 9am-5pm, Sat: 9am-4pm
Dance for all ages from three years up, this is a school for serious dancers – though how you know at three is a question.

Stagecoach

Varndean School Balfour Rd, Preston Park, Brighton BN1 6NA. T: 01273 747072
www.stagecoach.co.uk/brighton
hove@stagecoach.co.uk
Sat: 10am-1pm, 2.30pm-5.30pm, Sun 10am-1pm
Acting, singing and dancing classes for 4-16 year olds with inspiring performances at the end of term. It's expensive but three hours of weekend classes means that at least you get some time off from the little lovelies, and we've seen proof that it's a great way for budding stars to develop their performing arts

abilities confidently. Classes are also available in both Brighton and Hove.

Wendy Whatling School of Dance

74-76 Dyke Rd, Seven Dials, Brighton BN1 3JD
T: 01273 735 834
Mar-Sep: 9am-2pm, Oct-Feb: 10am-12pm
Great facilities which are slightly cramped, but extremely professional, with mirrors and Barres around the dance studio. Shows are put on regularly and pupils get the chance to audition for other stage productions outside of the classes. Wendy Whatling is very inspiring and fun, although she doesn't hold the other classes such as singing, drama, yoga, street jazz, belly dancing, pilates and flamenco herself.

FITNESS

Brighton and Hove Gym Club

St Agnes Church, Newtown Rd, Hove BN3 7DE
T: 01273 776209
Proper gymnastics for kids from one year and up with trampolines, monkey bars and a whole team of enthusiastic young gymnasts to inspire your kids. Classes are split between one to three year-olds, three to five year-olds and older kids, and take place throughout the day.

Brighton Health and Racquet Club

Village Way, Falmer, Brighton BN1 9SG. T: 01273 667800
www.esporta.co.uk
Mon-Fri: 6.30am-11pm, Sat-Sun: 8am-10pm
Tennis, badminton, yoga and an

T: 01273 327509
minimusic.
users@btopenworld.com
**Mon, Tue, Thur and Fri: 9.30am-
12.30pm**
Music classes for babies,
toddlers and pre-schoolers in
Hove, Portslade, and Steyning. The
classes in Hove are held at the
Cornerstone Community Centre
which is located on the corner of
First Avenue and Church Road. They
also provide entertainment for
private parties for young children
in Brighton and Hove and the
surrounding area.

Sing and Sign
91 Western Road, Brighton
BN1 2NW. T: 01273 700163
www.singandsign.com
info@signandsign.com
**Fri: 9.45am-10.30am, 10.45am-
11.30am**
Babysigners, the baby signing
people, are running classes where
parents can learn how to use sign
language with their babies before
they can talk. With songs, puppets
and stories, these playgroups are
based on Dr Joseph Garcia's award
winning programme.

indoor and outdoor pool that gets
packed with holidaying kids in the
summer. The supervised swims for
over-seven's and kids camps mean
that there can be life after kids.

**Mon: 9.30am, 10.30am, 11.30am,
2pm, 3pm, Tue: 9.30am, 10.30am,
11.30am, 1.15pm, 2.15pm.**
Music classes in Brighton and Hove
for kids at various venues.

LITTLE KIDS
Baby Signers
57 Bates Rd, Preston Park,
Brighton BN1 6PF
T: 01273 230956
www.babysigners.co.uk
Mon, Thurs and Fri: 9.30am-12pm
Baby signing is the new craze among
parents. This will help your baby
to tell you exactly what he or she
wants. Apparently.

Fiddlesticks Music
Garton House, Stanford
Avenue, Brighton BN1 6AA
T: 01273 273398
www.fiddlesticksmusic.co.uk

Happy Clappy
Church of the Good
Shepherd, Dyke Rd, Brighton
BN1 5AE. T: 01273 231428
www.happyclappymusic.com
Fri: 10am-12pm
£21 for 6 sessions. Groups are 6
months - 18 months, 2-4 years.
Combination of music, dance,
colour and parachute games.
Mums and dads are allowed in
and rewarded with tea and coffee
afterwards.

Mini Music
Holy Cross Church Hall,
Tamworth Rd, Hove BN3 5GZ

Tumble Tots
15 Lyndhurst Rd., Hove BN3
6FA. T: 01273 723511
www.tumbletots.com
Excellent mini gym sessions
mixed with singing and movement
for the under 4's. Classes are
held in Preston Park, Hove,
Haywards Heath. Morning and
evening classes are available.

Twinkle Twinkle

Bishop Hannington Church
Neville Avenue, Hove BN3
7NH. T: 01273 416360
Friday afternoon
Kids' music classes also held at the
Church of the Ascension in Hove.

PARTIES

Monkey Puzzle

39 Salisbury Rd, Hove BN3
3AA. T: 01273 725333
Mon-Fri: 4.30pm-6.30pm, Sat-Sun:
11am-6.30pm
Our favourite party venue for the
4-6 year group, this is bouncy castle
fun with the irrepressible Jamie to
keep the kids in check, providing all
the entertainment into the bargain.
Making birthdays really special, he
gets the kids to crawl into a cave to
sing to the birthday boys and girls.

Nosebag Arts Ltd

4 Rock St, Brighton BN2 1NF
T: 01273 623379
Mon-Fri: 9am-7pm
Party entertainers who bring out
the creative side of your kids with
hobby horse making and imagination
fuelling activities.

Paint and Pottery Café

31 North Rd, North Laine,
Brighton BN1 1YB
T: 01273 628952
www.paintingpotterycafe.co.uk
Mon-Sat: 10am-8pm, Sun: 11am-6pm
A great idea that has caught on
big time in B&H; buy the basic pot,
cup, plate or whatever you desire,
and spend the afternoon painting
it. Items start at £3, and you'll be

charged a firing fee of £4, which
brings it up to an expensive way of
entertaining the kids, but time it for
birthdays and Christmas and you're
laughing. On the first Thursday of
every month, late-night opening
times and a free buffet is on offer
to assist you in creating your
masterpieces.

Paint Pots

39 Trafalgar St, North Laine,
Brighton BN1 4ED
T: 01273 696682
Mon, Wed and Fri: 11am-7pm, Tue
and Thur: 11am-10pm, Sat: 11am-
6pm, Sun: 12pm-5pm
Painting pots isn't just for arty
kids; you can book your hen night,
birthday party or night out with the
girls and bring your own wine in too.
Owner, Vicky Rawlinson bakes and
glazes the pottery for you and you
pick it up 48 hours later.

PLAY

Brighton Pier

Brighton Pier, Seafront,
Brighton BN1 1TW
T: 01273 609361
www.brightonpier.co.uk
Mon-Sun: 10am-9pm
Show time every hour from 12.30-
5pm on Saturdays and Sundays starts
at Easter which consist of comedy
sketches, balloon and arty stuff, as
well as bags of old style fairground
attraction.

Candy Castle

Enterprise Point, Melbourne
St, off Lewes Rd, Brighton BN2
3LH. T: 01273 276060

www.candycastleplay.co.uk
info@candycastleplay.co.uk
Mon-Sun: 10am-6pm
Ear-splitting screams and vague
smells of wee are all part of the
charm of this bouncy castle in the
sky. Kiddy parties are catered for, but
mostly it's a top place to meet your
mates, get that document written or
read Hello while your kids go puce.

Deep Sea Pirates Den

The Saltdean Tavern Saltdean
Rd, Saltdean BN2 8SP
T: 01273 304614
Bouncy castles and fizzy drinks
attached to a pub perched on the
edge of a park. Bang next to the
Saltdean Lido and opposite the
beach, this could make for a top day
out for the whole family. Sessions
from 9.30am throughout the day up
till about 7pm and 9pm on Saturday.

SKIL: Sports for Kids in Laughton

Laughton Community
Primary School, Church Lane,
Laughton, Lewes BN8 6AH
T: 0774 0474477 T: 01273
812841
jim_gardiner@beeb.net
Holidays: 9.30am-3pm
James Gardiner is a fully qualified
primary school teacher. In the
holidays he provides children with a
fun and energetic alternative to the
play station in a rural environment.

Westows

Unit A, School Rd,
Hove, BN3 5HX.
T: 01273 711944 F: 01273 721338

CD Warehouse
163, Western Road 01273 731310
Possibly the best shop for CDs in Brighton. Stocks chart CDs at a reasonable price, and also some older music for as little as £5. Definitely worth a trip!

Churchill Square Shopping Centre
Whatever you're shopping for, whatever your tastes, you can't go wrong in Churchill Square. The greatest shopping centre around!

www.westows.com
info@westows@com
An adventure play area and bouncy castle for children with supervision. Staff are all trained in first aid and there are FA qualified coaches who will play footie with your littlies.

Teens
by Lara Hassell

The teens (and tweens!) of today's Brighton and Hove City will definitely squeeze the best out of it. But how should you do that? These juicy pieces of information should help you.

The Beach
The best place to be, and it's absolutely free! There are basketball courts, various cafés and, in the summer, you can swim. Also in the summer, of course, there's the sunbathing...

The Brighton Centre
Located on the seafront, this is an

ideal place to take advantage of what Brighton and Hove City has to offer. Possibly the best part has to be the indoor ice-rink, which occasionally hosts ice shows from time to time.

Brighton Palace Pier
A great place for an afternoon out! Rides for all ages, an arcade and food stalls, with fresh American doughnuts! A little on the expensive side, at 50p a token, but definitely worth it.

Brighton Youth Orchestra
The Brighton Youth Orchestra reaches its Diamond Jubilee in 2004. Features several different orchestras, so if you're a talented musician, check this out! 01273 643350

Brighton Youth Theatre
Arts and theatre arts workshops offered to 11-19 year-olds. Especially focuses on drama, dance and music. 01273 673211

The Marina
This is a fantastic place to go for the day. It's a long walk from the town centre, but you can catch a bus. There's a bowling alley, a few shops, and also some inexpensive restaurants.

Odeon Cinema
Kingswest, West Street
0870 5050006
In need for a bit of a clean, really, but if you want to catch the latest films, then this is the place to go. Add in great food, and you've got yourself a great time out!

Pavilion
Pavilion Buildings 01273 292822
Open all year round, this grand palace often hosts competitions and creative activities. You can also wander round, looking at the historic features. Definitely check out the gardens too—possibly the most beautiful and relaxing in Brighton!

Pizza Hut
Western Road 01273 327991
If you've never been to Pizza Hut, you're missing out on a lot. Serves yummy pizzas, as well as great pasta, and, if you're going for a healthier option, salad. This branch also has the famous Ice-Cream factory, where you can get as much ice-cream as you'll eat! 81,

Prince Regents Centre
Church St, Brighton BN1 1YA
01273 685692
This is right near the Pavilion, and perfect whether you're into sports or not. The best part has to be the huge pool, with a separate diving area, and water flumes!

Rag Freak
15, Cranbourne Street, The Lanes
01273 775117
A Goth's paradise, with clothes, chunky jewellery and accessories for anyone who's in touch with their darker personality.

What's New
King's Road 01273 202881
Tiny, but definitely worth a visit. Full of strange gadgets for all ages.

Withit
150, Western Road 01273 777868
It's a small, sweet shop with fabulous stationary on sale, and loads of cute gifts for friends and family. It's a good shop to go to if you're strapped for cash.

TWEENAGE BRIGHTON
By Elly Novick (8)

Living in Brighton is really good fun because there are loads of really fun activities.

Bungee jumping on the seafront because when you're in the air you feel like you're flying and it's really exciting.

Trampolining on the Pier because it's really fun. You can do loads of good tricks, and it's really cool because when you're in the air you

can look over the sea.

Seven Sisters Country Park because you can hire a bike and go out with your family and it feels really good. There are lots of lovely wild creatures in the woods.

The Bear Factory in Churchill Square because there are loads of nice people and they treat the bears like they're alive and take really good care of them.

Rollerblading on the seafront because it's nice and flat and you can see the waves while you're skating.

My favourite restaurant is The Emperor of China in the Marina because the food is really good and they're really kind to children.

I like the puddings at Moshi Moshi and the children can run around outside while the mums and dads are in the restaurant.

I love St Lukes Juniors because the children are really fun and the teachers are really kind. We've got our own swimming pool and so we can get free swimming lessons.

SPORT AND LEISURE

Dance

All Saints

All Saints Church Hall, Eaton Rd, Hove BN3 3PB
T: 01273 736974
Tues: 60 plus: 2pm-3.30pm, all ages: 7.30pm-9.30pm
Line dancing classes for wannabe cowboys of all ages. Classes are £2.50 in the afternoon and £3.50 in the evening.

Circus Circus

Preston Circus, Brighton BN1 4QF. T/F: 01273 620026
www.circus-circus.biz
info@circus-circus.biz
Tues and Thurs: 7.30pm-10.45pm
Forties rock'n'roll dance lessons in Lindy Hop and Jive.

Club New York

Dyke Rd, Brighton BN1 3FE
www.club-newyork.co.uk
info@club-newyork.co.uk
Mon-Sat: 8pm-10pm
Two hour lesson before the club begins rocking at 10.30pm.

Dance Laines

83 Gloucester Rd, Brighton BN1 4AP. T: 01273 697115
www.dancelaines.co.uk
info@dancelaines.co.uk

Esther Juan teaches children and adults British Ballet Organisation syllabus in her own, beautiful dance centre in the heart of the North Laine. Esther is considered to be one of the best teachers around and has

done Pointe Shoe fittings for the Moscow City Ballet. She has spent her career developing a new kind of Pointe shoe that does not damage your feet. Lessons must be pre-booked and start at £6.

Tango Argentina

Southwick Leisure Centre, Southwick
T: 01273 772462
Get onto this craze early and you will be so cool when the rest of the UK catches on.

Hilal at Evolution

2 Sillwood Terrace, Brighton BN1 2LR. T: 01273 204204
www.evolutionarts.co.uk
info@evolutionarts.co.uk
To make an appointment: Mon-Fri: 10.15am-1pm
Egyptian contemporary dance with a half hour yoga warm up first, this is a really fun way to keep fit and let your hair down. Jane also holds classes at the University of Brighton

DO IT YOURSELF

Bowlplex

Marina Way, Marina, Brighton BN2 5UT
T: 01273 818180
F: 01273 606007
www.bowlplexuk.com
Mon-Sun: 9.30am-late

Huge, bright and brash, this is like walking inside a pinball machine – a real sensory attack – but for most of the kids who go there,

that's cool. Still, it's a fun day/night out – just remember to phone and book a lane. There are 26 lanes and a 2am licence six nights a week. Prices range from £3.45 to Friday and Saturday nights when everyone pays £4.80 and – they proudly announce – no hidden charges. Shoe hire is free and there are special student nights on a Sunday, when bowling costs £1.50. If you're interested in joining a team go along on a Monday or Thursday. There's a burger grill, pool tables and slot machines. What more could anyone reasonably ask?

Brighton and Hove Hockey Club

Preston Park Cricket Ground, Brighton. T: 01273 389945
www.brightonandhovehockeyclub.net
Open to all ages and abilities, whether you're an expert or just have dim memories of playing at school. If you're interested in joining, phone the number above or go along to meet them at Sussex University, where they play on astro turf every Wednesday night 8-10pm.

Brighton Rugby Club

Waterhall Playing Fields, Mill Rd, BN1 8YN. T: 01273 562729
www.brightonrugby.co.uk
email@brightonrugbyclub.fsnet.co.uk
Brighton Rugby Club was founded in 1868 making it one of the first recorded rugby clubs in the country. They run 4 senior teams and a vibrant, thriving youth section

that has been running since 1999. All standards are welcome. The facilities are superb and include 2 out of the 5 pitches being floodlit. The club is friendly and sociable, membership also being valid for Palmers Bar in the city centre (Queen Square), which is run by the club.

Cycle Training South East
St Margarets Place, Brighton BN1 2FD
T: 01273 729979/07814 257495
www.cycletrainingse.co.uk
info@cycletrainingse.co.uk
Cycle Training is a not for profit organisation dedicated to promoting good cycling practice serving the whole of East and West Sussex. They teach everyone from beginners to people who want to lean about cycle maintenance.

Life Cycle
The Tile House, Preston Park, Preston Rd, Brighton, BN1 6HN
T: 01273 542425
www.lifecycle.com
lifecyclist@aol.com
Life Cycle hire and sell bikes in Preston Park, and on a sunny day, there's nothing better than hiring a family bike that will seat up to five. They cater for all your biking requirements, from trikes to family bikes and mobility solutions for those with special needs they'll even think up a way for you to get you dog to work by bike.

The Regency Pool Club
West St, Brighton BN1 2RA

T: 01273 821888
Mon-Sat: 11am-11pm, Sun: 11am-10.30pm

Eight American pool tables, a bar, a huge Plasma TV screen for all those sporting must-sees and right in the centre of town. Membership was an introductory £5 as we went to press.

Sussex Ice Rink
Queens Square, Brighton BN1 3FD. T: 01273 324677
Tiny, grotty little ice rink which you can hire out for parties. You can almost hear its death rattle, as plans for the new ice world get under way at Black Rock.

Thunder Football
Waterhall Playing Fields, nr Brighton and Hove Rugby Club, BN1 8YU
T: 01273 596060
www.sussex-thunder.co.uk
gary.whitfield@sussex-thunder.co.uk
American football league for those who like their sport a little rougher. This team, which used to draw crowds of up to 3000 at Withdean has been through hard times recently but is on the up and up with new coach Warren Smart taking the helm, hoping to propel the team back to its former glory. Requirements for joining are simply interest, enthusiasm, dedication and Warren will do the rest. A yearly subscription is £170 with kit and membership to the Rugby Club included. There is a junior

team (7-15), a youth team under development and they are on the hunt for a cheer leading squad, so if mud and pain isn't your thing then get your pom-poms out.

GOLF

There are six golf clubs in the Brighton & Hove area which are all listed below, but if you need any further assistance, or you want to know about clubs in the county, contact the East Sussex County Golf Union on 01273 589791. For membership costs and green fees, see www.juicymapminder.co.uk

Brighton And Hove Golf Club
Dyke Road, Brighton BN1 8YJ
T: 01273 556482

Dyke Golf Club
Dyke Road, Brighton BN1 8YJ
T: 01273 857296

East Brighton Golf Club
Roedean Road, Brighton BN2 5RA. T: 01273 604838

Hollingbury Park Golf Club
Ditchling Road, Brighton BN1 7HS. T: 01273 552010

Waterhall Golf Club
Mill Road, Brighton BN1 8YN
T: 01273 508658

West Hove Golf Club
Church Farm, Hove BN3 8AN
T: 01273 419738

GYMS

For membership costs
and current deals, see
www.juicymapminder.co.uk

Alive

Castle St, Brighton BN1 2HD
T: 01273 739606 F: 01273 324075
www.alivehealth.co.uk
sales@alivehealth.co.uk
Mon-Fri: 7.30am-9.30pm, Sat-Sun:
9am-6pm

Fitness and natural health centre
with gym, sauna, sunbed and an
extensive range of classes including
yoga, aerobics and dance. Virtually
every complementary therapy is
on offer: aromatherapy massage,
shiatsu and cranial osteopathy.
Membership starts at around £30
a month, but there are loads of
different options.

Coral Health & Fitness

Orchard Rd, Hove BN3 7BG
T: 01273 731262 F: 01273 202058
sales@coralfitness.co.uk
Mon-Fri: 7am-10pm, Sat: 8.30am-
8pm, Sun: 9am-8pm

The facilities include cardiovascular
and weights area, squash courts,
aerobics, crèche, sunbeds, sauna,
health suite and lounge bar. Non-
members can pay £3.50 for squash
courts in off peak hours.

David Lloyd Leisure

Marina, Brighton BN2 5UF
T: 01273 666401/666405

www.davidlloydleisure.co.uk
Mon-Fri: 6.30am-11pm, Sat-Sun:
8am-11pm

Two years ago, this gym where you
can pump your inner thighs while
looking out to sea was rated 54th
out of the 58 David Lloyds around
the country by its customers. A
change of management and a
sharpening up of customer relations,
flexible rates and upgrading the
equipment and the staff has
catapulted it to number two. It's
probably not your choice if you've
got kids; Esporta is only up the road
and is kiddie heaven – which is why
if you haven't got any, so is this.

Dragons Health Club

St Heliers Ave, Hove BN3 5RE
T: 01273 724211 F: 01273 735860
www.dragons.co.uk
hove-sales@dragons.co.uk
Mon-Fri: 7am-11pm, Sat: 8am-9pm,
Sun: 9am-9pm

Said to be a favourite among
young singles (isn't that what gyms
are for?), the swimming pool and
beauty therapies attract a less iron-
pumping crowd off-peak. Crèche
facilities, ballet classes for members'
kids, resident osteopath and sports
massage mark it out plus the fact
that Peter Andre was spotted flexing
his abs here earlier this year.

Esporta (The Health And Racquet Club)

Village Way, Falmer, Brighton

BN1 9SG. T: 01273 667800
F: 01273 667878
www.esporta.com
membershipmanager.
brighton@esporta.com
Mon-Fri: 6.30am-11pm, Sat-Sun:
8am-10pm

Enormous and probably the best in
town. It's a bit of a drive for anyone
who doesn't live on campus at the
University of Sussex, but with its
top-of-the-range tennis and squash
courts, gym and swimming pool
(including an outdoor heated pool),
it's worth it. They welcome children,
with supervised swimming for able
over-sevens, tennis, badminton,
netball, kids camps, crèche facilities
and kiddie yoga on offer while you
work out. Unsurprisingly, it's packed
with families.

Fresh Start Fitness for Women

78 Queens Rd, Brighton BN1
3XE. T: 01273 220931
Women-only gym with no wet
areas, this is for yoga, aerobics and
workouts with the girls.

Gym and Tonic

Queen Victoria Avenue, Hove
BN3 6XA. T: 01273 505459
ialesliegt@yahoo.co.uk
By appointment
Ian Leslie is personal trainer to
Brighton's movers and shakers,
and it's almost impossible to get
an appointment. It's worth trying
though; his gym is well equipped
and just big enough for Ian and

his client – which means no distractions and full-on attention to those abs, glutes and pecs. Using a combination of Pilates and fitness training, he knows how to get your centre strong, and the rest of the body follows.

King Alfred Leisure Centre
Kingsway, Hove BN3 2WW
T: 01273 290290/01273 292990
www.kingalfredleisure.co.uk
Mon-Fri: 7.15am-11.45pm, Fri: 7.15am-10pm, Sat-Sun: 7.15pm-10pm

Open seven days a week but times vary each day with adults only, ladies only and kids fun sessions throughout the week. One of the draws is the swimming pool, complete with bridges and some serious (and we mean serious) flumes. There's also a cardiovascular gym and a sports hall for aerobics and badminton. Membership costs around £40 a month.

LA Fitness
Tower Point 44 North Rd, North Laine, Brighton BN1 1YR
T: 01273 685868
www.lafitness.co.uk
Mon-Fri: 6.30am-10pm, Sat-Sun: 8am-8pm

Dead handy gym bang in the centre of town. There are all the usual machines, wet areas and personal trainers.

Prince Regent Pool
Church St, Brighton BN1 1YA
T: 01273 685692
Mon-Fri: 7am-9.30pm, Sat: 9am-5pm, 9am-9.30pm

A swimming pool in the middle of town where there's a free crèche Tuesday and Thursday mornings – and that means you can have a stress-free swim. There are four pools and a health and fitness suite. Open from 7am-10pm on weekdays and 9am-6pm at weekends, but the times and types of session vary. There are lessons, exercise classes, sunbeds and a sauna. Adults pay £2.70 for a swimming session, children (between 4 and 17) £1.40.

Riptide
Kings Rd Arches, Brighton BN1 1NB. T: 01273 725444
www.riptide.co.uk
manager@riptide.co.uk
Mon-Fri: 7am-9pm, Sat-Sun: 8am-7pm

Situated on the beach between the piers at the bottom of West Street and open all week from 7am to 10pm. There's a fully equipped gym, classes including circuit training, crewing, T'ai Chi, yoga, sauna and a TV lounge area. There's no pool, but for the really keen, the sea is a few yards away. Spinning classes (aerobics on a bike) and crewing classes (aerobics on a rowing machine) are a speciality. In the summer the windows open onto a sea view.

Saltdean Lido
Saltdean Park Rd, Saltdean, Brighton BN2 8SP
T: 01273 880616
Opened in the 1930's by Johnny Weismuller, this is a good, proper lido just like they should be. The swimming pool is open from the end of May to the end of September, 7am-9pm Monday to Friday and 9am-6pm at weekends.

Withdean Sports Complex
Tongdean Lane, Withdean, Brighton BN1 5JE
T: 01273 542100 F: 01273 562699
Mon-Fri: 7am-10pm, Sat-Sun: 8am-10pm

Body combat, body pump, supple strength, power and all sorts of classes to get the body you've dreamed of as well as a fitness suite, health spa with wet areas and racquet courts. It's also home to the excellent Phoenix Running and Athletics Club. (www.brightonphoenix.org).

HORSE RIDING

Ashdown Forest Riding Centre
White House Farm
Duddleswell, Uckfield TN22 3JA. T: 01825 712108
F: 01825 712854

Set in the beautiful Ashdown Forest, this riding school offers lesson for adults and children, although our sources say they are better for adults. It specialises in riding for those with special needs. Lessons start at £13 for a group lesson, £20 for half an hour private lesson, £22 for one hours hack through the forest and there is the opportunity for children to go on Pony Days (£25 per day). All instructors are British Horse Society qualified and insured.

PARKS

Blaker's Park
Cleveland Rd, Preston Park, Brighton BN1 6HN
Lovely little kiddie-friendly park out in leafy residential Preston Park. There's a well-tended playground and two tennis courts in good nick.

Hollingbury Playground
Ditchling Rd, Brighton BN1 7HS
An odd playground with tennis courts backing onto it, set off one of the main thoroughfares into Brighton. The pile of old tyres with slide, pouring kids from top to bottom attracts boy racers – but they tend to be about 10 and on a Chopper.

Hove Park
Goldstone Crescent, Hove, BN3 7BF
Well kept park with a great children's playground, model railway, great café and tennis courts.

Hove Seafront Playground
The Ellipse, by the West Pier, Hove BN1 2LN
Kids climbing frames, sand pits and paddling pool on the seafront.

Peter Pan Playground
Madeira Drive, Kemp Town, Brighton, BN2 1EN
Part of Kemp Town's regeneration, this new playground has "magic fountains" and climbing frames for smaller kids. There's a café, and plans for toilets.

Queen's Park
Queen's Park, Brighton, BN2 2GA
Beautiful park with a lake, children's playground, rockery and café.

St Ann's Well
Nitzells Ave, Hove, BN3 1PR
Perfect park in Hove with two playgrounds – one with whizzy zip wires and big kid stuff, and another with sandpits and little kid stuff. A café, tennis courts, a well with a little bridge and squirrels for the dogs to chase – this is the life.

Stanmer Park
Lewes Rd, Brighton BN1 9PZ
Brighton's largest park, with woodland areas, an old manor house and gardens, small dairy farm, Brighton Council's greenhouses and a great café. Perfect for summer picnics under the cedar trees, and circular walks into the woods.

TENNIS

Council courts are in just about every park in Brighton and Hove. You can't pre-book, but most of the courts have clubs attached. The best bet is to turn up and someone will either kick you off or collect payment. The city is extraordinarily pro-active in promoting tennis to budding young Henmans and has its own tennis development officer at the Council. Call Nicky Salmon: 01273 292570 for a list of clubs attached to the council courts, or check out www. juicymapminder.co.uk

Badgers Tennis Club

Church Place, Kemp Town,
Brighton BN2 5JN
T: 01273 677795

Four tennis courts in a hidden little corner of Kemp Town. Kids can learn to play mini-tennis from four years old, with indoor coaching up the road at the Manor Gym. Members can take guests in for £5 per session up to six times a year.

Esporta (The Health And Racquet Club)

Village Way, Falmer, Brighton BN1 9SG. T: 01273 667800
F: 01273 667878
www.esporta.com
membershipmanager.
brighton@esporta.com
See Gyms section.

Preston Lawn Tennis Club

Preston Drove, Preston Park,
Brighton BN1 6LA
T: 01273 505731
www.prestonltc.co.uk
membership@prestonltc.co.uk
Six Macadam, two Astroturf and two grass courts at this private tennis club just next to Preston Park where kids and adult coaching is available.

WATCHING

Brighton and Hove Albion Football Club

Withdean Stadium, Tongdean Lane, Withdean, Brighton BN1 5JE. T: 01273 695400/776992
F: 01273 648179
www.seagulls.co.uk

seagulls@bhasc.co.uk
Mon-Fri: 9am-5.30pm

With a bit of luck – well OK, an act of God – by the time you read this, all the information here will be redundant. The football club will have a proper ground and will be treated like something Brighton's proud of. Well, we can dream. Without the financial support a proper ground would provide, there's little hope of progress. Right now The Seagulls are in the Second Division battling for promotion. They've got a good team and great support and if John Prescott would get his finger out...

Brighton Bears Basket Ball

Sports Centre, University of Brighton, Falmer, Brighton BN1 9RB. T: 01273 697400
www.brightonbears.com
info@brightonbears.com
A big and bright sport that's taken some of the American razzmatazz and transferred it to the rather less glitzy surrounds of the Brighton Centre. Going to the basketball is a fun way to spend an evening. It's exciting to watch, noisy and fast. You don't need to know anything about the game and it's over before you get bored. Prices range from £11 for an unreserved adult ticket to £32 for a two up, two down family ticket.

Brighton Racecourse

Freshfield Rd, Brighton BN2 9XZ. T: 01273 603580

F: 01273 673267
www.brighton-racecourse.co.uk
info@brighton-racecourse.co.uk
Mon-Fri: 9am-5.30pm and on race days

From April, flat racing kicks off. If you've got kids, make sure you go to the Family Fun Days on Sundays where you can flutter on the Arab stallions while the kids bounce on the bouncy castle.

Coral Greyhound Track

Nevill Road, Hove BN3 7BZ
T: 01273 204601
hove.stadium@coral.co.uk
Mon, Wed and Fri: 9am-5.30pm,
Tues, Thurs and Sat: 9am-10.30pm,
Sun: 10am-2pm

Racing takes place Tuesday, Thursday and Saturday evenings (£4 and £5), Wednesday afternoons (free) and Sunday lunchtimes (free).

Sussex County Cricket Club

The County Ground, Eaton Road, Hove BN3 3AN
T: 01273 827100
The home of cricket. When the weather's fine and you've got a bit of time on your hands, is there a finer way to spend an afternoon? For details of matches and times, check www.juicymapminder.co.uk If you want to get involved in village cricket and want advice on how to contact your local team, the Sussex Cricket Board at the County Ground will be able to help you out.

WATERSPORTS

Throughout the year, the sea is awash with surfers; that Surfers Against Sewage has opened its only branch outside Cornwall tells you how popular it is here. To the uninitiated the waves don't look enticing enough to get your kit off for in the middle of winter, but there are enough bottoms being hauled into wet suits on the beaches east of the Marina, around the West Pier and at Hotpipes behind the Old Power Station at Shoreham to prove us wrong. Surfing around the West Pier in probably the most laid-back, with the longer established East Marina surfies less likely to share their breaks. For a tide timetable, ring the Marina (01273 819919). A useful website is www. sharkbait.co.uk

Boost
Victoria Terrace, Kingsway, Hove BN3 2WB
T: 01273 721100 F: 01273 721100
www.boostsports.com
info@boostsports.com
Mon-Sun: 10am-5pm, closed on Monday outside summer time

The brains and energy behind Brighton's Kitesurfing championships, this is the place to get your gear, your lessons and to meet anyone who has anything to do with the sport. Seb and Paul will organise your weekend if you're coming down for the thrill, with weekends in Blanch House and Pelirocco, evenings at The Alibi and long days on the beach waiting for the waves.

Brighton Sailing Club
109 Kings Rd Arches, Brighton BN1 2FN. T: 01273 321802
www.brightonsailingclub.org.uk
infobrightonsc@yahoo.co.uk

You don't need your own boat to join, but as there are few crew places available it helps. The club meets every Wednesday after 8pm and races on Sunday mornings from late March to early November.

Hove Lagoon
Kingsway, Hove BN3 4LX
T: 01273 424842 F: 01273 421919
www.hovelagoon.co.uk
info@hovelagoon.co.uk
If you're a complete beginner in seagoing activities, it's probably best to learn the ropes at Hove Lagoon (01273 424842; windsurf@hovelagoon.co.uk) which – and this is the reassuring bit – is only four feet deep. Their fully trained staff teach RYA courses in sailing, windsurfing, canoeing and just about any other water sport you can think of. Local schools such as Varndean, Thomas A'Beckett and St Christopher's make good use of the facilities for their older kids.

Neilson Active Holidays
Lockview, Brighton Marina, Brighton, BN2 5HA.
T: 01273 666064/0870 909 9099
www.neilson.com
Neilson UK Sailing offer a range of RYA sailing courses on a fleet of six Sigma Eight yachts. Level one and two Keel boat course run over two days each, mainly at the weekends, and are the first two steps for getting you on the water. No experience or special equipment is required, just the urge to master the elements. Courses start from £195.

DAYS OUT

Blackberry Farm

Whitesmiths, Uckfield, E
Sussex BN8 6JD
T: 01825 872912
www.blackberry-farm.co.uk
info@blackberry-farm.co.uk
Summer: 10am-5pm, Winter:
10am-4pm. Entrance Fee: Adults
£4, children £3.50

Stroking, grooming and even feeding
small farm animals is a three-year-
olds idea of heaven, and the fact that
it's largely undercover is a parent's.
Blackberry Farm also offers camping
facilities and – get this – mini breaks
for 8-12-year-olds working with the
farmer, grooming and feeding the
animals and tacking the ponies. It was
in the process of being taken over
as we went to press so they weren't

taking any bookings until they can be
sure that the new owners can keep
the spirit of Blackberry alive.

Chessington World of Adventures

Chessington, Surrey KT9 2NE
T: 01372 727227
www.chessington.co.uk
Entrance Fee: Adults £26.00,
under-11s are free. There are all
sorts of family deals available,
Check www.juicymapminder.co.uk
for offers.

Fun for all the family as long as you
can afford the theme park price of
£19.50 for adults and a staggering
£15.50 for the 4-13's. It's only open
from April to October but kids love
Cartoonland and Dragon Falls.

Drusilla's Park

Alfriston, E Sussex BN26 5QS
T: 01323 874100
www.drusillaszoo.co.uk
info@drusillas.co.uk
Mon-Fri: Summer: 10am-5pm,
Winter: 10am-4pm. Entrance Fee:
Adult £9.99, over-13s £9.49

Fantastic small animal zoo with
creative workshops, train, and huge
picnic area with play apparatus
for bigger kids and play barn for
toddlers. And – top fun – a meer cat
enclosure you can 'get inside' through
an underground Perspex tunnel.

Fishers Farm Park

Newpound Lane, Wisborough
Green, Nr Billingshurst,
W Sussex RH14 0EG

T: 01403 700 063
www.fishersfarmpark.co.uk
info@fishersfarmpark.co.uk
Mon-Sun: 10am-5pm

Pony & Horse rides, tractor-trailer
& combine harvester rides, animal
barns and demonstrations, giant
trampolines, bouncy castles...
Fun for all the family. A nice
combination of farmyard stuff with
kids play activities.

The Bluebell Railway

Sheffield Park Station,
Sheffield Park, W Sussex TN22
3QL. T: 01825 722370
www.bluebell-railway.co.uk
info@bluebell-railway.co.uk
Entrance Fee: Unlimited travel
between Sheffield Park and
Kingscote for £8.50 for adults and
£4.20 for 3-16s

For steam enthusiasts of all ages, a
real life Thomas the Tank Engine is
great for birthdays and days out. Go
to the Griffin for lunch, or take a
picnic and get off along the way.

Observatory Science Centre

Hailsham, E Sussex BN27 1RN
T: 01323 832731
www.the-observatory.org
info@the-observatory.org
Mon-Sun: 10am-5pm,
Apr-Sept: 10am-6pm
Entrance Fee: Adults £5.80,
children £4.20

Originally the home of the Royal
Greenwich Observatory, this is just
the job for budding scientists.

Tulley's Farm

Turners Hill Rd, Turners Hill,
Crawley, W Sussex RH10 4PE
T: 01342 715365
www.tulleysfarm.com
shop@tulleysfarm.com
Mon-Sun: 9am-5pm
Entrance Fee: Free
Masses of seasonal activities
at this child friendly farm with
Easter hunts, Christmas grottos
and Halloween horrors as well as
a Maize maze in the summer. They
also do PYO crops.

Washbrook Farm

Brighton Rd, Hurstpierpoint, E
Sussex BN6 9EF
T: 01273 832201
www.washbrooks.com
Mon-Sun: 9.30am-5pm

500 yards from Hurstpierpoint,
there are animals in barns to feed, a
playground, tractor rides, a tea room
and seasonal excitement like Easter
egg hunts.

Ashdown Forest

Wych Cross, Nr Forest Row,
E Sussex RH18 5JP
T: 01342 823583/F: 01342 824177
Emergency: 01342 822846
www.ashdownforest.co.uk
conservators@ashdownforest.
fsnet.co.uk
Originally enclosed in 1296m this is
reputedly the place which inspired

AA Milne's Pooh sticks episode.
It's a beautiful place anyway, and a
lovely dog walk.

Borde Hill

Haywards Heath, E Sussex
RH16 1XP. T: 01444 412151
www.borde.hill.co.uk
Mon-Sun: 10am-5pm. Entrance
Fee: £3.50 adults, £3 children
200 acres of parkland, bluebell
woods and pirates adventure play
area, walks, lake and wood.

Devils Dyke

Devil's Dyke Rd, Brighton,
E Sussex BN1 8YJ
T: 01273 886200
www.devilsdyke.co.uk
The story goes that The Devil came
to a Brighton priest and said 'Priest,
I want your church and I will take it
if I must'. The Priest replied 'Devil,
you can have my church if, you
can dig your way to the sea before
the cock crows, but if you fail you
must promise to leave here and
never return'. The Devil agreed and
began digging. He was nearly at the
sea and the sun was about to rise,
so the old priest lit a candle and
prayed. He placed the candle in
the window of the church so that
the stained glass shone like sunrise.
When the cock saw this he began to
crow and The Devil was banished.
And that is how The Dyke got its
name. And God rewarded the priest
by making the Dyke a great place to
fly a kite. And that's a true story.

High Beeches Gardens

High Beeches Lane,

Handcross, W Sussex RH17 6HQ. T: 01444 400589
www.highbeeches.com
gardens@highbeeches.com
19th Mar-30th June and 1st Sep-31st Oct, Mon, Tues, Thurs, Fri and Sun: 1pm-5pm1pm

20 acres of enchanting landscaped, woodland and water gardens with winding paths and open glades and rippling streams and waterfalls. The gardens are not really suitable for wheelchairs but there are disabled facilities.

Lavender Line

T: 01825 750515
www.lavender-line.co.uk
Most Sundays throughout the year, 10am-5pm every weekend in summer, plus Saturdays in June, July-August and December
Twenties style train ride for steam lovers, The Lavender Line is part of the former Lewes, Barcombe, Isfield to Uckfield railway opened on October 18th 1858. In its heyday, this was the way to travel from London to Sussex.

Llama Trekking

Hassocks, E Sussex
T: 01273 835656
www.slt.uk.com
southdowns@llamatrekking.co.uk
Call to arrange
Treks cost £50 for 2 people and a llama, £35 for one person and a llama and, curiously, £20 for one person and no llama.

Llama trekking is big in Brighton. Not that we know anyone who's done it, but the leaflets are everywhere, and it's hailed by the Tourist folk as the thing to do, so what's a bit of hype between neighbours? It's not cheap but if you do it and if you really fall for it... there's an Adopt-A-Llama link on the website. There's also corporate days out: As it says "If you are stressed at work, come and be calmer with a llama".

Middle Farm

Firle, E Sussex BN8 6LJ
T: 01323 811411
www.middlefarm.com
info@middlefarm.com
Nov-Mar, Mon-Sun: 9.30am-5pm,
Apr-Oct, Mon-Sun: 9.30am-6pm
Entrance Fee; £1

£1 gets you in to see small animals, and watch the milking of the Jersey herd at 3.30pm. There's a kids wooden play area, teashop, cider barn, organic food store and craft shop with picnic tables outside. The Apple Festival in mid October has live music, hot mulled cider, a fairground, horse and cart races, toffee apple dunking and all things British and attracts about 3,500 people.

Paradise Park

Avis Rd, Newhaven, E Sussex
BN9 0DH. T: 01273 512123
www.paradisepark.co.uk
enquiries@paradisepark.co.uk

Mon-Sun: 9am-6pm

Garden centre with botanic gardens and water gardens as well a fossil collection, dinosaur exhibition and rides for the kids. And there's a café.

Seven Sisters Sheep Centre

East Dean, Eastbourne, E Sussex BN20 0DG. T: 01323 423207
www.sheepcentre.co.uk
info@sheepcentre.co.uk
Mon-Fri: 2pm-5pm, Sat, Sun and holidays: 11am-5pm.

Beautifully kept, all the animals are very well looked after, and the tea rooms are new. Stoneywish also boasts one of the biggest bunnies in Sussex.

The Cuckoo Trail
Polegate, T: 01323 442667
24 hours a day

Running from Heathfield to Polegate, this is bike ride or walkers' heaven. Cuckoos hide beneath or within each of the mileposts designed by Sussex artists to thrill small children. Park at Polegate or join at any point along the 11-mile trail.

Wakehurst Place
Ardingly, Haywards Heath, East Sussex RH17 6TN.
T: 01444 894066
www.kew.org
wakehurst@kew.org
Mon-Sun: 10am-dusk

Sheep, yes there are sheep, but if you also like pigs, goats, calves, rabbits and chicks fear not because they're here too. Kids - that is, children - can help with bottle-feeding the lambs.

Sheffield Park Gardens
Sheffield Park, Nr Uckfield, E Sussex TN22 3QX
T: 01825 790231
www.nationaltrust.org.uk/places/sheffieldpark
2nd Mar-31st Oct, Tues-Sun: 10.30am-6pm, Nov-Dec 23rd,

Tues-Sun: 10.30-4pm

Blissful landscaped gardens just opposite the Bluebell Railway laid out in the 18th century by Capability Brown. The centrepiece is the original four lakes, and gorgeous shows of stunning flowers throughout the seasons are worth the 40-minute trek out of Brighton.

Stoneywish Country Park
Spatham Lane, Ditchling, E Sussex BN6 8XH
T: 01273 843498
Mon-Sun: 9.30-5pm

Country estate of Kew Gardens and home to the new £80m Millennium Seed Bank project which aims to save thousands of endangered plant species from extinction. It's got an interactive exhibition to explain the project and the chance to look into the laboratories and see the scientists at work. Wakehurst has 180 acres of botanical gardens and wood. There's also the Elizabethan mansion, a gift shop, and restaurant.

Medieval adventures with battlements and 14th century games with real bows and arrows. Children can try on the armour and watch jousting in the summer.

Charleston Farmhouse
Firle, E Sussex BN8 6PA
T: 01323 811626
www.charleston.org.uk
info@charleston.org.uk
Apr-Oct, Wed-Sun and bank holidays: 2pm-6pm, July and Aug, Wed-Sat: 11am-6pm

Open from April to October, Charleston houses the astonishing collection of artworks that Vanessa Bell and Duncan Grant, her lifelong partner, amassed throughout their lives there. Look out for the Gouache table tops, experimental painting on the backs of doors and picnic plates, Picassos and Matisses abandoned in dark halls, and some of the first Post-Impressionist work casually scattered throughout the house, illustrating the spontaneous creativity, which characterised their lives. Sister to Virginia Wolf, Vanessa Bell and her avant garde pals summed up the spirit of The Bloomsbury Set.

Wilderness Wood
Hadlow Down, E Sussex TN22 4HJ. T: 01825 830509
www.wildernesswood.co.uk
enquiries@wildernesswood.co.uk
Mon-Sun: 10am-5.30pm or dusk if earlier. Entrance Fee: Adults: £3, Cons: £2.50, Children £1.80

A privately owned, family run woodland in an area of outstanding natural beauty. There are trails, picnic areas, a playground, BBQ's for hire, tearooms and a tea garden. The wood is stunning in April/May when the bluebells are out. Dogs are welcome if controlled.

Wildfowl & Wetlands Trust
Mill Rd, Arundel, E Sussex BN18 9PB. T: 01903 883355
www.wwt.org.uk
info.arundel@wwt.org.uk
Mon-Sun: 9.30am-5.30pm (4.30pm in the winter)

Founded in 1946 by artist and naturalist Sir Peter Scott to improve interaction between wildlife and people. There are ducks, geese and swans, one of the biggest reed beds in Sussex and an award winning visitor centre.

Battle Abbey
High St, Battle, E Sussex BN33 0AD. T: 01424 773792
www.eng-h.gov.uk/ArchRev/rev95_6/batabb.htm
info@englishheritage.co.uk
1st Apr-1st Nov, Mon-Sun: 10am-6pm (dusk in Oct), 2nd Nov-31st Mar, Mon-Sun: 10am-4pm

Guided tour through one of history's bloodiest moments in 1066, and the abbey ruins. Children's play area.

Bodiam Castle
Bodiam, E Sussex BN32 5UA
T: 01580 830436
www.nationaltrust.org.uk/places/bodiamcastle
Mon-Sun: 10am-5pm

Chartwell
Mapleton Rd, Westerham, Kent, TN16 1PS. T: 01732 868381
www.nationaltrust.org.uk
chartwellchartwell@nationaltrust.org

Stately home to Winston Churchill for more than 40 years.

Firle Place

Firle, E Sussex BN8 6LP
T: 01273 858307
www.firleplace.co.uk
gage@firleplace.co.uk
Sun, Wed and Thurs from June 2nd-September 28th

A beautiful old house, full of history. Right in the courtyard there's a cute little tearooms where you can get your smoked salmon sandwiches and teas. Perfect after a walk on the Downs.

Fishbourne Roman Palace

Salthill Rd, Fishbourne,
Chichester, PO19 3QR
T: 01243 785859
www.sussexpast.co.uk
adminfish@sussexpast.co.uk
Mon-Sun: 10am-5pm
The remains of a Roman villa found accidentally by a farmer who was ploughing his field and suddenly ploughed through an ancient mosaic (it could happen to anyone). The sight is still being excavated, but the majority of it is now undercover with wooden walkways enabling you to get the best possible view of the mosaics. The likelihood is that the house belonged to a local British dignitary who was bribed to Romanise his village. Scientists have re-created a Roman garden by

carbon testing the soil to find out exactly what plants would have been used. The villa is also a perfect example of early Roman central heating and archaeology types go nuts for it.

Foredown Tower Countryside Centre

Foredown Rd, Hove, E Sussex
T: 01273 292092
www.foredown.
virtualmuseum.info
Science, nature and breathtaking views across the Sussex Downs, with interactive displays and exhibitions, one of the country's only two camera obscurer in SE England, countryside research and scientific data.

Glynde Place

Glynde, E Sussex T: 01273 858224
www.glyndeplace.co.uk
1st June-30th Sept, Wed, Sun and Aug bank holidays: 2pm-5pm

16th century house in lovely little village near Lewes. A perfect day would start with lunch at the Trevor Arms.

Groombridge Place

Groombridge, Tunbridge
Wells, Kent, TN3 9QD
T: 01892 863999
www.groombridge.co.uk
office@groombridge.co.uk
1st Apr-6th Nov, Mon-Sun:
9.30am-6pm
HR Puff 'n' stuff type forest to thrill kids of all ages.

Lewes Castle and Barbican House

169 High St, Lewes, E Sussex
BN7 1YE. T: 01273 486290
www.sussexpast.com
Tues-Sat: 10pm-5pm, Mon and Sun: 11am-5pm (dusk in winter)

Ruined castle in the historic town of Lewes.

Michelham Priory

Upper Dicker, Hailsham, E
Sussex BN27 3QS
T: 01323 844224
www.sussexpast.com
Tues-Sun: 10.30am-4, 5, 5.30pm
(depending on season), closed
from Nov-Mar

Gorgeous Tudor mansion and
medieval priory with moat and
resident ghost. The gardens and
herb garden are beautifully kept and
modern sculptures are set against
old stone of the building. There is
a working mill, which dates back to
the 1100s which still provides flour
for the locals. There is a café and
restaurant and they also cater for
functions like weddings and balls.

Newhaven Fort

Newhaven, E Sussex BN9 9DS
T: 01273 517622
www.newhavenfort.org.uk
info@newhavenfort.org.uk
Mar-Oct, Mon-Sun: 10.30am-6pm

The massive walls, ramparts and
guns and many other original
features all fire the imagination
with other exciting glimpses into
England's dramatic wartime past. To
really get to grips with the times,
sights, sounds and even smells of
the period you'll find a host of
displays, exciting 'real-life' sets and
audio-visual presentations.

Rye Heritage Centre

Strand Quay, Rye, E Sussex

TN31 7AY. T: 01797 226696
www.visitrye.co.uk
info@visitrye.co.uk
Mon-Sun: 9am-5pm, times may
vary seasonally

Ghosts and smugglers in a walking,
talking tour of the history of
gorgeous old Rye.

West Blatchington Windmill

Holmes Avenue, Hove, E
Sussex BN3 7LF. T: 01273
776017
May-Sept on Sun and Bank
Holidays only, 2.30pm-5pm

Dating from the 1820s, this Grade II
listed building still has the original
mill workings in place over five
floors. Last open to millers in 1897,
this lovely old windmill is almost
in full working order with much of
the original bits and bobs still there.
Take the kids to see what life was
like in a rural milling town (such as
Hove?) and then treat them to tea
in the barn.

The Hungry Monk

Jevington, E Sussex BN26 5QF
T: 01323 482178
www.hungrymonk.co.uk
Mon-Sun: 6.45pm-9.15pm, Sun
lunch: 12pm-2pm

Gorgeous old thatched pub with
beams, roaring fires and the business
for a full on romantic evening with

your true love. Set in the middle of
a picturesque Sussex village, it's also
a good bet for a Sunday lunch and
walk. Said to be the originator of
the very first Banoffee Pie.

Bentley Wildfowl and Motor Museum

Halland, Lewes, E Sussex BN8
5AF. T: 01825 840 573
www.bentley.org.uk
barrysutherland@pavilion.
co.uk
15th March-31st Oct, Mon-Sun:
10.30am-5pm

On the face of it, an odd
combination, but I guess there's a
historic link between cars and birds.
You can see every kind of swan in
the world at Bentley and there are
over 115 species of waterfowl here.
The Motor Museum houses a fine
old collection of veteran, Edwardian
and vintage cars and bikes. There's
an adventure playground for kids
and miniature trains. Electric
wheelchairs for the disabled
are available free of charge. The
museum is desperately looking for a
buyer at the moment as the council
has pulled the plug on funding.

How We Lived Then

20 Cornfield Terrace,
Eastbourne, E Sussex BN21
4NS. T: 01323 737143
www.how-we-lived-then.co.uk
howwelivedthen@btconnect.
com
Mon-Sun: 10am-5.30pm
In this late-Regency town house,

built in the 1850, you'll see 100 years of shopping and social history captured in old shops, rooms and displays.

Regency Town House

13 Brunswick Square, Hove, E Sussex BN3 1EA. T: 01273 206306. www.rth.org.uk info@rth.org.uk
Phone for tour dates

Grade 1 listed building and heritage centre which transports its visitors into the heart of urban 1820's life in Hove. Note that this is not a kiddy friendly kind of place.

Steyning Museum

Church St, Steyning, BN44 3YB T: 01903 813333
Tues, Wed, Fri and Sat: 10.30pm-12.30pm, 2.30pm-4pm, Sun: 2.30pm-4pm
A celebration of Steyning's Saxon and Norman history focusing on the crafts and industries.

Brooklands Park

Brighton Rd, Worthing, W Sussex BN11 2HP
T: 07867 762106
www.worthing.gov.uk/Visitors/LeisureFacilities
parks@worthing.gov.uk
Open Daily
Eight acres of lakeside park and boats, miniature railway, go karts and trampoline plus an adventure playground. Tell us, what more do your kids want out of life?

Tilgate Park

Titmus Drive, Tilgate, Crawley, Surrey, RH10 5PQ. T: 01293 521168
tilgate@crawley.gov.uk
21 Mar-21 Oct, daily: 10.am-6pm, 22 Oct-20 Mar, daily, 10am-4pm, Closed 25, 26 Dec, 1 Jan
Three lakes, a waterfall, a maze and 400 acres of landscaped gardens have earned it an award for the top attraction in Sussex.

SUNDAY LUNCH IN THE COUNTRY

The Anchor Inn

Barcombe, E Sussex BN8 5BS
T: 01273 400414
Mon-Fri: 11am-11pm, Sun: 12am-10.30pm

Gorgeous old pub on the river, with boat rides and ice creams at the pub's kiosk after a few pints and good lunch. It's child (and dog) friendly with a family room with incredibly helpful and patient staff. If you fancy a good walk to and from your pub lunch, park at the car park on right hand side of the A275 just before Barcombe, and follow the river to the pub, crossing over at the only possible place. On a summer's day, it's heaven; in winter, it's a muddy but serene 40-minute walk.

The Bull Hotel

2 High St, Ditchling, E Sussex BN6 8TA. T: 01273 843147

Dating back to 1569, this is the kind of beamed hostelry you can take your American friends to and watch them faint. The garden is sweet with apple trees groaning with fruit in the summer, and the food has plenty of vegetarian options.

The Griffin

Fletching, E Sussex TN22 3SS
T: 01825 722890
Mon-Sat: 12pm-3pm, 6pm

Owned by yet another London refugee, James Pullan formerly of Draycotts and Joe's Brassiere, The Griffin is where the likes of Helen Baxendale and Raymond Briggs who managed to save up for a pile in the country, spend their spare cash on a plate of organic veal or smoked chicken and olive salad. Using produce from local farms, much of which is genuinely organic, the food here is worth making the half hour trip for, and as one of the few restaurants in the area which can boast a wine list featuring 50 bottles of great wines under £20, it's good value at around £30 a head. The Sunday lunch in the garden with spit roast and live jazz over views across Sheffield Park, or dinner on the new Indian sandstone terrace might even make you think about packing your bag and buying a pad in the Sussex countryside. There are rooms at the inn too for those who never want to leave.

The Half Moon

Ditchling Rd, Plumpton, E
Sussex BN7 3AF
T: 01273 890253
Mon-Sat: 12pm-3pm, 6pm-
11.30pm, Sun: 12pm-11.30pm

Walkers retreat and Sunday lunch
favourite, but arrive before 12.30pm if
you want to eat before 2pm. The bar
is always packed, hiking boots piled
outside the door, and if you're late,
you'll have to suffer the blaring TV
and billiards crowd in the annex. The
garden is paradise for children, maybe
the best in the area. If it's raining, the
smoke's too much and the bar is full,
it's only a five-minute drive to The
Jolly Sportsman at East Chiltington,
but the kids won't thank you.

The Jolly Sportsman

Chapel Lane, East Chiltington,
E Sussex BN7 3BA
T: 01273 890400
www.thejollysportsman.com
Mon-Sat: 12pm-2.30pm, 6pm-
11.30pm, Sun: 12pm-4pm

Posh, rustic restaurant with an
eclectic selection of neeps, tatties
and ciabattas mixed in with fine
Modern British dining. A few locals
still huddle the bar, while the
Guardian and Telegraph readers (and
writers) laze over the papers and
ponder whether to go for the haggis
(£6.90) or the chicken liver parfait
with onion marmalade (£4.85), while
parents consider what on Earth to
feed the kids. The garden may be a

haven for kids, but feed them before
you leave home. Expect to pay
around £25 per head for dinner.

The Juggs

The Street, Kingston,
East Sussex BN7 3NT
T: 01273 472523
Mon-Sat: 11am-11pm, Sun: 12pm-
10.30pm

In the heart of one of Sussex's
most gorgeous villages and only
10-minutes from Brighton, The
Juggs is extremely popular with
townies looking for the nearest
country pub. It's picture book pretty,
which means that it's packed with
Americans in the summer, and
the food is good too. There's an
adventure playground for kids, but
that's where the child friendliness
stops. If you don't like to feed your
children nuggets and beans, feed
them before you get here.

The Mermaid Inn

Mermaid St, Rye, E Sussex
TN31 7EY. T: 01797 223065
www.rye-tourism.co.uk
mermaidinnrye@btclick.com
Mon-Sat: 11am-11pm, Sun: 11am-
10.30pm

Gorgeous ancient pub with good
food and four posters in five of the
31 bedrooms (£75pp). A pricey treat
for a romantic weekend away.

The Ram Inn

The Street, Firle, E Sussex BN8

6NS. T: 01273 858222
Mon-Sat: 11.30am-11pm, Sun:
12pm-10.30pm

Classic cars and open tops crowd
the car park in this otherwise sleepy
village on Sunday lunchtimes and
misty evenings when the food is
hot, the music is live, and the fires
roar. Since it was taken over by the
landlord's offspring, it's hopping with
parents and their kids on a weekend.
The children's playground complete
with pirate ship and secret garden
and ball pond in the stables perhaps?
For a weekend walk, follow signs
from the pub to Firle Beacon, and
make sure you've got your kite.

The Royal Oak

The Street, Poynings, E Sussex
BN45 7AQ. T: 01273 857389
www.royaloakpoynings.com
Mon-Sat: 11am-11pm, Sun: 12pm-
10.30pm

Always packed, it might take an age
for your bangers and mash, Sunday
roast or Salmon Hollandaise but
what's the hurry? The kids can play
on the climbing frame in the large
garden and you can plan your walk
across Devils Dyke while you wait.

The Shepherd and Dog

The Street, Fulking, E Sussex
BN5 9LU. T: 01273 857382
Mon-Sat: 11am-11pm, Sun: 12pm-
7.30pm

If the Royal Oak is full (or vice versa), try this lovely old pub just down the road with little poo sticks stream running through the garden perched on the back of Devil's Dyke. A lane next to the garden leads up onto the top of the Dyke and affords some breathtaking views of the area. Book if you want a table for a weekend lunch. But they will not let kids into the bar even to buy a packet of crisps; so if you are a family, don't go in winter.

The Snowdrop

South St, Lewes, BN7 2BU
T: 01273 471018
It's had a bit of an image-makeover, but it's still hippy heaven at heart. Affectionately known as The Snowy, it's decorated in vibrant purple and blue. The girls' loos are Barbie pink and they have a great selection of odd sculptures that may have been salvaged from skips. It's worth a visit just to listen to their record collection, which ranges from Blue Note Jazz to Janis Joplin. Perfect for a Sunday lunchtime jaunt, they stock some organic beer and kids are welcomed with open arms. Expect great comfort style vegetarian food at weekends and an extensive collection of homemade pizza.

The Sussex Ox

Milton St, Alfriston, E Sussex BN26 5RL. T: 01323 870840
sussexox@aol.com
Mon-Fri: 10am-3pm, 6pm-11pm, Sun: 12pm-10.30pm

Great for kids with fantastic adventure playground. Perfect for a huge lunch before a walk to the Long Man of Wilmington.

The Tiger Inn

The Green, East Dean, E Sussex BN20 0DA
T: 01323 423209
Mon-Fri: 11am-3pm, 6pm-11pm, Sat: 11am-11pm, Sun: 12pm-10.30pm

A long summer afternoon treat: lunch at the Tiger Inn, then visit the Seven Sisters Sheep Farm before walking through the woods and down the wiggly path to the beach.

The Trevor Arms

The Street, Glynde, E Sussex BN8 6SS. T: 01273 858208
Mon-Sat: 11am-11pm, Sun: 12pm-10.30pm

Dogs, hiking boots and green wellies are littered around this delightful

proper country pub. The food is good too; Sunday roasts are hearty and no-nonsense.

The Vinyard Lodge

42 High St, Hurstpierpoint, E Sussex BN6 9RG
T: 01273 835000
www.vinyardlodge.com
Mon-Sat: 11am-3pm, 6pm-11pm, Sun: 11am-3pm

Large sofas and enough toys to keep anyone under the age of seven amused throughout a South Down Roast Lamb lunch, a garden with swings and views, and an ambience laid back enough to keep the punters in until closing time, the Vinyard Lodge (sic) is a welcome addition to the Sunday lunch chapter. With 26 wines on offer and locally sourced produce, come Springtime, there'll be a queue of food loving young parents up the A23 before you can say 'Mine's a Chardonnay'.

BODY AND SOUL

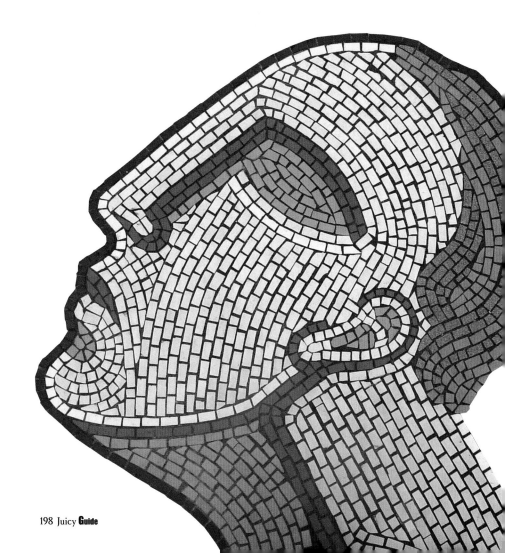

Brighton and Hove is the centre of alternative therapy and while that means that it attracts the right calibre of healer, it also means that there are a lot of flakes in the mix. What we've got here are some of those that we've used ourselves, or who come recommended by Juicy readers. Use the user review on www.juicymapminder.co.uk to tell us if you agree or disagree with our choice, and to suggest those you think should be on the list.

CLINICS

The Ardern Foot and Health Clinic
123 St James's St, Kemp Town, Brighton BN2 1TH
T: 01273 673964
Treatments get really holistic here; it's not just chiropody and reflexology, Indian Head Massage and Shiatsu, but also Geopathic stress and allergy testing, Earth Bound Energy checks and removal (that's ghosts and lost souls to you).

Brighton Natural Health Centre
27 Regent St, North Laine, Brighton BN1 1UL
T: 01273 600010
www.bnhc.co.uk
Mon-Fri 10am-3pm, Sat: 10am-1pm
Yoga, raqs sharqi, qigong, t'ai chi, Feldenkrais, shiatsu... This is the centre of Brighton's holistic universe.

Dolphin House Clinic
14 New Rd, Brighton BN1 1UF
T: 01273 324790

www.thechildrensclinic.org.uk
Mon-Fri: 9am-5.30pm, Sat: 9am-1pm
Dolphin House is a registered charity and has a sliding scale of donations, providing homeopaths, acupuncturists, nutritionists, auric healing, osteopathy and herbal treatments. The idea is to make complementary health available to everyone - particularly children. The same practitioners also run an adult clinic at normal prices.

The Drive Natural Health Centre
98 The Drive, Hove BN3 6GP
T: 01273 777509
Mon-Fri: 8.30am-5.30pm,
GP, osteopaths, herbalist, acupuncture, massage, homeopath, nutritionist, hypnotherapy and counsellors. Check out Rebecca and her kinesiology.

Dyke Road Natural Health Clinic
274 Dyke Rd, Brighton BN1 5AE
T: 01273 561844 F: 01273 561845
www.brightonosteopaths.co.uk
Mon-Fri: 9am-1pm, 2pm-5.30pm,
Sat: 9am-1pm
Alexander technique, homeopathy, acupuncture, osteopathy, physiotherapy, shiatsu, sports therapy and other alternatives to the doctor at this excellent clinic.

Evolution
2 Sillwood Terrace, Brighton BN1 2LR. T: 01273 204204
www.evolutionarts.co.uk
To make an appointment: Mon-Fri: 10.15am-1pm
All kinds of yoga for all levels plus wide variety of workshops.

Natural Bodies
28-29 Bond St, Brighton BN1 1RD. T: 01273 711414
www.naturalbodies.org.uk
info@naturalbodies.org.uk
Classes in Yoga from 8.45am until 9pm with a focus on 'undoing' the spine rather than a competition in postures. There are 23 different classes going on each week.

Planet Janet
86 Church Rd, Hove BN3 2TD
T: 01273 748234/01273 738389
www.planet-janet.com
Mon-Sat: 9am-8pm, Sun: 9am-6pm
All sorts of healing and yoga classes, as well as a café specialising in organic juices. Shiatsu, Therapeutic Massage, Hypnotherapy, Aromatherapy and Crystal Healing, as well as Sunday talks on alternative healthcare.

ACUPUNCTURE

Dave Bennett
Marine Clinic, 12 Marine Drive, Rottingdean BN2 7HQ
T: 01273 307001
Dave Bennett's Japanese needles and healing skills are legendary. Take your frozen shoulder, your lower back pain or your policeman's heel to him and he'll not only explain just why your body appears to have given up on you (which is always half the magic), but brings your pulses back to where they should be and your energies flowing back to all those depleted centres. He uses Five Element acupuncture, which sees a complaint as being rooted in an underlying energetic imbalance. Get to the core of the issue and

Philip Perry at Maximize People

Flat One, Calthorpe House, Lewes Crescent, Brighton BN2 1FH. T: 01273 626040
www.maximizepeople.com
philip@maximizepeople.com
Philip Perry's psychology background gives him a rare insight into his clients, allowing him to tease out their potential and help them to believe in themselves enough to get there. Using a variety of techniques including psychotherapy, NLP and positive psychology, as well as his experience as a life and business coach, he's got what it takes. Juicily recommended.

EASTERN MEDICINE

Ayurvedic Health Clinic

18 Mallory Rd, Hove BN3 6TD
T: 01273 298286
F: 01273 298286
www.ayurveda-asmita.co.uk
asmita.jani@ntlworld.com
Mon-Fri: 9.30am-5.30pm
Ayurveda is one of the most ancient and most holistic sciences. A detox is an essential precursor to any treatment that is going to work but if done properly, can sort out anything from skin problems to infertility. It's also deeply relaxing; listening to the rain beat down on Dr Jani's Conservatory while lying in her coffin-like steamer after a massage, is a top way to start your weekend. If you ask nicely – and pay appropriately – she'll do things with a length of rubber tubing that'll

profound healing takes place. He's also excellent with kids, and often doesn't need to use the sharper needles with them at all.

Elaine Gibbons

Unit 4 Natural Health Centre 20-26, Roundhilll St, Brighton BN2 3RG. T: 01273 562676
Acupuncturist with particular interest in pregnancy.

Steve Guthrie

Dyke Rd Natural Health Clinic, 274 Dyke Rd, Brighton BN1 5AE
T: 01273 561844
www.brightonosteopaths.co.uk

The head honcho at Dolphin House is there Monday, Wednesday and Friday – but you'll have to wait weeks before getting a session.

COUNSELLING

Patricia Holden

Marine Clinic,
12 Marine Drive, Rottingdean BN2 7HQ
T: 01273 307001
Patricia is the only hypnotherapist who came highly enough recommended to get into the Juicy Guide. She also practices The Abbey Clinic in London's Harley Street.

bring a tear to your eye.Dr Jani also teaches ayurvedic cooking courses and sells ayurvedic products.

The Chinese Medicine Centre
122 St James St, Kemp Town, Brighton BN2 1TH
T: 01273 699852 F: 01273 699852
Mon-Fri: 10am-5pm
Chinese medicine boosts the immune system and gets the body back on track, and correcting disorders in the vital organs. Jane is the front of house and works with the old Chinese doctor, translating the questions and the diagnosis in the strangest consultation in town. But if you ask the many who have experienced miracles at their hands, you'll shake your head and wonder... and trust.

HERBALISM

Sarah Furey
270 Eastern Road, Brighton BN2 5TA
T: 01273 621841
furey@waitrose.com
Modern herbalists combine the knowledge and wisdom from centuries of use of plant remedies with valuable information gained from modern scientific research to provide a therapy which is both safe and effective. Sarah gives lots of talks locally about how to avoid the menopause and some Western diseases through herbs, and if you want to look like her when you're her age, you'll book now.

HOMEOPATHY

Tim Couzens
Grove Lodge, 104 Preston Drove, Preston Park, Brighton BN1 6EW
T: 01273 558838/01825 840966
Tim holds a veterinary surgery in Brighton one Wednesday a month at Grove Lodge, and offers acupuncture, herbal medicine as well as homeopathic alternatives to vaccinations.

The Diamantopoulo Practice
1 Vale Rd, Portslade, BN41 1GD
T: 01273 419272
www.arnica.com.au
kate@arnica.com.au
This is Mission Control for The Kate Diamantopoulo Group Practice International, where Kate, Juicy homeopath and former nurse and midwife, can be contacted. After setting up the Steiner School, The Dolphin Clinic and her own practice of 15 years, Kate left Brighton for Perth, Australia two years ago. In a radical move, she now offers advice by email and twice yearly appointments to the many patients who couldn't believe that she was about to go. And it works. For those preferring personal contact on demand, there are now four practitioners at the Diamantopoulo Practice in Brighton, all trained by Kate. Kate has also developed a range of top quality Australian arnica products (see website), which are a must for any bathroom cabinet.

Trevor Gunn
Dyke Rd Natural Health Clinic, 274 Dyke Rd, Brighton BN1 5AE
T: 01273 561844 F: 01273 561845
Tues and Thurs
Trevor Gunn is one of the most prolific homeopaths in Brighton, possibly because he gives lots of talks and has such strong views on the issues of vaccination.

Jan Matthews
37 Southdown Ave, Fiveways, Brighton BN1 6EH
T: 01273 388857
Jan is one of Brighton's most popular homeopaths, and seems to have a lot of success with teenagers.

ASTROLOGY

Jessica Adams
Saint Margarets, High Street, Rottingdean
or 80/56 Gloucester Road, Kensington London SW7 4UB
T: 01273 300353/ 07748490386
www.jessicaadams.com,
jessicacadams@aol.com.
Jessica is the psychic for Cosmopolitan and the astrologer for Vogue in Australia and Asia. You can book a reading with her in London or Brighton.

INTUITIVE HEALING

Sohani Gonzalez
The Dyke Rd Clinic, 274 Dyke Rd, Brighton BN1 5AE
T: 01273 561844 F: 01273 561845
sohani@sohani.fsnet.co.uk
Allergy testing.

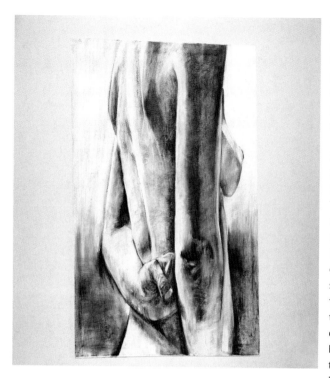

Philippa has a wide knowledge and network of holistic therapies and believes that successful treatment often involves working with a range of other complementary therapists, including herbalists, osteopaths and nutritionists.

Helen Noakes

28-29 Bond St, North Laine, Brighton BN1 1RD
T: 01273 711414
www.naturalbodies.org.uk
info@naturalbodies.org.uk
Indian rope massage is an experience everyone needs to try. The rope is suspended above the body to assist the masseur to use his or her weight to get into those little nooks and crannies, with foot, elbow and palm. Patients are encouraged to breathe through it, which brings on a natural high. Helen Noakes is, as far as we know, the only practitioner in the city.

Watering Hole

Meeting House Lane, The Lanes, Brighton BN1 1HB
T: 01273 778877
www.wateringhole.com
Mon-Fri: 10am-6pm, Sat: 10am-6pm, Sun: 12pm-5pm
Aqua massage is apparently quite the rage in the USA with machines in petrol stations and shopping malls. It hasn't quite caught on in the same way in Brighton, but if you fancy a fully clothed pummel by tonnes of pulverising water held only by a fine membrane, it's all yours in the heart of The Lanes. 36 water jets that pulsate up and down the body. Costs £7 for six mins, £20 for 20 mins.

Sally Roberts

Holistic Health Clinic, 53 Beaconsfield Rd, Brighton BN1 4QH. T: 01273 696295
Sally is a trained nurse who spends half the week healing people on the NHS and the other using colour therapies, Reiki and intuitive healing to heal her more holistic clients. She's effective with children, using angels and colours to heal their night fearsand other imbalances.

Nikki Wilson

35 Norfolk Square, Brighton BN1 2PE. T: 01273 728053
An extraordinary tarot reader and psychic, Nikki tunes into guides in the way that less enlightened folk tune into Eastenders. The dramas, the past lives, the lessons, they're all there. One of the best we've come across.

MASSAGE THERAPY

Kathryn Chapman
Shoreham BN43 6HS
T: 01273 269852 Mob: 07044 016484
kathychapman@supanet.com
Grab yourself an hour with Kathy Chapman and bliss out. Kathy specialises in hand and reflexology treatments for all sorts of problems. She visits homes and offices.

Philippa King

The Clinic, 69 Gordon Rd, Preston Park, Brighton BN1 6PE
T: 01273 232629
t.p.king@ntlworld.com

MEDITATION

Bodhi Garden Dharma Centre
7a Ship St Gardens, The Lanes, Brighton BN1 1AJ
T: 01273 557610
www.brighton.shambhala-europe.org
Meditation classes include meditative dance.

Bodhivsattva
3 Lansdowne Rd, Hove BN3 1DN
T: 01273 732917
www.meditateinbrighton.com
Mon-Sat: 2pm-4.30pm
Meditation centre which offers children and adults meditation, singing and drawing classes.

The Float Space
38 Gardner St, North Laine, Brighton BN1 1UN
T: 01273 572204 F: 01273 572101
www.hocuspocus.co.uk
info@hocuspocus.co.uk
Above Hocus Pocus, the witch shop in Gardner Street is The Clinic Upstairs where you can retreat back into the womblike like world of sensory deprivation in a floatation tank. Claustrophobics beware, but this is powerful relaxation for those who can give into the experience.

NUTRITION

AK Bicom Clinic
3 Eaton Gdns, Hove BN3 3TL
T: 01273 733620/01273 220908
www.healthaccess.co.uk
Mon-Fri: 9am-5pm

Andrew & Myriam use a combination of Applied Kinesiology, Bioresonance Therapy, Nutrition, Vibrational remedies to meet the individual needs of the client. They specialise in smoking (one session is good enough for most people), allergies, hay fever, asthma, eczema, emotional trauma, preventive treatment of Anaphylaxis and pain reduction. The machine that they use looks like something out of a Brave New World, but the effects are exceptional.

Lucy Pook
Holistic Health Clinic, 53 Beaconsfield Rd, Brighton BN1 4QH. T: 01273 696295 F: 01273 696295
www.holistichealthcentre.org
Mon-Fri: 9am-5pm
Lucy uses the five elements of Chinese Medicine to understand how the vital organs might be under-functioning. She also teaches the Gerson Technique which has been proven to be effective in dealing with cancer.

OSTEOPATHY

Rex Brangwyn and Associates
98 The Drive, Hove BN3 6FL
T: 01273 775559
A range of osteopaths and related therapies. Rex himself has a reputation for being great with kids.

Jonathon Hutson
Arden House, Dyke Rd Natural Health Clinic, 274 Dyke Rd,

Brighton BN1 5AE
T: 01273 561844 F: 01273 561845
www.brightonosteopaths.co.uk
Mon-Fri: 8am-7pm
One of the best osteopaths we've ever come across, Jonathon almost completely relies on cranial work to restore the body naturally.

Alexandra Luzzatto
Ardern House, Dyke Rd Clinic, 274 Dyke Rd, Brighton BN1 5AE
T: 01273 561844
www.brightonosteopaths.co.uk
Working closely with the exceptional Jonathon Hutson, Alexandra's gentle approach to osteopathy has made her particularly popular with young children. She works Monday, Wednesday and Saturday.

Liz Pegg
12 Buxton Rd, Brighton BN3 1AW. T: 01273 504340
Liz Pegg has been away having babies for the last couple of years, but is back on the scene again with her healing hands. Even the most brilliant osteopaths in Brighton and Hove don't seem to be able to fix bodies as quickly as Liz does (which saves a lot of money). We reckon she's a white witch in a white coat. Her cross training in reflexology, osteopathy and naturopathy means that she can choose the best way to work with your ails.

Andrew Rayment
28 Park Crescent Terrace, The Level, Brighton BN2 3HD
T: 01273 570352
Excellent cranial osteopath whose

explanations of how the body fixes itself are not patronising and empowering. Andrew is also available at Ardern House, Dyke Road Natural Health Centre (see Jonathon Hutson and Alexandra Luzzatto)

Sue Van Emden

Dyke Rd Natural Health Clinic, 274 Dyke Rd, Brighton BN1 5AE
T: 01273 561844 F: 01273 561845
Sue specialises in osteopathy for pregnant women, working with them throughout the term and after for both mother and child. Works Monday, Tuesday, Wednesday and Thursday.

PAMPERING

Aveda

8 Dukes Lane, The Lanes, Brighton BN1 1BG
T: 01273 720203 F: 01273 823102
www.aveda.com
Mon-Sat: 10am-6pm, Sun: 12pm-5pm
Leaders in haircare products including vegetable hair colours. Travel sized bottles to try if you need convincing first. Great line in quality inexpensive make-up.

Bay House Aromatics

88 St George's Rd, Kemp Town, Brighton BN2 1EE
T: 01273 601109 F: 01273 601174
www.bay-house.co.uk
enquiries@bay-house.co.uk
Mon-Fri: 9am-5.30pm
One of the best places in the South

East to buy essential oils. They'll also make up soaps, creams and treatments for you.

Boudoir Baby

97 Queens Rd, Brighton BN1 3XF. T: 01273 711101
www.boudoirbaby.co.uk
Mon-Sat: 9am-6pm
Just opened, Boudoir Baby is for beauty queens who love to be spoiled. Redefining the idea of holistic treatment, the super-camp staff will be concentrating on pampering the soul. Glass of wine and couple of chocolates with your Brazilian, Madam?

L'Occitane en Provence

23 East St, The Lanes, Brighton BN1 1HP. T: 01273 719171
www.loccitaine.com
Mon-Sat: 9am-6pm
Presents a plenty at this branch of the gorgeous Provencal goody chain. Soaps, shower gels, massage oils, hair and skin stuff all made out of the best lavenders and essential oils Provence can produce.

Lush

41 East St, The Lanes, Brighton BN1 1HL. T: 01273 774700
www.lush.co.uk
Mon-Sat: 9am-6pm, Sun: 10am-5pm
In a few years, Lush has gone from being an esoteric soap shop to (almost) a national institution. Going inside is a bit of a sensory-overload – so many smells all shoved together are a little overpowering – but on their own they are subtler. Try the

Bath Bombs, they come with glitter, rose petals and are really fun!

Neal's Yard

2a Kensington Gdns, North Laine, Brighton BN1 4AL
T: 01273 601464
www.nealsyardremedies.com
Mon-Sat: 9.30am-5.30pm, Sun: 11am-4pm
Heavenly apothecary. Medicinal herbs, lotions and potions in the famous blue and purple bottles. Alternative books. too.

Pink Pamper

1 St James St, Kemp town, Brighton BN2 1RE
T: 01273 608060
www.thepinkpamper.co.uk
enquiers@thepinkpamper.co.uk
Tues-Sat: 10am-6pm, Thurs: 10am-8pm
Relocated to a larger space in the heart of St James's, but still leading the way for Kemp Town beauty queens with five floors of white leather, Italian slate and Venetian mirrors. It's glamorous, it's indulgent and just so Kemp Town.

Retail Therapy

101 Gloucester Rd, North Laine, Brighton BN1 4AP
T: 01273 691720
Mon-Sat: 11am-6pm, Sun: 11am-5pm
Gifts and fun stuff for people into tarot. The treatment room at the back provides services such as aromatherapy massage, Indian and Thai head massages, performed by friendly, relaxed and chatty staff.

Saks Hair and Beauty

18 Ship St, Brighton BN1 1AD
T: 08000 341 248
www.sakshairandbeauty.com
Mon: 10am-5pm, Tues: 10am-6pm,
Wed: 9am-7.30pm, Thurs: 9am-
8pm, Fri: 9am-6pm, Sat: 9am-
6.30pm
Mark and his top team of tress-
trimmers come with a Vidal Sassoon
pedigree and beauty salon to match.
Oriental bodywraps, Japanese facials,
revolutionary tanning systems
and state of the art hair removal,
manicures and pedicures – a world
of pampering right in the centre of
The Lanes. They also have a branch
in Brighton Marina.

The Treatment Rooms

21 New Rd, North Laine,
Brighton BN1 1UF
T: 01273 818444
info@thetreatmentrooms.com
Mon-Fri: 9am-8pm, Sat: 9am-
5.30pm, Sun: 11am-5pm
There are plenty of places to get a
good treatment in Brighton
and Hove. Waxing is waxing,
massages are only as good as
the therapist, and occasionally
you'll get something weird and
wonderful like LA Stone therapy
which uses hot and cold stones to
bliss you out. But there's only one
place that we've found where
the environment is inspired by
Balinese spas, where the pastoral
pre and after care is as relaxing as
the treatment, which is probably
why you'll pay more for your
massage here, and have to book
three weeks ahead.

PREGNANCY AND BIRTH

Active Birth with Karel Ironside

365 Ditchling Rd, Preston Park,
Brighton BN1 6JU
T: 01273 277309
Active Birth is a philosophy which
encourages you to be positive about
the birth. The yoga will make you
more supple and Karel's print-outs
on active labouring are essential
when things don't go quite to
plan. The ante-natal classes start
at around three months, are great
for meeting other parents and to
spend some meditative time with
your bump.

Crowborough Birthing Centre

Southview Rd, Crowborough
TN6 1HB. T: 01892 654080
www.esh.nhs.uk/
crowborough
Crowborough Birthing Centre is
a small unit, located adjacent to
the Crowborough War Memorial
Hospital. It has six beds, is open
24 hours a day and is run entirely
by midwives. The Centre offers
complete ante-natal care, tests
(with an ultrasound scanner
available), parent education classes,
as well as many birth choices.
Birthing pools are available and
the midwives are sympathetic
to alternative therapies such as
acupuncture and aromatherapy.

Gentle Water

50 North Way, Lewes BN7 1DJ

T: 01273 474927
www.gentlewater.co.uk
If you're thinking of a home birth,
do yourself a favour and get a pool.
It's private, warm and a great pain
relief. And it's the most natural
way for a baby to be born without
intervention. You can get your pool
delivered from here.

YOGA

Bikram Yoga

Unit 9, The Old Perfume
Factory Off Fonthill Rd,
Hove BN3 6HA.
T: 01273 721944
F: 01273 725829
www.bikrambrighton.co.uk
info@bikrambrighton.co.uk
Mon: 10.30am and 7.30pm, Tues:
1pm and 6.30pm, Wed: 10.30am
and 7.30pm, Thurs: 1pm and
6.30pm, Fri: 10.30am and 6.30pm,
Sat: 10.30am and 5pm, Sun: 11am.
Hot yoga is the latest craze
sweeping the world, and
the idea is to challenge all your
senses at once. You sweat like
you didn't know you could sweat,
but just think of all those toxins
flooding out of you.

Dynamic Yoga

King Alfred Leisure Centre,
Kingsway, Hove BN3 2WW
T: 01273 727792
yogistuart@yahoo.co.uk
Yoga isn't about going for the burn,
but this will make you sweat. Hot
Yoga like Bikram's, but with more of
an Astanga approach, this is not for
the faint hearted.

NEIGHBOURS AND NEIGHBOURHOODS

FINDING YOUR TRIBE

The "villages" of Brighton and Hove are as distinct as they are in any city and different tribes gather tightly within their boundaries. This is the key to finding a home rather than a house, and any estate agent who asks how much you want to spend before he asks who you want to live next to should be rapped over the head with your Juicy Guide. The Greek statues on the front lawns of Withdean's castles might let on that there's money in them there hills, but if you're looking for the local pub or a late-night grocer, this is not your patch. Kemp Town with its bohemian reputation won't seduce many born and bred families with its patio gardens and three-storey houses, but its increasingly Boho feel has tempted the likes of Cate Blanchett and Supergrass frontman, Gaz Coombes.

If you're coming from London, the chances are you'll find your tribe somewhere along the seafront or the streets running off it from Arundel Street in Kemp Town right down to Wish Road in Hove, the streets stretching back from Western Road to Seven Dials, Queens Park and some roads in Hanover. Increasingly the city centre's groovy loft apartments are attracting the younger moneyed end of the buying market, impressed by the arrival of the Conran hotel, The Argus Lofts and Jubilee Street development in The North Laine.

Take some time out to sit in the cafes, pubs and parks to ponder where exactly you want to buy. More than anywhere, parks are where you will find your particular tribe. Eavesdrop or join in at St Ann's Well or Queen's Park, cheer the football teams at East Brighton and Preston Parks and reminisce about the old days with Hove's born and bred at Hove Park café. People watching is never more fun than when kids are involved, and the parenting skills of St Ann's Well media dads is the stuff of sitcoms. It may seem as if all the best properties are being snapped up, but relax and enjoy the varying vibes of Brighton and Hove before you ring an estate agent.

If you're driven by the need to have a garden, get yourself an ordnance survey map to see exactly where the gardens are. The roads around New Church Road off Hove seafront and in suburban areas such as Patcham, Westdene, Hangleton and Woodingdean are where most gardens are to be found, as well as Arundel Road in Kemp

Town, both with easy access to the sea and City centre. Once in the centre, you'll get little more than a yard or, if you're lucky (and loaded), a roof terrace. But before you dismiss the idea of a backyard, visit the gardens shown off as part of the Open Houses scheme in May's Brighton Festival (see The Season for details). The creativity is inspiring. There are also plenty of allotments available, so ring the Council for details.

Estate agent Paul Bonett suggests that families who want gardens, garages and community could look at Patcham and Westdene, both of which have strong communities linked to the primary and junior schools. "I sold a gorgeous 18th century cottage in Patcham Old Town and a lovely flint-fronted wing of a 17th century mansion house. The family who bought it had moved from Queen's Park to get more of a garden. And they've got access to the best baker in town, Patcham Bakery, which sells the best doughnuts and curry pasties you've ever tasted!"

Portslade is also a good place to look for cheaper properties now that Hove is officially full. "A new three-bed semi with a garage and garden will cost you around £195,000," says Bonett. "And it's two minutes away from the A27 and about 15 minutes into the centre of Brighton." Saltdean, a three-mile hike from Brighton and Hove is becoming increasingly popular, particularly with families who want to buy a bigger house. Three bed-roomed houses with views over The Downs are currently going for around £300,000, but two-bedroom detached bungalows with loft extensions, front and back gardens and plentiful parking, on or off road can go for as little as £200,000.

Shoreham is the next place to watch if the growth of Brighton-style restaurants and bars is anything to go by. Two-bed, three-storey fishermen's flint cottages behind the High Street are on the market for about £200,000 although three-bedroom homes could be as much £400,000.

Shoreham Beach is a strange little shanty town of art deco and retro properties right on the waterfront. Because there's only one way in and one way out, the community is tight and houses not often for sale. When they are, the three-four beds go for around £500,000-£600,000. Rope Tackle is a Barclay Homes development

with a range of town houses and flats - all with river views. And one for the real property speculators: Hastings. You don't believe us? Have a look into the South East Economic Development Agency's closely clutched purse, and don't say we didn't warn you.

MONTPELIER

Aesthetically, Montpelier is one of Brighton's most appealing areas in a city with so much stunning architecture. Large white houses lurk in streets of pastel hues lending an atmosphere of style rather than wealth, a feel of Mykonos rather than Belgravia. Montpelier is about as close to central Brighton and Hove as you can get. The luvvy of Brighton neighbourhoods, it buzzes

all year round, leaving little peace for its chic, funky residents. But that's why they choose to live here: this is where the action is, and most have the money to pay for it. Montpelier is small enough to negotiate and close enough to everything for access. Soho apart, it's rare to find a community feel in the centre of a city, but Montpelier pulls it off.

In the Clifton Conservation area, a large four-bedroom house could cost over £850,000, a medium-sized, three-bedroom house will go for between £300,000 and £400,000 or more. You will be lucky to find even a two bedroom for under £250,000. Powis Square, with its elegantly distressed balustrades and peeling white paint, still has a Georgian grandeur and attracts a hip but wealthy

of the high ceilings and large rooms are magnificent. Beware the shamelessly chopped-up Eighties developments, though. A one-bed in the ever-popular Chatham Place will cost around £125,000. If you want real Regency style with balustrades and balconies, you might just pick up a two bed maisonette in Compton Avenue for around £215,000 plus.

PORTHALL

Sometimes known as Prestonville, the residential area at the back of Seven Dials is possibly the most popular area among Juicy relocators. The two/three bed terraced houses with gardens big enough for little more than a sandpit and tricycle or two are packed with families who borrow each others' sugar and invite their kids to parties at the Community Centre in Exeter Street. The kids go to Stanford Infants and Juniors or to BHASVIC while the parents walk to the station and head off to Cape Town on a photographic shoot, or cycle down to The Dolphin House Clinic for a shiatsu. Four to five bed houses with big gardens here are not cheap at £450,000 although good value compared to the same size a couple of streets away in St Ann's Well.

THE NORTH LAINE

The hippy heart of Brighton, the antique centre of the South East and the arty den in which Brighton's creatives work on their scripts and practice their punch lines, living in the North Laine is a buzz. In some of the quieter roads such as Over Street and Queen's Gardens, the residents find their tranquility in their Tardis like homes – a top buy this year with the development of Jubilee Street at around £260,000. The new Jubilee Centre with the children's library attached to the Prince Regent swimming pool, Conran Hotel and Argus Lofts will make a big difference to the area, although this is still where old Brighton comes for its cuppa. It may be the age of Aquarius in this new city, but the old towners (those who moved from London more than five years ago) still practice a very hippy version of 'them and us' apartheid). A small terraced house might cost anything from just under £260,000 to £385,000. A family house in Pelham Square will cost around £350,000 plus.

resident. Set in the heart of the Montpelier/Clifton area, the five-storey houses (some with 30-foot gardens) are worth £700,000 plus and the no longer neglected central communal garden is a much-loved play area for the local toddlers. Flats and converted maisonettes are a better buy and go from £160,000 to £200,000.

SEVEN DIALS

Only minutes away from Brighton station, Seven Dials has become a prime location for commuters. Almost all the Regency and Victorian houses have been divided into flats. This year, the wannabe roads are still Vernon Terrace where you'll find a two-bedroom flat for £185,000 and the busy Denmark Terrace where some

KEMP TOWN

Kemp Town is undergoing a sea-change in its culture and environment. London media types, the gay crowd, local families and trendy young things of all gender persuasions are the kind of neighbours you'll find in this community. And it's only two minutes from the beach and five from The Downs.

Once a village of beautiful facades where the grimmer reality behind the front doors spilt into the streets around St James's, Kemp Town has been known for its drugs and anti-social behaviour for the last 20 years. But Europe has been generous with its regeneration funding and St James's Street, like many of its residents, has had a facelift. This time, its beauty is more than skin deep and the new shops, cafes and bars have added a new dynamic that has successfully attracted new business and new residents to the area and galvanised the existing community.

Stretching east from St James's Street and St George's Road, is some of the most beautiful Georgian architecture in Brighton and Hove. Designed to house the aristocrats who followed the Prince Regent down to Brighton to "take the waters" on the advice of Brighton's most influential alternative therapist, Dr Richard Russell, Kemp Town was built to be grand and includes one of the most famous examples of Regency architecture, Sussex Square. Its lower lawns which spread down into Lewes Crescent, even hide a secret rose garden with its own tunnel leading to the beach. Expect to pay up to £160,000 for a ground-floor, one-bedroom flat and watch out for maintenance payments on these Grade 1-listed buildings. You can add zeros as you add bedrooms - something which won't be helped by The Independent listing it as one the most desirable places to live in England. A five-storey Regency house will set you back anything from £750,000 to £3 million.

QUEEN'S PARK

Queen's Park has been called the heart of Brighton - and you can see why. It's a family place; couples move here who have grown out of their flats and want more space for the kids with easy access to both Kemp Town and the centre of town. The park was designed and built as an ornamental garden in 1824, flanked at each end by two formal arches and is sweetly laid out, with a wild garden, lake, tennis courts and bowling green. There's also a children's playground and café that heaves in the summer.

Some of the biggest gardens and most expensive properties are here. East Drive and West Drive, which curve around the park, are the area's best addresses with their large, semi-detached Victorian houses and some of the biggest gardens in Brighton. Expect to pay in the region of £500,000 plus. Even the more recently built Thirties houses have increased in value as this area becomes ever more popular. Canning Street, home to the band The Levellers, falls in the middle of Queen's Park and Kemp Town area. Popular with families, the Victorian three-bed houses here range from £260,000 to £300,000.

HANOVER

Developed back in the 1860s to accommodate the train and carriage labourers working at Brighton station, the small terraced houses of Hanover has been dubbed The Muesli Belt and the "The People's Republic of Hanover", because the kids who grew up here became an army of teachers and social workers, musicians and students who spend more than an average amount of time debating life's challenges in any one of the pubs. In the middle of August, Hanover closes to cars and a good, old-fashioned street party takes place, and in October, the annual Hanover Beer Festival keeps the party going.

Hanover is well placed for schools, with access to Queen's Park, Elm Grove and St Lukes which keeps the kids in the community. Not so long ago, Hanover was a haven for first-time buyers, but the prices are moving swiftly upwards and a two-bedroom in Stanley Street will cost upward of £195,000. Hanover Crescent, which is part of the Valley Conservation area, is the smartest road in Hanover with its 24 listed buildings. Houses start at around £500,000.

ELM GROVE

As Hanover's property market reaches saturation point, first-time buyers are looking at Elm Grove, the area on the other side of the hill behind Brighton racecourse. From Elm Grove's lofty peaks you can clamber up on to the South Downs and look out to sea, or take a surprisingly beautiful walk through to one of the cemeteries. Although Elm Grove doesn't zing with community spirit, it's a deceptive area, and within its boundaries lie some lovely streets. In De Montfort Road the larger houses with substantial gardens are worth looking at. A house here will set you back upwards of £280,000.

PRESTON PARK

The well-heeled who care not a jot for a sea-view can make their way to the Victoriana of Preston Park. The large park has a clock tower, a scented garden for the blind, a playground, a cycle track where kids can learn to throw away the stabilisers and enough squirrels to keep the dogs happy. The area tends to attract professional couples and parents-to-be moving down from London. For most buyers here, the huge pull are the local schools. Balfour infants and junior schools and Dorothy Stringer secondary school are said to be the best (academically) in Brighton and they can – and do – pull the net tightly around the local area.

The triangle from Preston Park to Preston Drove and Stanford Avenue are where the biggest houses with gardens are to be found. A two-storey, two-bed house with 25-50 foot garden will go for around £240,000, while a house with loft conversion in Cleveland Road overlooking Blakers Park, might go for about £425,000.

Neighbouring Florence, Rugby and Surrenden Roads with houses ranging from £350,000 minimum to £700,000 or even more, depending on size and garden, can accommodate the bigger families. The prices come down again for the slightly smaller Victorian terraced houses (from £245,000) in the Preston Drove area, and the people tend to be a little less precious. Estate agents will tell you that the Preston Drove divide will cost you £30,000, with the neat rows of well-maintained homes on the Blaker's Park side lending a more genteel air.

PRESTON VILLAGE

This is not what we expect from a village these days with no shops, village square or real sense of community. In fact, it is no more than six roads off the London Road, stretching from South, Middle and North Roads with their older Victorian cottages and gardens worth between £190,000 and £245,000, to Clermont Road and Terrace at the back of Preston Park station, where substantial houses can set you back anything from £375,000 to as much as £675,000. A hop and a skip from a commuter station, it's beginning to attract more London buyers.

FIVEWAYS

Stretching from one end of Ditchling Road to the other, Fiveways refers to the junction of Stanford Avenue, Preston Drove and Hollingbury Road, and is where the Kemp Town and Hanover families tend to move to when they have more kids, a move hastened by the reputations of local schools Downs and Balfour school, Dorothy Stringer and Varndean.

The community is children-oriented with a distinct lack of focal points from shops or pubs, but someone could (and will) make a fortune by opening a deli/café. Zel have already spotted the gap and filled it with The Open House, a lounge lizard of a pub with mosaic patio for Sunday barbecue lunches.

With former head at Somerhill, Wenda Bradley now at Hertford Primary, the area is bound to attract more families. David Andrews of Raymond Beaumont Estate Agents says that they should look at the number of Edwardian houses with 45 foot gardens just north of Fiveways. At between £220,000 and 260,000 for a two bed, and £275,000 for a three bed, and within the much coveted Balfour catchment, these are a steal.

HOVE

Until fairly recently, Hove was Brighton's rather well kept back garden, a place to retreat to after you've enjoyed the action. Maybe it will give you an idea of Hove's past to say that there's a local by-law which states that houses in Brunswick Square – one of the magnificent Regency squares that characterise Hove's seafront – must be repainted in Regency Beige every five years. (Of course what this means in real life is that there's always loads of scaffolding up, but let's not get bogged down in detail).

Brighton's quieter, more refined sister is only a stone's throw from the main action, but by the time you've marvelled at the Peace Statue and the manicured lawns which mark the boundary, an air of tranquillity really does seem to descend. The breathtaking architecture of Brunswick and Palmeira Squares leaves the showy, gaudy anomalies of Brighton's seafront such as the Brighton Centre and the tacky eateries paling into insignificance. It all looks impossibly grand.

Hove has many faces – the shabby chic of Brunswick, the family filled tree lined avenues off Portland Road, the suburban money of Hove Park and the young marrieds of Poets Corner to name a few – and how could we not smile when Portslade Station is to be renamed Portslade and West Hove. Time for a Botox.

BRUNSWICK

If you're young(ish) and single with a bit of disposable cash, you're likely to go for the area north and south of Western Road around the Brighton/Hove boundary at York Road. The prices might have risen since Nigel Richardson immortalised the area in his book Breakfast In Brighton, but it's still well worth a look. Most properties are converted flats - some with lovely little patio gardens.

In the last five years, most of the people who have moved to this part of town are likely to have sold their one-bed flat in London, made £100,000 on the deal and ploughed it into their £170,000 one-bed or £240,000 two-bed flat. They buy their interiors from the shoppers' heaven that is the North Laine and build an architectural garden out of nothing more than a slab of east-facing concrete and some serious creativity.

The Regency two-bed flats in Brunswick or Palmeira

Squares, push the property prices into the 3% Stamp Duty over £250,000 bracket. A rare four-bed without a garden will go for £300,000. Bargains are hard to find, but you can get a really good first floor flat with a balcony for £275,000, while a roof conversion in the same building will go for £200000, and both will look out over the Channel. A big bow fronted four bed with two receptions in Brunswick Road will go for around £500,000.

NEW CHURCH ROAD

It may seem a bit suburban, but the difference between buying in Hove and buying into Terry and June suburbia is that you can walk along the seafront to some of the best clubs in the country. Teenage kids can get a cheapish cab home, parents can walk their younger kids to school, and you can save a fortune on petrol because Brighton and Hove thinks it's a good deal bigger than it is.

The wide, tree filled avenues off New Church Road are quickly becoming home to London relocators who have a bit more cash to spend on their kitchens than most. Some of the houses around Westbourne Gardens are enormous with four floors and endless rooms pushing prices up to £450,000 and beyond. Others such as Hogarth Road may be smaller inside but have huge gardens and are a bargain at around £295,000. "It's an odd area" says Bonett, "People moving from the Dials won't go beyond Sackville because they think the semis are too suburban" – but there are some huge gardens to be had if you blaze the trail and head towards Portslade a few roads down.

POETS CORNER

The Bohemian area of Hove which leads from the station to Clarendon Villas, as far west as Alpine Road and down to Portland Road, is still up and coming. It is the place where the first time house buyer in Hove usually starts with a two-to three-bed Victorian middle terrace houses for between £210,000 to £245,000. You can pick up a small one bedroom flat for between £120,000 plus and two bedders are about £155,000. East of Sackville are some two and three-storey Victorian houses which are going for about £240,000. It's a foothold on the market, and the starting point for many families who might move to New Church Road when the kids get too big to share.

Hove has a few parks dotted around this area, and uses the beach as its playground. It's only when you get up to Hove Park and across to Preston Park and Queen's Park that you'll find the buzz, the trees, the bigger playgrounds and the cafes which a good park should be about.

ST ANN'S WELL GARDENS

This is the area of leafy and not so leafy streets that border Montpelier, Seven Dials and central Hove. It is one of the genuine communities in Brighton and Hove, largely because at around 8.45am and 3pm, the streets are awash with parents and kids trekking to and from Davigdor, Somerhill, Brighton and Hove High School for Girls, Cottesmore, Cardinal Newman, Blatchington Mill and Hove Park. The area is dense with schools and people rather than the shops, pubs and clubs which characterise the rest of Brighton and Hove, and its heart is in St Ann's Well Gardens where the community comes to play.

Houses here vary from late Edwardian semis to large, detached Thirties buildings. One of the best selling points of the area is the size of some of the gardens that average between 50 to 100 feet in Somerhill and Nizell Avenues. But it does mean that they're not cheap, ranging from £335,000 to between £450 and £500,000.

HOVE PARK

Hove Park, according to some estate agents and the people who live there, is the best place to live in Brighton and Hove. The park itself is a large, rolling, well-kept expanse of space hedged by the Old Shoreham Road. It is designed to please with a family run café, kiddies' playground, bowling green and recently revamped tennis courts. The miniature railway is run by volunteers and is open in the summer, and the cycle track makes it a perfect stroll for those with buggies and wheelchairs.

Mallory Road, Shirley Drive, Woodland Drive and Woodruff Avenue are Hove's idea of budget housing, and four bed homes with large gardens are going for between £500,000 and £700,000. "Money is cheap these days" says Glen Mishon of Mishon McKay. "People are selling for around £350,000 and looking to move to one that's going for £450,000 should easily be able to find a mortgage of £100,000 to suit their lifestyle, and they're going for it".

SCHOOLS

Schools. The whole issue is a minefield. Ask one parent and she'll tell you that her son is in the school band, taking his Maths GCSE early and talks easily to girls of his own age. Talk to another, and his 15-year-old will have been so badly bullied by a group of teenage girls in the same school in full view of teachers that she's been moved to an independent school in the countryside.

This year's secondary school of the moment (Stringer) was last year's third choice; last year's school of the moment (Varndean) is this year undersubscribed. Hated heads are replaced by Superheads, specialist status injects new funds and nightmare year groups disappear into the big wide world leaving a calmer more co-operative school in their wake.

Ofsted only tells part of the story, as do the head teachers and their staff. They all do the best they can to give us guidance on one of the most important decisions of our children's lives, but what we aim to do is to give another side of the story – the parents'.

We also talk to professionals who work with the schools and who can tell us about the mentors and the magic teachers. They can also tell us about a school's involvement with community arts and music, a sure-fire stress release for both a year seven who has just left Juniors, and a 15-year-old who is buckling under peer group and exam pressure.

One of our partners online at www.juicymapminder.co.uk is The Good Schools Guide which will tell you yet another side of the story. Map it all together and we hope you make the right choice. If your school isn't in our selection, use the user review online to tell us why it should be.

Alternative

Brighton and Hove Montessori

67 Stanford Avenue, Preston Park, Brighton BN1 6FB
T: 01273 702485 F: 01273 702485
www.brighton-montessori.org.uk
brighton.montessori@ntlworld.com
Mon-Fri: 8.45am-3.15pm
A good option to a posher independent school for children from 2-11. Montessori teaching is purposeful with activities very rooted in the real world; polishing shoes, washing up, cleaning, rather than water and sand play. The idea is that children learn how to be comfortable in their world and grow at their own pace. This year the school hopes to see the fulfilment of a dream to start moves into the state sector, becoming the first free Montessori School in the country. At the beginning of the year the Government announced that the money was available, and work to achieve it continues.

The Dhama School

149 Ladies Mile Rd, Patcham, Brighton BN1 8TB
01273 502055
Mon-Fri: 8.40am-3.15pm
The Dhama School has graduated from its humble beginning; front room in Queens Park with 8 students, to a beautiful Art Deco building in Patcham. 80 students are now taught the National Curriculum in a Buddhist environment. The aim of the school is to "Give the children confidence in their ability to learn and to not be afraid of learning". Even the Tiny members of the Dragonfly nursery attend Puja every morning for reflection and meditation. The children are honoured to have the Dali Lama as their patron; Peter Murdock has just taken over from Kevin Fossey as head and the school continues to flourish under his guidance.

The Brighton Steiner School

Roedean Rd, Kemp Town, Brighton BN2 5RA
T: 01273 386300 F: 01273 306313
www.brightonsteinerschool.org.uk
enquiries@brightonsteinerschool.co.uk
Children work in a disciplined

environment but are allowed to learn about the world in an organic and non-competitive way, preserving their natural hunger for knowledge. The Brighton school is a teenager in the world of Steiner and has attracted mixed opinion. But the parents are some of the most committed in the city and the shared vision tends to build a very cohesive community among adults and children. Michael Hall, the oldest Steiner in the country and set in the most glorious surroundings, is a school bus ride away in Forest Row near East Grinstead and a very different option to Brighton's own school.

Nursery

The Orchard Nursery
89 Queen's Park Rd, Brighton BN2 2GL. T: 01273 622883
Mon-Fri: 8am-6pm
Morning and afternoon sessions or all-day care available. Kids bring their own lunchboxes, but tea (beans and soup in winter, sandwiches and fruit in summer) is prepared and cooked onsite. Be aware that it has a very long waiting list.

The Royal Spa Nursery
Park Hill, Brighton BN2 0BT
T: 01273 607480 F: 01273 607480
Mon-Fri: 9am-11.30am, 1pm-3.30pm

Tarnerland
St John's Place, Kemp Town, Brighton BN2 0BT
T: 01273 607651
Mon-Fri: 9am-11.30am, 1pm-3.30pm

These two are worth a mention for being the only State-funded independent nurseries in the whole of East Sussex. Many of the primary schools have nurseries attached, but these two stand alone. Both The Royal Spa and Tarnerland come highly recommended and have great locations with The Royal Spa nestling next to the playground in Queen's Park and Tarnerland situated just off the Queen's Park Road. The Royal Spa was purpose-built and the huge garden within the park provides a lovely environment for young children. Classes are large, with 40 per class, but pastoral care is good. The emphasis is on learning through play, and children develop good social skills.

Primary

Balfour Infants
Balfour Rd, Preston Park, Brighton BN1 6NE
T: 01273 500617 F: 01273 565808
www.balfourinfbrighton-hove.sch.uk
office@balfourinf.brighton-hove.sch.uk
Mon-Fri: 9am-3.15pm
Balfour Infants is one of the most sought after schools in the city, and set in a leafy middle class area, it's very hard to get in. It's well respected and gives children a very positive start to school life. The big criticism from parents has been the emphasis on academia over creativity but

the introduction of dance groups, theatre groups and an artist in residence have made a greater impact in the last year. Because of its academic reputation, it's very oversubscribed so unless you live on the doorstep, you're unlikely to get in. The exceptionally pro-active parents association organises well attended events, and raises £6000 in its annual fireworks display alone.

Balfour Juniors

Balfour Rd, Preston Park,
Brighton BN1 6NE
T: 01273 553521 F: 01273
559648
www.balfourjun.brighton-hove.sch.uk
office@balfourjun.brighton-hove.sch.uk
Mon-Fri: 8.55am-3.20pms
Academically one of the best. If art and music get pushed out to accommodate the highly structured curriculum, maybe Balfour can get away with it because its parents tend to be able to pay for the after-school art classes at Beacon Arts and the private piano or violin lessons. New head, Louise Parsons has a background in art and fashion and has injected a more creative feel. Parents report that the school has become much more open.

Cottesmore St Mary's Primary

The Upper Drive, Hove BN3 6NB
T: 01273 555811 F: 01273 555423
www.cottesmore.brighton-hove.sch.uk

office@cottesmore.brighton-hove.uk
Mon-Fri: 8.50am-3pm
The local infant and junior school in Upper Drive is a large-halled, stone building with a rather traditional interpretation of the school curriculum. It is one of the handfuls of Roman Catholic schools in Brighton and Hove and feeds the gorgeous-looking Cardinal Newman secondary school, which sits on the other side of the road. So committed was Cottesmore's magic teacher, Mr Butler to the Adopt an Author Scheme which the Festival encourages in all schools, that his weekly email dialogue between his kids and their adopted author was held up as an example to the rest of the country.

Davigdor Infants School

Somerhill Rd, St Anne's Well,
Hove BN3 3 1RG
T: 01273 731397 F: 01273 324038
www.davigdor.brighton-hove.sch.uk
Mon-Fri: 9am-3.15pm
One of the reasons that families are flocking to the deli and café community of Seven Dials and the borders of Hove is Davigdor. It's a small, family environment that doesn't put children off education for life, and the teachers really do listen to parents. It's now vastly over-subscribed so don't even think about it if you don't live on the doorstep.

Downs Infant School

Ditchling Rd, Preston Park,
Brighton BN1 6JA

T: 01273 500146 F: 01273 700504
Mon-Fri: 9am-3pm
Downs Infants and Junior schools have an artier profile than Balfour, being a little closer to Fiveways with its arty community. The head teacher is Miss Kruger whose commitment to the children is shown through her lateral interpretation of the numeracy and literacy hours. Downs works closely with Same Sky, the art organisation behind The Children's Parade and Burning the Clocks.

Downs Junior School

Rugby Rd, Preston Park,
Brighton BN1 6ED
T: 01273 558422 F: 01273 330769
www.downsjunior.org.uk
Mon-Fri: 9am-3.15pm
An enormous school by primary standards (500 pupils), and that can lead to some disorganisation and more traditional approaches to teaching and discipline. There's a lobster climbing frame in the playground, an amphitheatre for kids' own plays as well as the African tribal dancing and storytelling which is part of the cultural curriculum, and rubberised ball areas. For working parents, the Breakfast and After School clubs are handy, and fun for kids with arts and crafts, chess clubs and basketball. The whole school is very creative and works closely with Same Sky, the arts organisation behind The Children's Parade and The Burning of the Clocks.

Elm Grove Primary

Elm Grove, Hanover,
Brighton BN2 3ES. T: 01273

708004 F: 01273 708300
www.elmgrove.brighton-hove.
sch.uk
Mon-Fri: 9am-3.15pm
One of the most popular primary
schools in Brighton. The previous
Headmistress transformed its ailing
reputation by working in partnership
with parents and the local
community, and super-head John
Lynch, now into his third year at the
helm, is continuing to develop this,
with parents' special needs support
groups among the initiatives.

Hertford School
Hertford Rd, Hollingdean,
Brighton BN1 7GF
T: 01273 552931
www.hertfordinf.brighton-
hove.sch.uk
Former Somerhill head, Wenda
Bradley has taken over the reigns of
Hertford and pulled it onto a level
playing field alongside Downs and
Balfour. It's too early to tell, but
her magic touch should encourage
parents in the Fiveways area to go
and have a look.

Mary Magdalene
Spring St, Brighton BN1 3FH
T: 01273 327533
F: 01273 327259
office@stmarymagsbrighton-
hove.sch.uk
A Roman Catholic city centre
school with a wide range of
different nationalities, this is a very
cosmopolitan school and encourages
the kids to understand different
cultures and languages. It's small and
friendly and the kids are met every

morning by Jack the caretaker in the
playground, which is always buzzing
with laughter. Only one class intake
a year along with a 'buddy' system
for the younger children means that
all of the kids know each other and
all of the teachers.

Middle Street Primary School
Middle St, The Lanes, Brighton
BN1 1AL
T: 01273 323184
F: 01273 724769
www.middlestreet.org
admin@middlestreet.brighton-
hove.sch.uk
Mon-Fri: 9am-3.15pm
Right in the heart of old town
Brighton this is an example of how a
school can be. The school achieves
excellent results, and has a wide
range of active links with the local
community, integrating its very
diverse mixed-ability multicultural
intake, which includes significant
numbers of refugee and minority
group children. Mr Dyer is a cutting
edge IT wizard – check out his
school website. His wife runs the
nursery for 3 and 4-year-olds, and
is another of those special teachers
you remember forever; imagine a
teacher giving your child a poem
she'd come across at home just
because it reminded her of him.

Peter Gladwin Primary
Drove Rd, Portslade BN41 2PA
T: 01273 294959
Jane Bentley is the kind of head
who should be teaching at Steiner
instead of a State school, but if you

don't mind the fact that she's quite
likely to cancel a maths lesson and
take the kids to the beach to write
poetry, this is a dream of a school.
Exceptionally well connected in
the city's arts network, Jane can
get the best illustrators, artists,
photographers and dancers into the
school to run inspiring workshops.
It's also based in a beautiful location
overlooking the sea.

Queen's Park
Park St, Queen's Park,
Brighton BN2 0BN
T: 01273 686822
Mon-Fri: 9am-3.30pm
Queen's Park school has a fantastic
location, perched at the bottom of
the park and within skipping distance
of the park playground. Unlike its
neighbour, St Luke's, Queen's Park has
a separate nursery and a two-form
entry. The school also has a lower
intake than the others and so the
class sizes are smaller, and since
Queen's Park has become extremely
popular, entrance is difficult unless
you live very close by.

St Luke's Infants
Queen's Park Rise, Queen's
Park, Brighton BN2 9ZF
T: 01273 699924
F: 01273 674268
admin@stlukesinf.brighton-
hove.sch.uk
Mon-Fri: 9am-3.15pm
Divided into infants and juniors,
St Luke's is the largest primary
school in the area with a three-class
intake. Pastoral care in the Infants is
a top priority under the guidance of

the head, Nesta Saunders, and even the tiniest of children seem to settle in happily. Expectations are high and met easily without distracting the kids from their main purpose at this age, which is play and friendship. A very popular after school club has recently been set up for the Infants and Juniors, and a new playground with climbing frames is due to be built later this year.

Stanford Infants

Highcroft Villas,
Brighton BN1 5PS
T: 01273 555240 F: 01273 551826
www.stanford-inf.brighton-hove.sch.uk
office@stanfordinf.brighton-hove.sch.uk
Mon-Fri: 9am-3.15pm
On the whole, Brighton is big on the arts, and at Stanford the infants make pottery masks in the school kiln and learn about multi-cultural arts within a broader curriculum. Arts include dance and music, and are used in numeracy and literacy hours. Stanford parents are infamous in the city for their pro-active anti school run campaign; a walking bus takes the kids to school, with some parents taking turns to lead the procession and others barring the ends of the Stanford Road to cars at 8.50 and 3.15.

Somerhill Junior

Somerhill Rd,
St Anne's Well,
Hove BN3 1RP
T: 01273 739659

F: 01273 733614
admin@somerhill.brighton-hove.sch.uk
Mon-Fri: 8.55am-3.25pm
Somerhill's star has fallen since the departure of Wenda Bradley (now at Hertford Juniors). The word is that the pastoral side of the school is not as hot as it once was which leads to stress among the kids and anxiety among the parents. It shares its huge field for football, baseball and other sports with its little sister, Davigdor.

St Andrews (Church Aided) Primary

Belfast St, Hove BN3 3YT
T: 01273 294800
Primary school serving Hove's Church going community (and many of those who join the Church in order to get into the better schools in Brighton and Hove), the feel is cosy and caring. And for the cynical, we can report some real conversions along the way too. Residential field trips start at Year 4, and unusually there are three male teachers, one of whom was nominated for teacher of the year last year. The new Tesco built the school a new sports field, external play areas and new buildings as part of the deal to bring the superstore to Church Rd.

St Bernadette's RC Primary School

Preston Rd, Preston Park,
Brighton BN1 6UT
T: 01273 553813 F: 01273 563213
mail@stberns.brighton-hove.sch.uk
Mon-Fri: 9am-3.15pm

A highly recommended primary with, unsurprisingly, a heavy Catholic bias (99% of the pupils are Catholic), where the teaching, discipline and ethos comes from the religion. Montessori has influenced much of the teaching, a legacy from the former deputy head who trained as a Montessori teacher, so expect a high level of independence from pupils.

St Luke's Juniors

St Luke's Terrace, Brighton BN2 9ZE. T: 01273 675080
F: 01273 625473
admin@stlukesjun.brighton-hove,sch.uk
Mon-Fri: 9am-3.15pm
Arty, sporty (despite the lack of green fields) and impressing the Ofsted inspectors last year with its 'unusually cohesive and motivated team which expects high standards (and gets them) from their students', St Luke's is one of the most popular Junior schools in Brighton. Ron Guilford leaves as head this year after 37 years at the school, and will be sorely missed by the children whose good behaviour has been rewarded by his fairy cake tea. Kay Berny, currently deputy and already part time acting head, will make sure that the kids continue to be inspired by visiting theatre groups and ex pupils such as the founders of Stomp.

Stanford Juniors

Stanford Rd, Brighton BN1 5PR
T: 01273 565570 F: 01273 566031
www.stanfordjun.brighton-hove.sch.uk
office@stanfordjun.brighton-

hove.sch.uk
Mon-Fri: 8.55am-3.30pm
A happy school where the social mix is less diverse than many of the other schools in the city, which means there's more cohesion in and out of school. Parents have raised a lot of cash to do up the playground and make it more interesting, and head teacher Martin Thorne is old school, but is really working hard for better resources. Catch the Winter Panto to see what Stanford parents look like in tights.

Secondary

Blatchington Mill School
Holmes Avenue, Hove BN3 7BW. T: 01273 736244
F: 01273 739615
www.blatchingtonmill.org.uk
office@blatchingtonmill.org.uk
Mon-Fri: 8.30am-3pm
On the north side of the Old Shoreham Road in Hove, this is one of the better secondary schools and sixth form colleges and was awarded performing arts status. Its music teacher Steven Jeffries is one of those magical teachers children will remember forever, and is rewarded for his inspiring ways by the fact that this year there are three pop bands in Year 7 alone. The bands and the orchestra play international tours and are very involved with the Brighton Festival.

Cardinal Newman
The Upper Drive, Hove BN3 6ND. T: 01273 558551
Mon-Fri: 9am-4pm

So good that people even convert to Catholicism to get in, it's the best alternative, according to parents at the school, to going private. It has an excellent record for both pastoral care and exam results, with great effort made in introducing the Year Sevens to life at "Big School"; without the rest of the school there for their first two days, the new eleven year olds can run around the school as if they own it. Although a Catholic school, church going Protestants are also welcome.

Dorothy Stringer High School
Loder Rd, Preston Park, Brighton BN1 6PZ
T: 01273 852222
F: 01273 852310
www.stringer.brighton-hove.sch.uk
office@stringer.brighton-hove.sch.uk
Mon-Fri: 8.45am-3.05pm
This year's school of the moment, the school is known for its drama and music departments; Stringer children have sung both with The Brighton Youth Orchestra at Glyndebourne and at the London Palladium. Parents have mixed opinion on the vocational training for the less academic kids and argue furiously about whether schooldays are for maths and English or hairdressing placements. Word is that it's a sink or swim school, both academically and socially; 'Stringer Mingers' with their push up bras and low slung jeans are the subject of

Brighton teenage boys' dreams and nightmares, and those who don't fit in have been known to go for the much more suburban Patcham High.

Hove Park
Hangleton Way, Hove BN3 8AA. T: 01273 295002/3
www.hovepark.org.uk
Hove Park, under its previous head, was a real no no. Even the teachers were too demoralised to go to school, but things have changed under the inspiring headship of Tim Barclay who joined last September from an inner city school in Tower Hamlets. Now a specialist language school with excellent facilities, the students can learn Japanese, Russian and Chinese among others, and students are very involved in and passionate about global projects.

Longhill School
Falmer Rd, Rottingdean BN2 7FR. T: 01273 304086
www.longhill.brighton-hove.sch.uk
With gorgeous views over the South Downs and away from the urban streetwise schools of inner city Brighton and Hove, Longhill is a steady secondary where kids get on with life. Mr Ellis leads a tight ship with discipline and attendance a high priority, but if the hand is firm, parents report that it's unlikely to light any fires. A news sports hall, and a nursery attached to the school give it a good community feel, and bullying is dealt with systematically and thoroughly.

Patcham High School

Ladies Mile Rd, Patcham,
Brighton BN1 6PZ
T: 01273 503908
www.patchamhigh.brighton-
hove.sch.uk
office@patchamhigh.brighton-
hove.sch.uk
Mon-Fri: 8am-3pm
Patcham High School has established
itself as an award winning school
with a reputation for innovation
and recently has been given Media
Specialist status. The only secondary
in the area to have achieved both
the national GOLD Artsmark and
GOLD Sportsmark (with a new
recommendation for distinction),
it is chosen frequently to pilot
national initiatives like summer
schools. Liz Fletcher is the kind of
head who knows all the students
and whom they view with affection
and respect.

Varndean School

Balfour Rd, Preston Park,
Brighton BN1 6NP
T: 01273 561281 F: 01273 564614
www.varndean.brighton-hove.
sch.uk
school@varndean.brighton-
hove.sch.uk
Mon-Fri: 8.55am-3.05pm
Varndean has an excellent reputation
for secondary academic education. It
shares a very large site with Dorothy
Stringer and the Balfour schools,
and has a healthy competition with
Stringer. It has specialist Technology
College status, and is also a Beacon
school (good enough to be a role
model for other schools). The music

and drama is very good, and its
Samba Band is one of the highlights
of the Children's Parade. An email
system between tutors, pupils and
parents means that the fact that the
head himself is reported to be more
of an unapproachable businessman
than an inspiring mentor, doesn't
have to hinder communication.

Sixth Form

BHASVIC

205 Dyke Rd, Hove BN3 6EG
T: 01273 552200
F: 01273 563139
www.bhasvic.ac.uk
webmaster@bhasvic.ac.uk
Mon-Fri: 8am-5pm
Brighton and Hove's sixth form
college, where the brainiest kids
from here and Lewes vie for places.
This college is particularly good for
sciences.

Varndean College

Surrenden Rd, Preston Park,
Brighton BN1 6WQ
T: 01273 508011
F: 01273 542950
www.varndean.ac.uk
office@varndean.ac.uk
Mon-Fri: 8am-5pm
Varndean College is situated in the
leafy suburbs of North Brighton with
about 1,000 full-time 16 to 18-year-
olds taking mainly advanced level
courses. It has a national reputation
for the quality of its exam results
and, particularly, for its 'value-added'
achievement where it was recently
ranked as the top college in the
whole country.

Independents

Brighton and Hove High

Junior School Radinden Manor
Rd, Hove BN3 6NH
T: 01273 505004
F: 01273 505006
Mon-Fri: 8.35am-3.30pm
Senior School Montpelier Rd,
Brighton BN1 3AT
T: 01273 734112 F: 01273 737120
www.gdst.net enquiries@gdst.
net
Mon-Fri: 8.30am-3.45pm
Placed firmly at the top of the
Sussex league tables, Brighton and
Hove was one of the first schools in
the country to provide high quality
education for girls, and early pupils
were among the first women in
England to go to university. It is
deeply selective, and will only take
in girls who are already at the top
of their class. Significantly, this is
the first year that The High School
is taking part in the Brighton Festival
Children's Parade.

Brighton College Upper School

Eastern Rd, Kemp Town,
Brighton BN2 0AL
T: 01273 704339 F: 01273 704204
www.brightoncollege.org.uk
Mon-Fri: 8.30am-5pm
Brighton College is less selective
than its main competitor,
Brighton and Hove High although,
academically, there's little to
choose between the two schools.
It beats the High School in some
league tables, and has smaller class
sizes and a broader curriculum. Dr

Anthony Seldon is an inspiring head who believes in and promotes the Howard Gardner idea of the seven forms of intelligence: linguistic, logical, physical, spiritual, aesthetic, emotional and interpersonal.

The Drive Prep School

101 The Drive, Hove BN3 6GE
T: 01273 738444 F: 01273 738444
www.driveprep.co.uk
enquiries@driveprep.brighton-hove.sch.uk
Mon-Fri: 8.30am-4.30pm
The Drive Prep believes in each child's individuality and aims to raise him or her to their maximum potential. With very small classes (16 in the prep, 12 in pre-prep and 7 in the nursery), It is obvious that pastoral care is integral.

Mowden School

The Droveway, Hove BN3 6LU
T: 01273 503452
F: 01273 503457
www.mowdenschool.co.uk

info@mowdenschool.co.uk
Mon-Fri: 8.30am-5.30pm
Sporty and academic, this is the kind of place which turns out plenty of self motivated high achievers. Although it stands in extensive grounds it is actually a relatively small school, which means there are great communication links between staff, pupils and parents and always a friendly vibe about the place. The school is very hot on manners and good behaviour and it achieves good levels of discipline by emphasising pupils' achievements, praising strengths and focusing on rewards rather than punishments. The ethos of the school is firmly based in family values and Christian traditions although children from all faiths are welcomed. Although it's now co-educational, the majority of its pupils are boys and it has become clear that it will be a few years before the ratio of boys to girls becomes more balanced.

Newlands School

Eastbourne Rd, Seaford BN25 4NP. T: 01323 892334
F: 01323 898420
www.newlands-school.com
newlands1@msn.com
Mon-Fri: 8.30am-5.20pm, Sat: 8.30am-12.30pm
An independent day and boarding school from 3 to 18 set on a picturesque site. The school has excellent sports and recreational facilities and is known for a superb theatre arts programme. The school does not select pupils but achieves very good academic results, and the Gannon Centre on site provides extra tuition and support for children with a range of special needs.

Roedean

Roedean Way,
Brighton BN2 5RQ
T: 01273 603181 F: 01273 676722
www.roedean.co.uk
Mon-Fri: 8.30am-5pm, Sat: 9am-12pm
The famous ivory tower on the

hilltop with its own tunnel down to the sea has managed to keep hold of its reputation as top gels' school, while joining the 21st century. Set up by early feminists, it has always been keen to encourage girls to get ahead and provides exceptional facilities to help them get there.

St Aubyns

76 High Street, Rottingdean BN2 7JN. T: 01273 302170 F: 01273 304004 www.staubynsschoolbrighton. co.uk office@staubyns-school.org.uk
Mon-Fri: 8.10am-5.30pm
A traditional co-ed Christian prep school in the heart of Rottingdean run by a husband and wife team whose children all went to the school. The performing arts studio and extensive sports facilities including fencing and horse-riding are par for the course in independent schools, but the homely feel marks it out. Don't be put off by its out of town location; day pupils of all ages commute from Brighton and Hove on the school bus. Flexi boarding is also available.

St Bedes At The Dicker

Upper Dicker, Hailsham BN27 3QH. T: 01323 843252 F: 01323 442628 www.stbedesschool.org enquiries@stbedesschool.org
Mon-Fri: 8.30am-5.20pm, Sat: 8.30am-12.30pm
St Bedes is an independent, mixed, day and boarding school with a very positive atmosphere and

philosophy, and is often chosen when other schools fail. It is set in the beautiful Sussex countryside and aims for high standards in academic and social development. In the afternoons the children choose from over 140 activities including horse riding, go-cart building, cookery and a wide variety of sports. There is an extensive facility for children with learning difficulties and a well-developed Arts department. There's a very clear bullying policy; once and you're on the red carpet, twice and you're out.

St Mary's Hall

Eastern Rd, Kemp Town BN2 5JF. T: 01273 606061 F: 01273 620782 www.stmaryshall.co.uk enquiries@stmaryhall.co.uk
Mon-Fri: 8.30am-4.30pm
An independent, day and boarding school for girls of three to 18 with extensive music, art, drama and sports facilities, and a philosophy which supports educating the 'whole person'. The small classes mean that there's a great deal of personal attention, and some parents report teachers going the extra mile to accommodate a child's particular passion despite 'administrative inconvenience'. Pupils agree that the lower school is wonderful but there are also reports of bullying, particularly in the upper school. This is par for the course among teenagers, but some parents have not been impressed with the school's efforts to deal with it.

Windlesham School

190 Dyke Rd, Hove BN2 5JF T: 01273 553645
Mon-Fri: 8am-6pm
A homey environment for 3 to 5-year-olds extending out the back into a warren of classrooms, lawns, swimming pool and sports courts. Parents report that the pastoral care with difficult children can sometimes leave something to be desired.

Special Needs

Jeanne Saunders Centre

31, Palmeira Avenue, Brighton BN3 3GD
T: 01273 294944 F: 01273 294942
Mon-Fri: 9am-4.30pm
Children are generally referred here by a doctor or educational psychologist. Classes are held on site with separate facilities for children with physical handicaps. Classes consist of no more than six and there is an 'off site' team who go into nurseries to work with children.

ASD Support, Hearing Impaired

Downs Park, Foredown Rd, Portslade BN41 2FU
T: 01273 424963 F: 01273 424963 www.education.brighton-hove.gov.uk
Mon-Fri: 8am-5pm
There's a special facility for children with severe hearing impairment at Bevendean Primary, and an ICAN centre (for children with speech and language difficulties) at Carden Primary school.

Health

Brighton and Sussex University Hospital
Eastern Rd, Kemp Town,
Brighton BN2 3FE
T: 01273 696955
www.bsuh.nhs.uk

Brighton General Hospital
Brighton General Hospital, Elm
Grove, Brighton BN2 3EW
T: 01273 696011 F: 01273 673530
www.southdowns.nhs.uk

Royal Alexandra for Sick Children
Dyke Road, Hove BN1 3JN
T: 01273 328145
www.bsuh.nhs.uk

Listed below are the only hospitals with A&E facilities:

Royal Sussex University Hospital
Eastern Road, Kemp Town
T: 01273 696955

Southlands
Upper Shoreham Road,
Shoreham
T: 01273 455622

Victoria
Nevill Road, Lewes
T: 01273 474153

For health and dental care
for registered NHS patients,
phone 0800 665544

SERVICES

Late night chemists

Ashtons
98 Dyke Road, Seven Dials
T: 01273 325020
9am-10pm

Westons
6 Coombe Terrace, Brighton
T: 01273 605354
9am-10pm

Libraries

Brighton Central Library
New England St,
Brighton BN1 2GW
T: 01273 290800 F: 01273 296965
www.citylibraries.info
Mon, Tues, Thurs and Fri: 10am-
7pm, Sat: 10am-4pm
Good children's section, audio books,
videos, music and internet access.

Hollingbury Library

Carden Hill, Brighton BN1 8DA
T: 01273 296906
www.citylibraries.info/
branches/hollingbury.html
Mon & Thurs: 10am-1pm, 2pm-
5pm, Sat: 10am-1pm, 2pm-4pm

Moulsecoomb Library

The Highway, Brighton BN2
4PA. T: 01273 296910
www.citylibraries.info/
branches/moulsecoomb.html
Tues: 10am-1pm, 2pm-7pm, Thurs-
Fri: 2pm-6pm, Sat: 10am-1pm,
2pm-4pm

Moulsecoomb Toy Library

Hill View Annexe, Brighton
BN2 3LR. T: 01273 679735
www.citylibraries.info
Mon-Fri: 11am-5pm

Westdene Library

Bankside, Brighton BN1 5GN
T: 01273 296922
www.citylibraries.info/
branches/westdene.html
Mon, Tues and Wed: 10am-3pm,
Fri: 10am-5pm

Whitehawk Library

Whitehawk Rd, Brighton BN2
5GD T: 01273 296294
www.citylibraries.info
Tues-Fri: 9.30am-1pm, 2pm-5pm,
Sat: 9.30am-1pm, 2pm-4pm

Woodingdean Library

Warren Rd, Brighton BN2 6BA
T: 01273 296928
www.citylibraries.info/
branches/woodingdean.html

Mon: 10am-1pm, 2pm-5pm, Thurs:
10am-1pm, 2pm-7pm, Sat: 10am-
1pm, 2pm-4pm

Places of worship

Churches

Church Of Christ the King
New England Street, Brighton
T: 01273 747687
www.cck.org.uk office@cck.
org.uk

St Bartholomews Church
Ann Street, Brighton
T: 01273 685142
C of E Grade 1 listed building which,
say the children of Brighton, is the
real Noah's arc upside down.

St Paul's
West Street, Brighton
T: 01273 739639
Astonishingly laid back local church
which is packed to the gills every
Christmas as families come to show
their kids what church should be like.

St Peter's
York Place, Brighton
T: 01273 682960
Austere C of E church with proper
job choir in frilly collars and organ.

Synagogues

Middle Street Synagogue
Middle Street, Brighton
T: 01273 888855
The oldest and most splendid
of synagogues in the area. It's an
Orthodox working shul but open

to the general public on the first
Sunday of every month from March
to November. During the May
festival, it's open every Sunday.

Hove Hebrew Congregation
Holland Road, Hove
T: 01273 732035

**Brighton and Hove New
Synagogue**
Palmeira Avenue, Hove
T: 01273 735343
Reform synagogue.

**Brighton and Hove Progressive
Synagogue**
6 Lansdowne Road, Hove
T: 01273 737223
Rabbi Elizabeth Tikvah Sarah has
recently taken over from the truly
progressive Paul Glantz who went
out of his way to welcome mixed
families into the Jewish community.

Quaker

Religious Society of Friends
Friends Meeting House, Ship
Street, Brighton
T: 01273 770258
www.brightonquakers.net
admin@brightonquakers.net

Mosques

Islamic Centre & Mosque
150 Dyke Road, Brighton, BN1
5PA. T: 505247

Al Medina Mosque
24 Bedford Place, BN1 2PT
T: 737721

Jehovahs Witness

Brighton Central Congregation of
Jehovahs Witnesses
2 Osmond Road, Hove, BN3 1TE
T: 01272 329505

Police

For all non-emergencies, call
Sussex Police on 0845 6070999.
This is a central number that deals
with all Sussex. (Obviously, if
things are a little more urgent, you
should call 999).

Lost property: 01273 665510
The front desk at Brighton Police
Station (John Street, Kemp Town) is
open 24-hours.

Post

The post depot on North Road has a
late collection at 8pm.

Tourist Information

10 Bartholomew Square,
Brighton. T: 01273 292599
Open Mon-Fri 9am-5pm, Sat 10am-
5pm, Sun 10am-4pm

Useful Numbers

Brash (youth scheme) 01273 293632
Brighton Media Centre
9 Middle Street, Brighton BN1
1AL. T: 01273 384200
Mon-Fri: 9am-8pm

Brighton Relate
T: 01273 697997

Citizens Advice
T: 01273 772277

County Court
County Court, William Street,
Brighton BN2 2RF
T: 01273 674421

Family Planning Clinic
T: 01273 242091

Gay Brighton
The Gay switchboard on 01273
204050 offers help and
advice and also helps find
rooms in gay-friendly
accommodation. There are
also some specifically gay hotels/
B&Bs in the Accommodation
chapter of this book.

Magpie Recycling Co-operative Ltd
Saunders Park View, Brighton
BN2 4AY
T: 01273 677577

24-Hour Helplines

Animal welfare: 0870 555 5999
Environment Agency:
0800 807060
Childline: 0800 1111
Samaritans: 0845 7909090

Where To Go Later

Brighton Borough Mortuary
Lewes Rd, Elm Grove, Brighton
BN2 3QB
T: 01273 602345
Mon-Fri: 9am-5pm and Sat and Sun:
10am-3pm

Downs Crematorium
Bear Road, Brighton BN2 3PL
T: 01273 601601
Mon-Fri: 9am-4pm, Sat and Sun:
10am-4pm
Beautiful crematorium set in wood
and parkland.

Woodvale Crematorium
Lewes Rd, Brighton BN2 3QB
T: 01273 604020
Mon-Fri: 9am-4.30pm, Sat and Sun:
11am-4.30pm
Beautiful crematorium set in wood
and parkland.

Petrol Stations

Asda, Marina Village
Asda, Crowhurst Rd
BP, 100 Lewes Rd
Tesco Express, Highcroft,
239 Dyke Road, Hove
BP, 49-57 Hollingdean Rd
BP, Lewes Road, 58-62
Lewes Rd
BP, University Way, 100 Lewes
Rd (24 hour)
BP, 134 Ditchling Rd (24 hour)
BP Express, 373 Kingsway,
Hove (24 hour)
Hove Station, Denmark Villas
(24 hour)
Q8, Mill Road, Patcham
(24 hour)
Shell, 132 Old Shoreham Rd,
Hove
Shell, 193 Preston Road
(24 hour)
Tates, 27 Old Shoreham Rd,
Portslade
Total, 236 Eastern Rd,
Kemp Town (24 hour)

Map from www.mapminder.co.uk © 2004 NavTeq

Map from www.mapminder.co.uk © 2004 NavTeq · **Brighton & Hove** 235

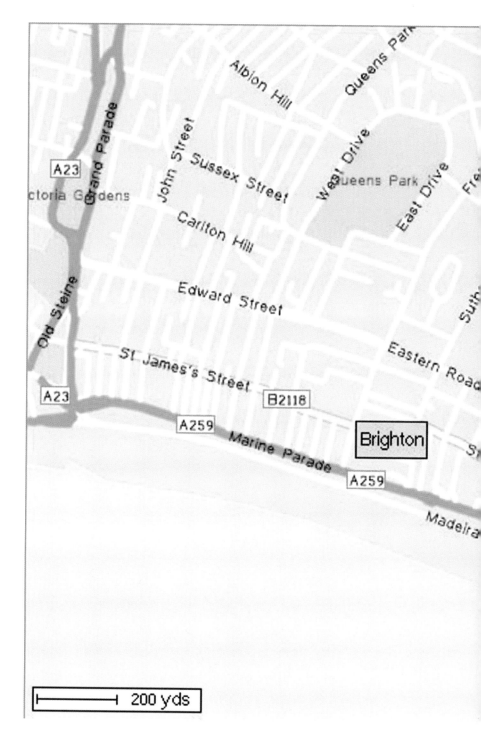

200 yds

Map from www.mapminder.co.uk © 2004 NavTeq

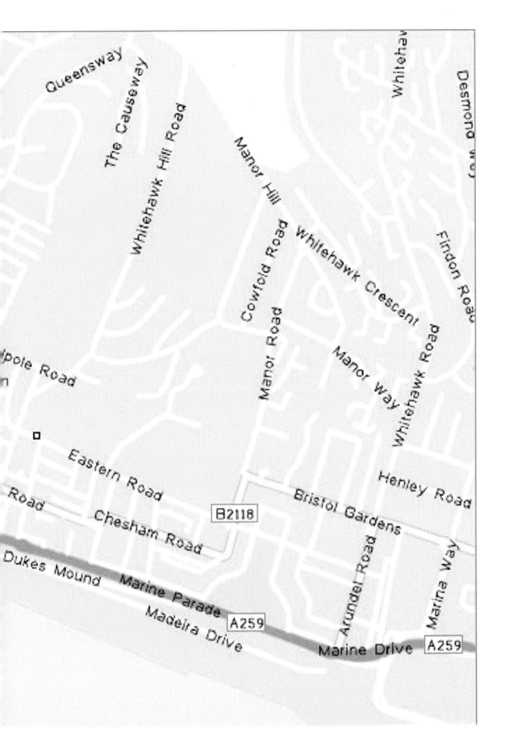

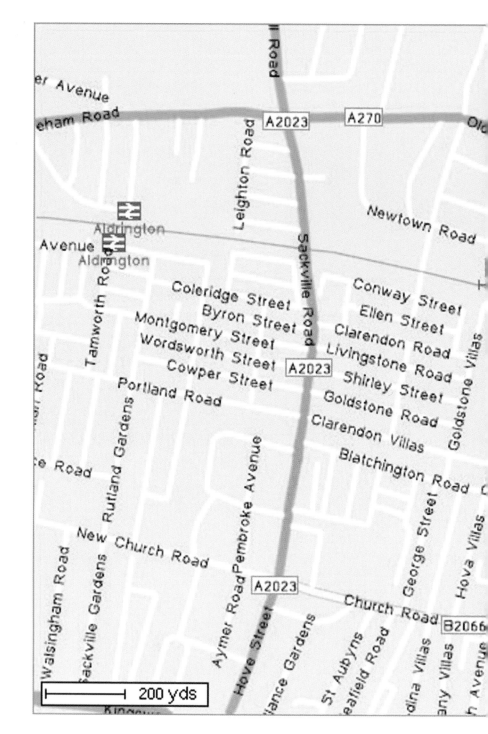

Map from www.mapminder.co.uk © 2004 NavTeq

200 yds

Map from www.mapminder.co.uk © 2004 NavTeq

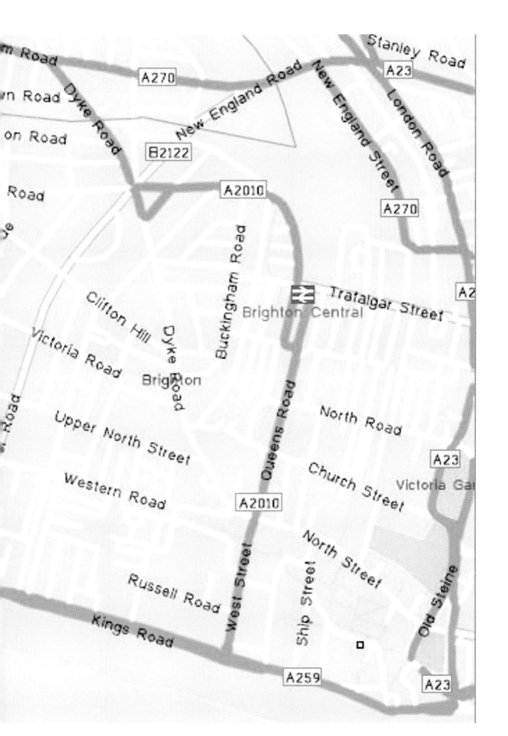

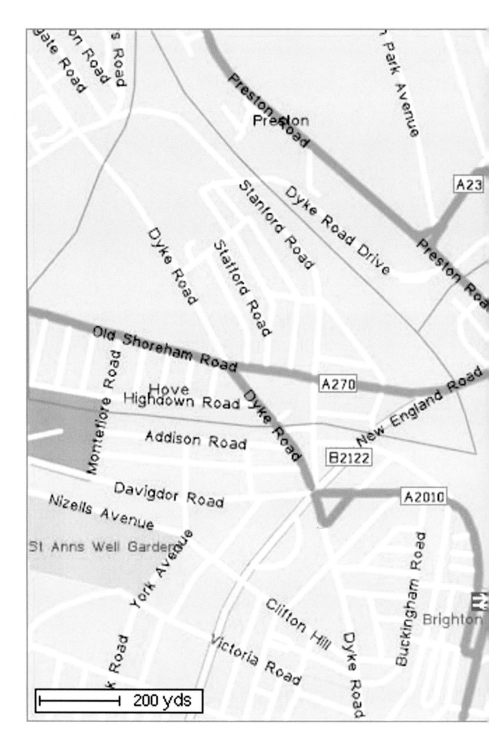

Map from www.mapminder.co.uk © 2004 NavTeq

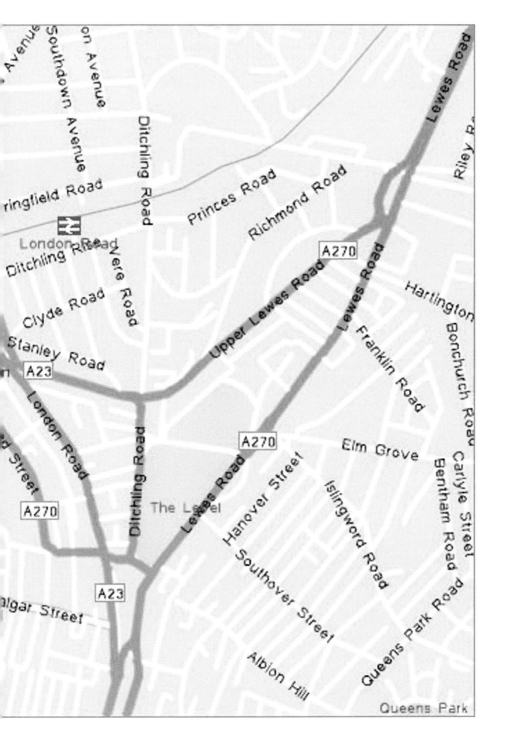

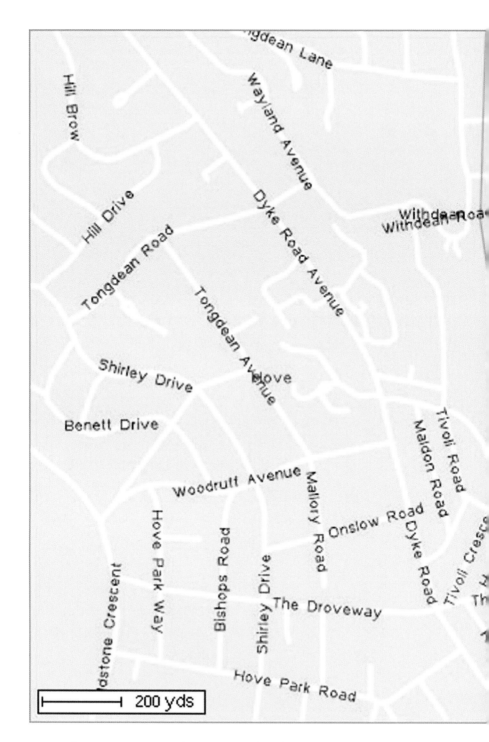

200 yds

Map from www.mapminder.co.uk © 2004 NavTeq

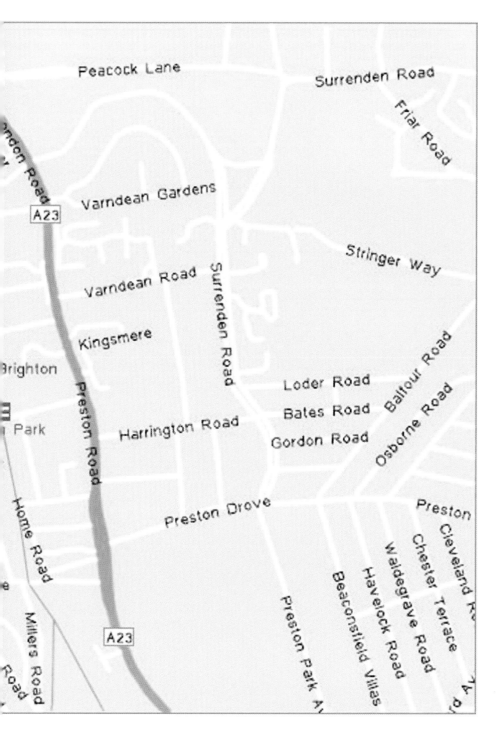

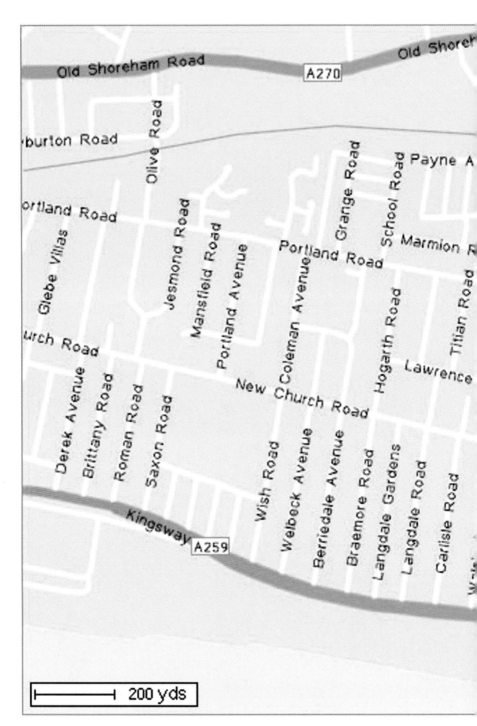

200 yds

Map from www.mapminder.co.uk © 2004 NavTeq

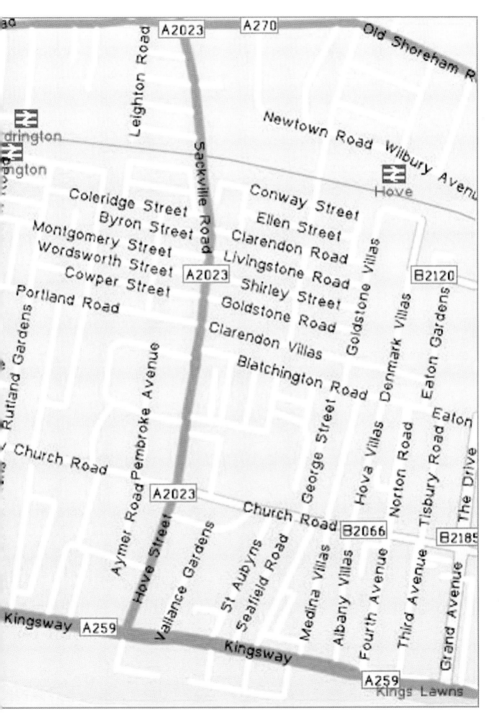

HOTELS

RESTAURANTS

INDEX

The Bath Arms, 95

The Black Lion, 95

The Bristol Bar, 95

The Caxton Arms, 95

The Charles Napier, 95

The Colonnade, 95

The Constant Service, 95

The Cricketers, 95

Doctor Brighton's, 95

The Dragon, 96

The Druid's Head, 96

The Eagle, 96

The Earth and Stars

The Eddie, 96

The Fiddler's Elbow, 96

The Fishbowl, 96

The Fortune of War, 96

The Freemasons, 97

The Full Moon, 97

The Geese Have Gone, 97

The Great Eastern, 97

The Greys, 97

The Hampton, 97

The Hanbury Arms, 98

The Hand In Hand, 98

The Hanover, 98

The Heart In Hand, 98

Hectors House, 98

The Hop Poles, 99

The King and Queen, 99

The Lion and Lobster, 99

The London Unity, 99

The Mash Tun, 99

Mrs Fitzherberts, 99

The Nelson, 99

The New Vic, 99

The Office, 99

The Open House, 100

The Pond, 100

The Prince Albert, 100

Princess Victoria, 100

The Prodigal, 100

Pub With No Name, 101

The Pull and Pump, 101

The Queen's Head, 101

Regency Tavern, 101

The Roundhill, 101

Royal Pavilion Tavern, 101

St James's, 101

Shakespeare's Head, 102

Shakespeare's Head, 102

The Sidewinder, 102

The Slug and Lettuce, 102

The Smugglers, 102

Star of Brunswick, 102

The Station, 102

The Sussex, 102

Three Jolly Butchers, 102

Victory Inn, 103

The Waggon and Horses, 103

The Walkabout Inn, 103

The Walmer Castle, 103

The Western Front, 103

The White Horse, 103

William IV, 103

The Windmill, 103

CLUBS

Arc, 120

Audio, 120

Babylon Lounge, 120

The Beach, 120

Brighton Gloucester, 121

Casablanca, 121

Club Mango, 121

Club New York, 122

Concorde 2, 122

Core Club, 122

Creation, 123

Enigma, 123

Envy, 123

The Event II, 123

Funky Buddha Lounge, 124

Funky Fish Club, 124

Hanbury Ballroom, 124

Harlequin, 124

Honey Club, 124

The Jazz Place, 125

The Joint, 125

Midnight Blues, 125

The Ocean Rooms, 125

Penthouse, 125

Po-Na-Na, 125

Pressure Point, 125

Revenge, 126

Royal Pavilion Tavern, 126

Sumo, 126

Volks Tavern, 126

Zap, 126

SHOPS

Abstract, 139

Acacia, 134

Across the Tracks, 153

Adam Flude Rugs, 146

Air Born Kites, 159

All That Glitters, 152

Amaryllis, 141

Ananda, 146

Appendage, 152

Art Asylum, 130

Art Republic, 130

Arts and Crafts Home, 147

Audrey's Chocolates, 142

B.Right.On, 142

ARTS

DAYS OUT

SPORT AND LEISURE

SUNDAY LUNCH

BODY & SOUL

PICTURE INDEX

A big thanks to all the venues that allowed us to use their images, and to the local galleries who lent us their artists. A huge thank you to Alexis Maryon (01273 672185) and to Brighton and Hove Visitor and Convention Bureau for allowing us to use their gorgeous photographs. We have credited the Bureau here as B&HV&CB.

Win a trip for two to Paris

Tell us your top three things to do in Brighton and Hove, and you could win a trip for two to Paris.

Simply contact us at www.juicymapminder.co.uk or write to us at 13 Arundel Rd, Brighton, BN2 5TE with your full postal details, and we'll enter you in the draw. Your choices will be listed on JuicyMapminder, and could be in the next Juicy Guide.